Urban Sociology

Urban Sociology

Satish Mittal
Sushil Kumar Saxena

Commonwealth

Urban Sociology

Edition 2024

ISBN 978-81-311-0368-5

Published by :
COMMONWEALTH PUBLISHERS (P) LTD.
4831/24, Govind Lane,
Ansari Road, Darya Ganj,
New Delhi - 110002
Ph. : 23272541, 23242541
e-mail : commonwealthpublishers2016@gmail.com

Distributed by :
ARJUN PUBLISHING HOUSE
4831/24, Govind Lane,
Ansari Road, Darya Ganj,
New Delhi - 110002
Ph. : 23272541, 23242541
e-mail : arjunbooks2001@gmail.com

Laser Typesetting by :
Dimple Computers
Delhi

Printed at :
Milan Enterprises
Delhi

Preface

Urban sociology is the sociological study of social life and human interaction in metropolitan areas. It is a normative discipline of sociology seeking to study the structures, processes, changes and problems of an urban area and by doing so providing inputs for planning and policy making. Urban sociologists use statistical analysis, observation, social theory, interviews, and other methods to study a range of topics, including migration and demographic trends, economics, poverty, race relations, economic trends, etc.

After the industrial revolution, sociologists such as Max Weber, and particularly Georg Simmel in works such as *The Metropolis and Mental Life,* focused on the increasing process of urbanization and the effects it had on feelings of social alienation and anonymity. The Chicago School is a major influence in the study of urban sociology. Many of their findings have been refined or rejected, but the lasting impact of the Chicago School can still be found in today's teachings.

The present book provides an indispensable introduction to urban sociology. It not only includes clear explanations of theories and evidence, but also covers the most cutting-edge research, data, and debates. Written in a lively and accessible style, the book has been specially designed to support students' understanding, and to develop their critical responses to the literature.

Authors

Contents

1

Urbanisation and Urban Development

Urbanisation is an integral part of the process of economic growth. As in most countries, India's towns and cities make a major contribution to the country's economy. With less than 1/3 of India's people, its urban areas generate over 2/3 of the country's GDP and account for 90% of government revenues.

Urbanisation in India has expanded rapidly as increasing numbers of people migrate to towns and cities in search of economic opportunity. Slums now account for 1/4 of all urban housing. In Mumbai, for instance, more than half the population lives in slums, many of which are situated near employment centers in the heart of town, unlike in most other developing countries.

At present approximately 307 million Indians lives in nearly 3700 towns and cities spread across the country. This is 30.5% of its population, in sharp contrast to only 60 millions (15%) who lived in urban areas in 1947 when the country became Independent. During the last fifty years the population of India has grown two and half times, but Urban India has grown by nearly five times. In numerical terms, India's urban population is second largest in the world after China, and is higher than the total urban population of all countries put together barring China, USA and Russia.

Table 1. India: Urban Population 1901 – 2001

	Urban population (million)	Percentage of Urban to total population	Decadal growth rate (percent)
1901	29.9	10.8	—
1911	25.9	10.3	0.4
1921	28.1	11.2	18.3
1931	33.5	12.0	19.1
1941	44.2	13.9	32.0
1951	62.4	17.3	41.4
1961	78.9	18.0	26.4
1971	109.1	19.9	38.2
1981	159.5	23.3	46.1
1991	217.6	25.7	36.4
2001	306.9	30.5	41.0

At the 1991 census, two-third of the country's urban population lived in Class-I cities with more than 1,00,000 population.

Table 2. Distribution of urban population by size class of towns

Class	Population Range	No. of Towns	Share of urban Population
I	1,00,000 & above	300	65.20%
II	50,000 to 99,999	345	10.95%
III	20,000 to 49,999	947	13.19%
IV	10,000 to 19,999	1,167	7.77%
V	5,000 to 9,999	740	2.60%
VI	Less than 5,000	197	0.29%
	All Classes	3,696	100%

About one-third of Urban India (71 million) lives in metropolitan cities (million plus). The number of such cities in India has increased from 1 in 1901 to 5 in 1951 to 23 in 1991 to 40 in 2001. Out of the total increase in the country's urban population of 58 million between 1981 and

1991, 44 million were added to Class I cities alone. 28 million persons were added in metropolitan cities.

Urban areas are the engines of productivity and growth in the country. This is manifest in the increasing contribution of urban sector to national income.

Table 3. Urban contribution to national income

Year	Percentage of Urban to total population	Estimated contribution to national income
1951	17.3	29%
1981	23.3	47%
1991	25.7	55%
2001	30.5	60%

Growth of employment (main workers) in urban India during 1981-91 was recorded at 38% against 16% in rural areas and 26.1% in the country as a whole.

ENVIRONMENTAL IMPACTS OF URBANISATION

Some of the chief forces driving urbanisation today are shifting of jobs from agriculture to industry and the concentration of economic opportunities in the urban areas. Urbanisation is associated with higher incomes, improved health, higher literacy, improved quality of life and other benefits. Yet along with the benefits of urbanisation come environmental and social ills. Since with urbanisation the concentration of people is increasing in cities so is the demand for basic necessities like food, energy, drinking water and shelter. The result is in terms of poor quality housing, lack of water supply and sanitation facility and lack of proper waste disposal facility leading to spread of communicable diseases.

Urbanisation affects the environment in three major ways: implications due to urban poverty which is a result of migration, stressed infrastructure and management systems and finally incresing consumerism. These problems warrant major concerns on three accounts. Firstly the prevailing pattern and trend of Urbanisation is more material and energy intensive. Secondly the discharge of pollutants and generation of solid waste in cities is particularly harmful because it is uncontrollable and thirdly the financial, institutional, technological and infrastructure systems available for help to control these problems in the region at present are inadequate.

Urban Waste

Increasing urbanisation is resulting in the generation of increasing amounts of solid waste. It is estimated that 20-50 percent of the solid waste generated remains uncollected. In New Delhi, 3,880 tons of garbage is produced per day, yet only 2,420 tons is collected for disposal. Even if collected, municipal solid waste remains a problem in many cities.

As the living standards are rising the organic content in the waste is reducing and non-biodegradable wastes like metal, plastic and glass are on a rise. Urbanisation and increasing trend of consumerism in cities are the main factors leading to generation of more waste.

Urban Water Quality

Ever increasing urbanisation and their growing amounts of waste have over taxed the natural recycling capabilities of local rivers and lakes. Of the many problems associated with urban effluents, nutrient loading or eutrophication of local waters is one of the most serious problems. Poor water resource management too contributes to water problems.

Urban Transportation

Transportation systems are a major contributor to the decay of urban environment and reduced quality of life in the metropolitan areas due to their contribution to atmospheric emissions, noise and risk of accidents. Increasing vehicular pollution in major urban centers is becoming an area of growing concern. Poor maintenance of vehicles, degraded condition of roads and use of un-pure fuels primarily precipitate the problems of air and noise pollution arising from operation of motorised vehicles.

Urban Air Quality

Urban air quality has deteriorated largely on account of growth in industrial activity, transportation needs and energy production. In India, ambient air quality status derived from a network of 290 stations covering 90 towns and cities in recent years indicates that while suspended particulate matter (SPM) is consistently critical in many cities, the concentration of nitrogen oxides and sulphur dioxide is also increasing and is already transiting from moderate to high to critical levels. As estimated, 2000 metric tones of air pollutants are emitted into the atmosphere everyday, vehicular sources contributing the maximum.

Energy demand: Urbanisation has profound effect on the amount and type of energy consumed. Along with population growth, economic development and industrialisation, urbanisation is one of the principal forces driving the increase in energy demand. Although the traditional rural societies rely heavily upon the human and animal energy and on nearby wood or fuel, today urban societies are characterised by their reliance on fossil fuels and electricity. These patterns of energy use lead to different environmental impacts.

Water Demand

India although has enormous reserve of water, but it still suffers from urban water supply problems. The growing demand of water, along with poor water resource management and mounting pollution levels contributes to water supply problems in and around cities. Urbanisation is leading to change in lifestyle and consumption pattern, which is leading to increased demand for water. As number of people in urban area increases, so does the demand for food and hence for irrigation in agricultural areas close to cities. These pressures can quickly result in demand for water that surpass local water supply.

Poor water management practices exacerbate local water shortages. Inefficient water distribution system is another major source of water loss. Water scarcity is closely linked with water quality. Freshwater lakes and rivers provide affordable and easy accessible water, but uncontrolled discharge of domestic sewage and industrial effluents has left many urban rivers heavily polluted and their water is unsafe for use. Already struggling with uneven distribution of water resources and local water scarcity, the total water demand is projected to double by 2025 in India.

Responses

Rapid urbanisation accounts for most of the renewable and non-renewable resource consumption and waste generation. These long-term ecological concerns are relevant to urbanisation as they grow and prosper, their consumption of resources and generation of wastes will rise accordingly, unless action is taken now to promote the efficient use of resources and minimisation of waste. The challenge is to seek new management approaches that provide both for the needs of urban residents and protect environmental resources on which human life depends. Environmental Management Systems (EMS) is a new management approach for urban local bodies that can lead cities towards eco-cities.

India has entered the new century with a whopping 300 million urban population. Urbanisation continues to increase steadily bringing with it both the benefits of infrastructure growth and the environmental ills. The administrative units of small towns/cities, municipal towns and industrial townships are expected to satisfy a broad spectrum of citizens' needs to provide various facilities and services. It has been observed that within their levels of jurisdiction they are unprepared to address the complex environmental challenges that are confronting them.

Operation and development of urban areas involves:

- Infrastructure development
- Resource utilisation
- Availability of support systems to sustain ever growing population

Therefore, to achieve sustainable development, each operational unit in an urban area needs to manage the environmental aspects arising from its activities and services in a systematic procedure. The EMS framework integrates the environment into everyday business operations, and environmental stewardship becomes part of the daily responsibility of employees and citizens across. At different levels of townships, the relevance of EMS is:

- *At the township administration level:* To integrate environment management and promote the use of a systematic standard procedure in township administration.
- *At the facility level:* To establish a management system in their day to day operation of the facility to minimise the environmental impacts, optimise resource utilisation and manage the waste in a standarised and continual procedure.
- *At the residents level:* To involve all residents in a participatory manner for minimising the environmental impacts arising out of their use of the facilities and in the process of designing, establishing, implementing

and maintaining the management system in a continual manner.

Till date, EMS as per ISO 14001 was widely accepted by industries. Realising the requirements of the management and the residents of the municipalities/towns/townships, Development Alternatives initiated facilitation of EMS in three Industrial townships of India and all the three has been certified for their ISO 14001 implementation. Implementation of EMS in townships is a good role model for other urban local bodies to replicate.

Implementation of EMS for township is much different from implementing EMS for the factory; primarily because the processes in factory are known and the same have controllable parameters measurable on certain yardstick. The processes in township are only partially controllable as the inputs having environmental impacts are generated at individual level (at household level) and the commitment to a cause is unlikely to be uniform. Organisational structure can modulate the output through methodologies adopted, but unless inputs have regulated performance which, could be otherwise inconsistent.

Sustainable Urban Development

Sustainable development means attaining a balance between environmental protection and human economic development and between the present and future needs. It means equity in development and sectorial actions across space and time. It requires an integration of economic, social and environmental approaches towards development. Sustainable urban development refers to attaining social equity and environmental protection in urbanisation while minimising the costs of urbanisation.

UN General Assembly convened a conference on the "human environment" at Stockholm in June 1972, which came out with guiding principles on "human environment". It emphasised that man has the fundamental right to environment of quality and also that he has a responsibility towards protecting the environment for present and future generations. It also maintained that natural resources of the earth must be safeguarded for the benefit of present and future generations.

About a decade later, to address the issues concerning continuing depletion of natural resources and unsustainable development, the World Commission on Environment and Development was created in 1983. Popularly known as Brundt land Commission, it described sustainable development as *"development that meets the needs of the present without compromising the ability of future generations to meet their own needs"*. After twenty years of Stockholm Declaration, the UN Conference on 'Environment and Development' (also known as 'Earth Summit') was held at Rio-de Janeiro in 1992 that adopted an action plan, popularly known as 'Agenda 21'. The agenda 21 promised to reduce poverty, provide clean water and health care, and protect the natural resources and so on.

Also to be noted that some of the Millennium Development Goals have urged for ensuring environmental sustainability and reduction of the percentage of the population under extreme poverty. Similarly, explaining implications of climate change for sustainable development the Intergovernmental Panel on Climate Change notes (IPCC) the importance of social and environmental equity in development. Thus all the major world conferences and initiatives taken so far on environment and development have stressed on economically viable development, socially equitable development and protection of the environment for attaining sustainable development. Sustainable *urban* development specifically means achieving a balance between the development of the urban areas and protection of the environment with an eye to equity in employment, shelter, basic services, social infrastructure and transportation in the urban areas. With rapid expansion of urban population around the world there has arisen a wide awareness about minimising the environmental costs of urbanisation. Concerns are raised at environmental damages and depletion of non-renewable resources and rising levels of pollution in urban areas. In recent times cities have become places of urban environmental degradation and wasteful use of resources, which is proving to be costly to generations present and future. In order to mitigate the problem we require to minimising the depletion of non-renewable resources and resort to environmentally sustainable economic development. But this has to be done in ways that are socially, economically and politically acceptable. While planning for sustainable development of the towns, we should also take into account the factor of climate change. According to this, ensuring environmental sustainability means taking steps, which include

a) integration of the principles of sustainable development in the policies and programmes of the country,
b) reversal of loss of environmental resources,
c) reduction of the proportion of people without sustainable access to safe drinking water,
d) improving the lives of slum dwellers.

Role of Environment and Climate Change in Sustainable Urban Development

While planning for sustainable development of the towns, we should also take into account the factor of climate change. Explaining implications of climate change for sustainable development the Intergovernmental Panel on Climate Change notes "*Sustainable development represents a balance between the goals of environmental protection and human economic development and between the present and future needs. It implies equity in meeting the needs of people and integration of sect oral actions across space and time.*" One of the greatest challenges that the world is facing today is climate change.

Climate change is the variation in the earth's global climates over time. It involves changes in the variability or average state of the atmosphere over durations ranging from decades to millions of years. These changes can be caused by dynamic process on earth, external forces including variations in sunlight intensity and more recently by human activities. Human influences can be by increase in CO_2 levels due to combustion of fossil fuels, aerosols, cement manufacture etc. Other factors like ozone depletion, animal agriculture and deforestation also change climate. The effect of climate change can be found on among other things, on rising sea level that may accelerate coastal erosion, on increasing temperature, on increase in intensity of natural disaster, and very importantly on vector borne diseases. There has been an increasing trend in the annual mean temperature in India. In recent decades the east coast has been experiencing fewer rainy days while the northwest has been experiencing heavy summer monsoon. There have also been some extreme climatic events like heat wave, intense rain, floods and droughts in India.

Researchers have documented the increase in frequency of hot days and multiple-day heat waves in the past century. There has been record rainfall in Mumbai, India on 26 to 27 July 2005, which led to loss of large numbers of lives. Consecutive droughts between 2000 and 2002 caused crop failures, mass starvation and affected millions of people in Orissa. Also, increased water stress poses to be a major problem for India. Accelerated glacier melt is likely to cause increase in the number and severity of glacial melt-related floods, slope destabilisation and a decrease in river flows as glaciers recede. The researchers have predicted that with the current trend in the melt of glaciers, the Ganga, Indus, Brahmaputra and other rivers could likely become seasonal rivers in the near future and affect the lives of people residing around them.

Thus, it is likely that climate change will hamper sustainable development of India as it increases the pressures on natural resources and the environment associated with rapid urbanisation, industrialisation and economic development. In order to reduce the effect of climate change, we need to include climate-proofing concepts in national development initiatives. Urban areas mostly face problems of air quality pollution, green house gases, unsustainable consumption and of inadequate sanitation and water supply.

Thus translated into policy initiatives, environmental sustainability of urban form should aim at energy efficiency in transport and buildings, optimal planning solutions in terms of locations, distances and spaces, which will reduce air and noise pollution. It should also aim at sustainable management of sanitation and water supply, promote equity in provision of services and of course reduce deforestation. The recently announced National Action Plan on Climate Change by the Prime Minister in June 2008 visualises to make economic development of India energy efficient.

All these concerns, questions and initiatives about sustainable environment and climate change have resulted in experiments and debates over city forms that are sustainable. Before discussing the relevant city forms it would be pertinent to discuss the sustainable management of urban basic services and the inefficiency in the land policy in India and its implications for sustainable city form and development in India, which is done in the next part.

Deficiency and Options for Sustainable Management

Deficiencies

Sustainable city planning should aim at achieving social and environmental equity while improving the lives of the people. For that to happen we need to have a sustainable city form as well as provision and proper management of the services. Thus, in order for a city or urban area to be sustainable it needs to produce and manage basic services like water, waste, energy, and transportation in a way that it conforms to the principles of sustainable development. In other words, the city should be able to produce and distribute the services in an economic, environment friendly and equitable way.

Cities in the developing countries are deficient in the provision of basic services that pollute the environment. It is to be noted that though there are some differences between cities and between rich and poor nations, in general urban infrastructure systems are designed without much attention to environmental and social impacts. Mostly the delivery of the services like water, energy, waste, transportation, are based on non-renewable energy sources. Moreover, the inequality in the provision of these services is very high. Indian cities are characterised by high density of population, deficiency in services and air pollution.

Let us see the status regarding these in India. In urban India in 2001, 69 per cent of the households had safe drinking water, 61 per cent of the households had their latrine facilities within their houses and only 35 per cent of the households had closed drainage facilities. Eighty eight per cent (88%) of the urban households had electricity and only 0.2 per cent had solar energy in 2001. In Delhi, the capital city of India, 77 per cent of the urban households had tap as source of drinking water, 63 per cent had their latrine facilities within their premises and 52 per cent of the households had closed drainage facilities. Delhi generated 5922 tonnes of solid waste per day in 2004-05. Air pollution has become a major problem in Indian cities. Taking the case of Delhi, we find that there are around 54 lakh vehicles in Delhi. Around 70 per cent of the air pollution in Delhi happens to be due to vehicles. It has been found in a World Bank study based on 1994-95 air quality data that around 10,000 people die every year prematurely due to air pollution in Delhi alone.

According to Delhi Medical Association the incidence of asthma in Delhi is ten times the national average (Centre for Science and Environment). Densities of Indian cities are very high. Management of the basic services should be done keeping in mind the deficiency in the services, the environmental impacts and the inequality in the provision of the services. Thus we have two issues here, the first one is covering the deficiencies in services and the second one involves how to provide the services in an environment friendly way.

Sustainable Management of Urban Basic Services

Management of Water Supply

The effect of climate change on water supply will be negative in almost all the countries. Thus care should be taken that energy efficient alternative systems are innovated. As for efficient practices, water consumption can be limited by using raw water, recycled water for gardening and landscaping. In the state of Vermont, U.S.A., a waste-water treatment system uses a series of tanks containing plants and other organisms to naturally clean waste-water that serves 500,000 people per year. There have been other scattered evidences of use of waste-water but the example of a city doing it on large scale is rare. In India the water from Sewage Treatment Plants (STP) in factories are used for landscaping and gardening. However, in developing countries the main challenge is to provide clean drinking water to all the urban residents adopting sustainable water management practices. Rainwater harvesting has its possibilities for partially managing water supply. Conservation of old water bodies like lakes, ponds can be made for increased and sustainable water supply. It has been considered as an optional reform under Jawaharlal Nehru National Urban Renewal Mission (JNNURM) in India. In Delhi itself, one after another marsh lands and water bodies are being converted in residential areas, garbage dumps, petrol pumps and so on, the latest victim being the Jahangirpuri marsh land. Marsh lands recharge ground water substantially. Much is yet to be done regarding this in India. Other environmentally sustainable methods can be explored.

Management of Waste

Waste management practices should be started from the production and distribution stages of economic activities through reuse and recycling. Reuse of things like metals, glass, paper, plastic, textiles, organic waste and water will reduce demand for energy, raw materials, fertilisers and fresh water sources. However, care should be taken that hazardous wastes do not go for recycling. Plastic should be used less. In Delhi more than 5000 tonnes of municipal solid waste is generated everyday, which is disposed of in land-fills. Too much land is being consumed for disposal and is creating danger of ground water contamination. As such the department of environment of the government of India recommended that other 'best practices' in waste management should be adopted in a large scale. The practices include, vermi-culture, pelletisation, aerobic composting and so on. A research study by NEERI has recommended mechanical composting as the viable option for such a huge amount of waste. The Supreme Court of

India, hearing public interest litigation on solid waste management of Delhi directed the Municipal Corporation of Delhi to improve the system.

Management of Energy

Energy management practices should be encouraged in the planning of buildings and the city form. Buildings and city forms that are energy efficient and use sustainable energies like solar and wind energies should be considered. There are fragments of evidences in India of settlements using solar power, water recycling techniques and waste management practices. But in general the environment friendly techniques are yet to be practised in urban areas, especially in large cities where the differences would be felt. City forms should be such that it uses energy efficient transport. Coming to the financing part, it can be said that the policies should help energy efficient practices. The loans should be easily available and tax benefits provided for such practices.

Reduction in Inequality

Management of basic services in the cities should reduce inequality in services between rich and poor. The concept of commercial viability does not hold for social services always. City form should take into account social conditions also. The ability of urban poor to pay for the full cost of water supply would remain low in India. Thus reduction in grant of the government and introduction of private sector in this sector is likely to make the situation worse. It is also well known that much of the subsidised schemes in the past have gone to the middle and high-income areas. Apart from deficient, non-environment friendly and unequal basic services, the other major problem in developing a sustainable city form in India is inefficient land policy of the country, which we discuss next.

Inefficiency In Land Policy Of India

Land is an important input for producing goods and services for urban development. Under the conventional analysis, factors of production i.e. land, labour and capital flow to make goods and services but the social and environmental consequences are not reflected in such analysis. Sustainable urban development does take account of social and environmental effects and means balance between the development of the areas and protection of the environment with an eye to equity in employment, shelter, basic services, social infrastructure and transportation in the urban areas. For this to happen, one has to ensure that land is properly used to meet these objectives. Urban India is plagued by shortage of housing facilities and scarcity of land for social overheads like roads, footpaths, parks, schools and so on. The roots of these problems can be found in the inadequate, inefficient, iniquitous land policy of the country. This is why it is important to have an effective and appropriate land policy that would promote sustainable development.

National Commission on Urbanisation of India recognised the need for adequate supply of land, efficiency and equity in allocation of land and promotion of flexibility in land use. Thus it mentioned that the objectives of urban land policy should be:

a) to achieve an optimum social use of urban land,

b) to make land available in adequate quantity to both public authorities and individuals at reasonable prices

c) to encourage cooperative community effort as well as individual builders to develop land and construct houses,

d) to prevent concentration of land in few hands,

e) to use land to finance urban development,

f) to encourage socially and economically efficient allocation of land so that land development conserves resources and land utilisation is optimal,

g) to promote flexibility in land use in response to a growing city.

Also, the Eleventh Five Year Plan of India emphasises, "governments at appropriate levels including local authorities, have to strive to remove all possible obstacles that may hamper equitable access to land". It identifies failure to adopt appropriate urban land policies and land management practices as the primary cause of inequity and poverty. Thus the Eleventh Five year Plan calls for a flexible land policy which will make conversion from one use to another, cost efficient and promote equity. It judges that urban planning tools like master planning, zoning and regulations are not enough for the requirement of land supply for rapid urbanisation. The problem has also been addressed somewhat by Jawaharlal Nehru Urban Renewal Mission in India.

Sustainable City Form

Thus one side of the problem is inefficient land policy, which blocks supply of land for efficient and equitable housing, social infrastructure, basic services and transportation. The other side of the problem is how best or optimal the urban areas can be planned so that the *urban form* can be sustainable. In recent times cities have been found to pollute the environment and deplete the natural resources. This has prompted the need for finding an urban form that will be sustainable. Various ideas have come up with solutions. One such idea for sustainable urban form is compact city. This necessarily means a high density, mixed land use and efficient public transport planning, which encourages pedestrian oriented habitation. It may be high-rise like Hong Kong or low rise as suggested by National

Commission on Urbanisation (NCU) of India and so on. It should be remembered that "high density" is a relative term depending on the culture and the environment of the country.

The two important issues about high-density cities are the costs and benefits of the form and how dense should it be and "higher than what"? The two main benefits of compact city are reduced dependency on private cars and preservation of greenery while the main costs are more air pollution, noise, crime and overcrowding. A literature review of the various studies finds social and environmental benefits of compactness of a city. The benefits can be summarised as

a) protection of the countryside, green space and bio-diversity;

b) reduction of travel distance, emission, greenhouse gases and thus global warming;

c) reduction of materials for construction of infrastructure;

d) have economies of scale in providing social institutional services like hospitals, banks and

e) in having a better interactive community life.

The various costs have been found as

a) exploiting open and green urban spaces;

b) overcrowding;

c) traffic congestion;

d) ill health;

e) crime and

f) high-energy demand in compact high-rise buildings.

But the relationship is not so simple. The concept has been developed in relation to developed economies with sprawling areas but it has not been tested adequately on high-density developing countries. However, a study conducted in China measures the urban compactness of the city. This study may be somewhat relevant for Indian cities because both have high population densities and both are developing countries.

The study measures compactness by the non-agricultural population density in built-up area of the city. It tests the argument that urban compactness exploits the economies of scale for public services (e.g. schools, public buses, public utilities) and environmental resources (e.g. land, petrol and water). It also examines that too much compactness may cause negative environmental externalities. To examine the arguments in Chinese context 16 representative variables on environmental aspects were taken.

To implement compact city form policy, it is necessary to maximise the advantage and minimise the disadvantage. It finds that urban compactness of the 45 core Chinese cities will improve accessibility of services, reduce per capita domestic energy consumption and more or less promote infrastructure efficiency and use of public transport. But compactness i.e. high population density aggravates negative externalities, like, air pollution, noise and loss of green space. It also finds that environment efficiency is positive up to a level of approximately 168 persons per hectare. National Commission on Urbanisation (NCU) of India recommended low-rise high density (LRHD) built-form for Indian cities. It explains that such form is less expensive to maintain and has the advantages of security of neighbourhood protection.

Most important of all is that it satisfies the criteria of *equity*. It says "income profile and afford ability considerations suggest that a range of small and medium plot sizes, between 25 sq m to 100 sq m (with some plots perhaps up to 200 sq m) can satisfy the needs of over 95 per cent of the urban population". The Commission explains that this typology is more economical than apartments because no space is required for public circulation and lifts and also it provides much better living conditions. It would also reduce the disparities in our urban areas.

According to this form, a 50 sq m plot per family with five members will generate a net density of 1000 persons per hectare (i.e. a gross residential density of 500 persons per hectare). Similarly, a 100 sq m plot would generate a gross residential density of 250 persons per hectare. It also states that high gross densities found in inner city can be tackled by interventions in city structure and by adjusting land use allocation in within the city itself to create spaces for social overheads. Its recommendations for built form specifies that residential sites should be provided so that 1) 50 per cent of the lands are in plots between 25 to 100 sq m, 2) 25 per cent of the land are in the plots between 100 to 200 sq m and 3) 25 per cent of the land are in these or any other sizes. The Commission also recommended that, "these plots should be leased out not to individuals buyers, but to co-operative societies. Should the members of a cooperative society decide to pool their land and build group housing or apartments, they should be free to do so, provided the total number of dwelling units remains the same. This maintains the principle of urban equity and, at the same time, allows the construction of apartment buildings at higher FARs." The report also says that, "as long as our cities remain within density thresholds (i.e. neighbourhood densities of 250 to 1,000 persons /ha) there are efficient and cost effective solutions within our resources."

Talking about densities, it points out that the densification can be increased at selected nodal points depending on the holding capacity of the area. It should be related to the mass transport network. Though the net densities recommended by NCU seems to be on higher side, it would be worth mentioning that cities in India are rather densely populated. The cities of India are already compact if seen by the standard of densities. As concluded in the case of Chinese cities the negative externalities of high population density may be relevant for the cities of India as well. For example, high population density aggravates negative externalities, like, air pollution, noise and loss of green space. But like the high density Chinese cities high population density may improve accessibility of services, reduce per capita domestic energy consumption and more or less promote infrastructure efficiency and use of public transport. However, there is dearth of study to support this in the Indian context. Other options like *multi-modal urban region* may provide some solution with the help of transport, which can be environmentally sustainable. This will be discussed next.

Multi-modal Urban Region

Transport has an important role in meeting the goals of urban sustainability. One of the challenges of a sustainable urban form is to meet the economic performance objectives and environmental sustainability of a city at the same time. It may be useful to build multi modal urban region and supply transport to take care of the different urban and economic activities. For this to happen the land use and transport policies will have to match the demand of different activities. The idea is to create a city that performs well economically and conforms to the objectives of environmental sustainability. In order to be economically efficient a city needs to reduce production costs, e.g. costs of receiving inputs and distributing outputs. It also needs to reduce travel time between the different related companies, between the company and the workers' homes. At the same time the enlargement of the space of the urban labour market enables the companies to choose from a large pool of workers and also gives the workers a variety of jobs to choose from. An economically efficient city also creates economies of scale for services and housing markets. It has been argued by Prud'homme and Lee that actual extent of the spatial markets engaged in economic functioning rather than the city size is what matters. Also the jobs those are accessible rather than those showed in statistics that are significant. Two more factors namely, the speed of its transport system and the geographical spread of activities affect economic performance.

The combination of speed, size and spread determines the effective labour market according to Prud'homme and Lee. Ken worthy and Lobe comparing the data on speed and spread of 46 cities of the world found that, American cities use cars, have higher speed and travel distance and low land use density. On the other extreme, rich Asian cities like Hong Kong, Tokyo and Singapore use slow speed public transport, travel less distances and have concentrated land use density. European cities use public transport as well as cars and have moderate densities of land use. Thus the challenge is to find an urban form, which gives an effective size of urban market by combining land use policies and transport alternatives.

Two factors are important in this regard which are accessibility i.e. acceptable time and environmental sustainability i.e. reducing costs like CO_2 emissions, air pollution, traffic noise. One solution that has been offered in the literature is multi modal urban region. The idea is to create an environment friendly transport system and create activity places that are reachable within acceptable time limits. For this to happen, activity locations should be created which can be reached:

a) without moving, by walking, by cycling,

b) by public transport,

c) by energy efficient cars.

Land-use and transportation implications of this is to create:

a) multi-functional homes/work-places which does not need travel,

b) develop multi-functional neighbourhoods, which can be accesses by walking, cycling,

c) develop nodes having functional concentrations that can be reached by public transport and

d) develop multi-functional urban regions which can be reached by energy efficient cars.

In Randstad, the highly urbanised west of the Netherlands, modal specialisation are found to hold for relationships between different areas. In 1997, it was found that within the large city bicycle dominates the mode, the train is used considerably between the large cities while car is the dominant mode for other middle and long destinations. This also gives an indication of the possibility of polycentric developments in sustainable city form. However, much needs to be researched on to get an optimal solution and may be for different conditions.

National transport policy of India, 2006, advocated public transport and recommended to promote road transport, which are energy efficient, conserves environment and meets social demand. It noted that it is needed to promote public transport to reduce negative externalities, like air pollution and congestion. It also advised to promote Non-Motorised transport. The national policy recommended, "Transit Oriented Development" with high-density areas and urged for developing new satellite towns along major transport corridors. It also discourages sprawl through taxes and fees.

Like most of the developing countries, in India a large percentage of people travel by cycling and walking by compulsion as they are poor and cannot afford motorised transport. Walking and cycling has an inverse relation with city size in India. But then it varies among the large cities. For example, in Delhi walking and cycling is more common than in Mumbai and Kolkata. Perhaps Mumbai and Kolkata's better public transport explains the difference. Lack of good public transport in Delhi has resulted in use of private cars. It may be mentioned here that Delhi Transport Corporation (DTC) has recently introduced air conditioned bus services in some routes and is making profits. More such options in other routes may reduce use of private cars. One should keep in mind that low density sprawled development makes it difficult for public transport system to survive. This makes a case for high-density polycentric development with multi modal region.

2

Human Settlements in Peri-urban Areas

Third World cities are divided into two distinct sectors: formal and informal, or urban and peri-urban. Peri-urban and informal sector settlements are also commonly referred to as squatter settlements, marginal settlements, shanty towns, urban slums, or illegal settlements. A consensus definition of peri-urban areas or urban informal sectors has been difficult to achieve among practitioners and researchers; however, there is general agreement to include settlements that are marginal to the physical and regulatory boundaries of the formal city. In other words, local and national governments consider the urban formal sector legitimate, but do not approve of peri-urban/informal sector settlements.

Peri-urban settlements largely develop outside of government control and do not follow strictly formal and traditional urban planning and development processes. It is important to note, though, that the peri-urban sector is not monolithic and, more often than not, informal settlement development is a hybrid of formal and informal systems.

Peri-urban areas are characterised by uncertain or illegal land tenure, minimal or no infrastructure, low incomes, and lack of recognition by formal governments. Families who live in informal settlements build on the cheaper land outside city limits, on land within city limits that is not zoned for housing, on land that has not been urbanised with infrastructure, or on land considered dangerous or environmentally fragile. Many informal settlements begin as land invasions with families illegally squatting on the land.

Other informal settlements begin with the legal landowner illegally subdividing and selling the land without formal land registration or basic service provisions. Families often pay the former owner or occupant the full purchase price, but receive in return no registered title to the land. They generally do not participate in local government and are unconnected to the municipal service network. Finally, they tend to be ignored by municipal authorities, who find themselves overwhelmed by the informal sector sheer numbers and needs, which far outstrip the capacity of the local planners and government.

The peri-urban population should, therefore, be a focus of concern. Spatially, peri-urban areas are growing much more rapidly than formal urban districts; in many cities, the peri-urban sections are already bigger than the formal areas. Their rapid growth and informal status have resulted in low levels of sanitation services. The lack of these services in particular, inadequate excreta (human waste) management threatens the public health and environment of the peri-urban settlement, as well as the urban area as a whole. But even the few institutions that recognise the problem and want to do something about it find that little knowledge or experience exists about how to address this problem constructively.

Characteristics of Peri-urban Areas

This section identifies the common characteristics of peri-urban areas, especially those that distinguish them from rural and formal urban areas. It also identifies common sanitation practices in peri-urban settlements.

An estimated 600 million people in urban areas of the Third World now live in life and health threatening homes and neighbourhoods, primarily in peri-urban settlements. These homes and neighbourhoods share two characteristics that bear serious potential health effects:

1. The presence of pathogenic microorganisms (especially those in human excreta), caused by lack of infrastructure and related inadequate water supply to remove them
2. Crowded, cramped housing conditions The removal and safe disposal of excreta and waste water from washing, bathing, and other domestic uses in peri-urban settlements are critical health and environmental needs. Many rivers in Third World cities are literally large open sewers. Surface and ground-water contamination is widespread in many developing countries, and the resulting environmental degradation is more and more apparent along rivers and sea coastal areas.

Impact on Health and the Environment

Most urban areas (both informal and formal) in Africa and Asia, including many cities with one million or more inhabitants, have no effective means of off-site disposal of excreta (for example, water-borne sewage systems or collection and treatment systems for latrine contents). Rivers, streams, canals, gullies, and ditches are the destinations of most untreated human excrement and household waste. Such waste accumulates on streets, in open spaces between houses, in stagnant pools of water, and on wasteland.

Latin American cities are a little better off. The formal urban areas in most of these cities have some collection and distribution systems; however, most existing systems are in disrepair. The recent cholera epidemic in Latin America, for example, has been partly attributed to the contamination of water distribution systems by adjacent leaky sewage pipes. In addition, most water-borne sewage collected is disposed untreated into rivers that also serve as sources of water for drinking, bathing for families living in peri-urban settlements, and irrigation for farmers living downstream. Moreover, as in Africa and Asia, the growing peri-urban areas throughout Latin America, which often make up more than 50 percent of a cites population, lack sewerage or latrine collection systems (Table 1).

Table 1. Estimated Percentage of Third World Urban Population Without Sanitation Services (1987)

City	*Country*	*Present urban population without sanitation services*
Luanda	Angola	71
Lusaka	Zambia	66
Karachi	Pakistan	51
Bogotá	Colombia	45
Manila	Philippines	35
Nairobi	Kenya	35
Lima	Peru	33
Caracas	Venezuela	30
Mexico City	Mexico	30
Tunis	Tunisia	30
Ankara	Turkey	24
São Paulo	Brazil	22

The crowding of large numbers of people in peri-urban areas creates conditions very favourable to the rapid spread of a variety of infectious diseases, often in the form of disastrous epidemics such as the previously cited cholera outbreak in Latin America. Indeed, an increasing volume of literature suggests that health problems resulting from a lack of sanitation facilities (among other factors) are greater among the urban poor living in overcrowded peri-urban settlements than they are either in the rest of the urban areas or in rural areas. A recent World Bank study suggests that, in contrast to higher-income urban dwellers and some rural population, the urban poor have a lower life expectancy at birth and a higher infant mortality rate . A variety of intestinal parasites is usually present in poor urban population, with roundworms and whipworm often observed at higher levels of incidence than in corresponding rural population. Likewise, the accumulation of waste water as a result of the limited soil area to absorb it in densely settled urban areas has led to increased transmission of filariasis in many cities.

The fundamental reason for undertaking urban sanitation improvement programs is to improve health, but in general it has been difficult to demonstrate a causal relationship between the two, although a recent WASH study concluded at least that sanitation interventions in urban areas had a higher health impact than do water supply interventions.

In addition to threatening health, the lack of excreta management systems in Third World cities is having a tremendous negative effect on the environment contaminating surface and ground-water with organics, nutrients, and solids. Because of their current and growing size and density, and their lack of adequate infrastructure, peri-urban areas are the largest source of focal contamination in cities. Men, women, and children often defecate on open ground. Their faces wash down the hillsides through various neighbourhoods or through low-lying flood plains to a river or other water source. Many cities are literally awash in excreta.

Even in communities where widespread use of pit latrines has been achieved, human waste can still harm the environment. Unlike sparsely settled rural areas, peri-urban settlements have high population densities, and the sheer numbers of closely spaced latrines can overwhelm the carrying capacity of soils and pollute underground aquifers.

The lack of adequate sanitation systems for families living in these growing peri-urban areas is a major contributor to water pollution in the city. Removing and disposing of excreta in ways that prevent human contact are central to reducing the burden of disease and environmental degradation. This degradation uncontrolled and far reaching is in itself as compelling a justification for action as the impact of inadequate sanitation on health.

Population Growth in Peri-Urban Areas

The world is becoming increasingly urban. Urban areas of developing countries are growing faster than either the urban areas of developed countries or the rural areas of the developing world. The population of some urban areas doubled during the International Drinking Water Supply and Sanitation Decade (1981-90). Between 1980 and the year 2000, 85 percent of the worlds urban growth is expected to take place in developing countries. According to United Nations data, 1.3 billion people, or approximately 25 percent of the Third World population, now live in urban centres; by the year 2020, it is anticipated that more than 50 percent of the population in the developing world will be living in cities. The estimated annual growth rate of the developing worlds urban areas will range from 1.5 percent in Latin American cities to 4.8 percent in African cities. Between 75 and 90 percent of this growth will take place in the peri-urban or informal sector. By the year 2000, the exploding growth in Third World settlements that do not benefit from formal urban infrastructure could result in as many as one billion people living without adequate excreta disposal.

Characteristics That Set Peri-Urban Areas Apart

Peri-urban settlements have a number of unique characteristics that distinguish them from formal urban and rural areas; these characteristics are outlined below.

Poor Physical Site Conditions and Complicated Site Layouts

Poor urban families searching for a plot of land on which to build a home are strongly influenced by the existing market prices for urban land; inevitably the land that is most desirable for residential construction is the most expensive. The more affordable sites are areas that are undesirable for formal development, such as those located on steep slopes, along gullies and ravines, on soil that is too rocky to excavate easily, in desert lands, or in areas prone to flooding. Poor families move on to these lands because they are relatively cheap to purchase or because illegal occupation of such sites is less likely to be challenged.

Since informal urban settlers lack technical know-how and assistance, they often develop their areas haphazardly, without allowing adequate space for installing infrastructure lines. Urban settlers in parts of Africa and Asia build their houses according to village traditions that is, patterned according to family formation, with houses directly abutting their neighbours on all sides, with no room left for service right-of-ways.

Limited Water Availability

Most peri-urban settlements do not generally have piped water; instead, increasingly they have water vendors who sell water at market cost, which is significantly higher than what families in the urban formal sector pay. Not only is the cost higher on a per-liter basis, but it also consumes a higher percentage of family household income.

The vended water in peri-urban areas is mostly of poor quality, and because of its high cost, families can buy only a limited amount of it. The limited availability of water leads to major sanitation problems when purchasers are forced to set priorities that may compromise public health; for example, peri-urban families are not apt to purchase water to flush a toilet.

Some peri-urban families have access either to a standpipe nearby or to water piped into the house. But, in either case, this water is usually limited in quantity and is erratic in flow. This leads to low levels of personal and domestic hygiene and thus favours the transmission of excreta-related infections.

High-Density Population

Demographic data are lacking for peri-urban areas. Because these communities are illegal and for the most part are not recognised by the formal sector, municipal tax, health, or other records do not exist for most of them. Typically, however, peri-urban settlements have a high population density often greater than 400 people per hectare. High population density without basic infrastructure entails greater health and environmental risks than those found in rural and formal urban areas. Moreover, a growing number of peri-urban areas (especially in the Middle East) have vertical construction, that is multi-family, multi-story housing that increases population density dramatically.

Organisation of Communities and Social Characteristics

Peri-urban settlements, in general, are not homogeneous with respect to ethnic background, income level, language, and social norms. Residents have migrated to these settlements from various parts of a region or country or, in many cases, from other countries. This heterogeneity often leads to misunderstandings and distrust among neighbours and may result in minimal contact between neighbours. Consequently, a broad-based sense of community often is lacking in peri-urban settlements. Nevertheless, community organisations can and do exist, often formed around an issue of universal interest to the settlement, such as school construction.

Among important forms of organisation, at least in the early stages after a peri-urban community is established, are the neighbourhood associations created in response to the problems connected with the establishment of the communities, that is, the need for security of land tenure and for basic urban services. These associations serve the dual functions of coordinating neighbourhood self-help activities and of providing the link between the communities and government authorities.

In cases of settlement by organised invasion, the makings of such organisations already exist before the communities themselves are formed. In cases of settlement by encroachment and purchase, individuals initially make what arrangements they can with respect to transportation, lighting, water supply, excreta disposal, and so on. Eventually, small groups and communities begin to form to address common concerns, as the settlers realise that without organisation they stand little chance of obtaining services from the government or any other outside agency. An important aspect of the socio-demographic composition of peri-urban population is the fact that a large number of households are headed by women. A disproportionate number of these female-headed households also fall in the lowest-income brackets. In addition, a significant percentage of peri-urban population is made up of children.

Legal Land Tenure and Lack of Government Recognition and Services

In most countries, a strict application of development regulations denies the legality of land and buildings developed in peri-urban communities. Laws governing property rights, land acquisitions, registration and transfer of titles, development regulations, taxation of real estate, and municipal institutions often were introduced by former colonial rulers. These laws and urbanisation standards were essentially adaptations of European models of urban planning that may no longer suit modern conditions in developing countries. In most developing countries, the existing legal, formal land development market is grid-locked by overregulation and its corresponding costs. This has been a major contributing factor to the creation of an illegal informal land market that is unencumbered by controls.

Because prohibitive costs lock them out of formally developed areas, in most peri-urban communities, occupants are in violation of tenure laws and/or development regulations. Residents of peri-urban areas often do not have legal land tenure, and, in most cases, the site itself has not been legally urbanised. Therefore, governments generally do not recognise the legality of these settlements.

Low Income Levels and Reliance on the Informal Economy

As noted above, families settle in peri-urban areas for rational reasons, primarily because land prices or rents are low. A significant percentage of the population of Third World cities cannot afford the formal sectors housing, even when costs are cut to a bare minimum. The economic crisis in many developing countries has reduced the purchasing power of low-income families and limited even further their ability to pay for formal sector housing or services. Many households in peri-urban areas do not enjoy a regular income, and large numbers of peri-urban households are headed by single women who in turn tend to have the lowest income levels of all workers.

Families in rural areas are for the most part not in the cash economy. Their life is more agricultural subsistence. In contrast, in formal urban areas, most families do operate in the cash economy as workers and have access to steady jobs, pay taxes, and so on. In peri-urban areas, families are also in the cash economy but their workers rely mainly on the informal economy (for example, carpenters working out of their backyards or women selling tortillas in the market). Though poor, they nonetheless make and spend money. Because cash in the informal economy is unsteady and unreliable, residents are not deemed creditworthy and cannot get conventional bank loans.

The Role of Informal Businesses

Informal businesses play a significant role in the construction and urbanisation of peri-urban settlements, whereas in rural areas, the community provides self-help (free or donated labour) for construction (for example, the digging of latrine pits). Sometimes a local non-governmental organisation (NGO) is hired to do the construction, or a local formal sector contractor is hired. In peri-urban areas, the existing practice is that most sanitation infrastructure is built by local private builders or manufacturers in the informal sectors. For example, a local manufacturer might produce toilet seats in the families backyard workshop, and local carpenters or masons might be hired to construct latrines.

Limited Political Influence

Because peri-urban settlements are not recognised as legal areas, their community leaders and residents have limited political influence. People living in peri-urban areas are not illegal their houses are, but even though the people living in these settlements are not illegal residents per se, they are mostly economically poor, marginalised, and uneducated, and historically have held limited political power. Residents in formal urban areas, on the other hand, enjoy the status of being recognised as constituents to whose needs politicians must respond in order to stay in office.

A political change is beginning to occur in peri-urban areas, however. Peri-urban residents can represent an enormous voting block and can have a major influence on elections. Yet, after elections, their political clout becomes limited because they do not know how to use the system by organising into political pressure groups. Furthermore, given the heterogeneous nature of most peri-urban settlements, the united strength and community organising around local issues that are visible in many rural and formal urban areas are not as apparent in peri-urban areas. Peri-urban residents in most places are less visible and vocal to municipal leaders.

In theory, decentralisation and democratisation should give informal settlements greater leverage and visibility. Also, in theory, once the urban poor have voting rights and representation, they will keep in office those politicians who manage resources wisely and respond to their needs. At present, however, those holding leadership positions in most peri-urban settlements do not necessarily represent the interests of the wide range of subgroups in these settlements.

Common Sanitation Practices

Peri-urban communities overwhelmingly lack adequate arrangements for waste disposal. Waste water from bathing and washing is typically spilled right outside shelters, where it may soak into the ground or form stagnant pools in poorly drained areas. Where sewers exist, they are virtually always open drainage canals. The ground by the side of the shelters or in alleyways serves as a frequent substitute for urinals. In general, residents have improvised sanitation systems in peri-urban areas to satisfy their perceived needs (privacy and convenience, for example), and as materials and labour become available. Some of the most common sanitation practices in peri-urban areas are described below.

1. *No system:* Defecation occurs in open areas within the settlement, on the perimeter of the settlement, or in drainage ditches. The lack of any planned waste

disposal system is characteristic of most peri-urban areas.

2. *Latrines:* Use of latrines is the second most common sanitation practice in peri-urban regions. A wide range of latrines can be found in peri-urban areas, including bucket latrines, pit latrines, and ventilated improved pit (VIP) latrines. In Asia, some systems for excreta removal from latrine pits exist, either through buckets or vacuum trucks, but in other areas excreta removal is not common. Latrines in peri-urban areas are often poorly designed and maintained and may not be used by all family members.

3. *Pour-flush toilets/septic tanks:* In peri-urban settlements experiencing regular or even irregular water supplies, pour-flush toilets with soak-away or septic tanks may exist, relying either on household or community septic tanks. However, the septic tanks often are poorly maintained or undersised.

Peri-Urban Sanitation Challenges

Why should peri-urban areas be distinguished from rural and urban areas for sanitation improvement activities? This section addresses this question and presents the unique challenges to sanitation improvement in peri-urban areas.

Demand-Driven Sanitation Interventions

A major difference between urban and peri-urban program design challenges is that the former are supply driven, and the latter are demand driven. Supply driven is used here to denote the traditional/conventional urbanisation process whereby a supply of housing stock is developed and then offered to the public for sale. This process can be summarised as follows:

1. Land use rights are legally transferred (usually sold).

2. The land use is changed (usually from agricultural to residential).
3. The land is subdivided into plots or parcels.
4. The land is registered in the new owners name.
5. The land is developed by installing basic urban services such as water, sewage and drainage, roads, and electricity.
6. A house is built on the land.
7. The house is put on the market and sold.
8. The house is occupied by a family.

In a supply-driven urbanisation process, the human factor does not enter into the equation until the end of the process.

Demand driven is used here to denote the more common urbanisation process that exists in peri-urban areas. This process can be generalised as follows:

1. Individual families or a large group of families need housing.
2. Unserviced but affordable land is ?acquired@ either through invasions or through informal purchases.
3. Individual houses are built, usually with rustic building materials (these initial houses usually do not meet building standards and usually have no provision for basic sanitation).
4. Families use their new home base to enter into the informal economy and start accumulating capital.
5. The houses are incrementally improved according to household priorities and available capital; this stage may include the construction of an improved latrine.
6. Communities get organised and start ?demanding@ that municipal authorities provide them with basic urban services such as electricity, roads, water, and sewage.

7. After infrastructure is installed, land is then legalised and registered by municipal authorities.

In this demand-driven process, people move in before the water supply, sanitation, and other infrastructure exist. Once they are on the land and have a house, their demand for infrastructure evolves.

In the peri-urban sector, a controlled supply-driven process is not possible; people reside in the areas before any formal development takes place and they live in overcrowded conditions. Sanitation improvements are more critical in crowded urban areas where population densities are very high, diseases are more common, and the assimilative capacity of the environment has been exceeded. These areas require a demand-oriented government response, which is quite different from the controlled and orderly process of most formal urban planning and development. The government action should be responsive to the demands and needs of families already living in peri-urban areas and be tailored to the conditions of the settlements.

It is important to keep in mind, however, that the demand by the community for sanitation improvements may be low compared with the demand for water, electricity, drainage, roads, or solid waste removal. Residents in peri-urban settlements often have higher priorities than excreta disposal to which to allot their scarce financial and other resources.

Political Motives

To address these features and the peculiar needs they elicit, the project designer and implementer must deal with engineers, legal specialists, financial analysts, social scientists, urban planners, and a wide range of institutions, such as the water and sanitation utility, the Ministry of Health, urban development authorities, and municipalities.

Because of the high visibility of these urban slum areas, and their higher numbers of people, the involvement of politicians is greater than it is in rural or formal urban sectors. The result can be a scenario involving a clash of values for example, the A.I.D. Development planner or NGO community organiser who favours assistance to peri-urban areas versus the politicians who prefer to help formal developments. Therefore, the choice of intervention sites can become politicised. In other words, political interest can become a criterion in site selection, rather than need or feasibility.

Conflict of Interest or Goals

Similar to motives that surface in political conflicts, the donors interest or goal may be to improve sanitation for peri-urban residents, whereas municipal authorities may see a sanitation intervention in an illegal settlement as counter to their interest. In most cases, this interest is *not* to formalise peri-urban settlements and thereby make them more permanent. The fundamental issue is this: Unless project designers can in the beginning of the process get a political commitment from the mayor or other key decision-maker to agree to sanitation interventions in illegal settlements, or to make illegal settlements legal, any further work on project design could prove to be fruitless.

Lack of Data

In contrast to rural and formal urban areas, statistics relating to residents of peri-urban areas (and their needs) are not gathered in many Latin American and African countries. Thus it becomes extremely difficult to analyse overall data about peri-urban settlements. Without bank mortgages or building permits, who can say how many houses are built each year? When people in these settlements do not show up on employers payrolls, how can one tell how many are employed or what incomes they earn? Without health records, who can detect their mortality or morbidity rates? When they pirate water from public aqueducts, buy it from vendors, or use home-made septic tanks or pits, how can their water consumption and level of sanitation be assessed?

A lack of real data makes it difficult to determine how many peri-urban houses lack access to sanitation systems and what kinds of systems would be most appropriate to introduce.

Cheap Land/Expensive Infrastructure

Ironically, for very rational reasons the urban poor settle on the cheapest land, which also requires the most expensive infrastructure. It is more costly to put low-cost systems on steep slopes or in flood plains than to put them on dry, flat ground. Even pit latrines, a very low-cost option, can be more expensive to construct in peri-urban settlements than in rural areas.

Limited Technologies Appropriate to Peri-Urban Areas

Because of the unique characteristics of peri-urban areas, the technological lessons learned from sanitation interventions in rural and formal urban areas are not always applicable to peri-urban sites. To date, construction of latrines has been the main sanitation intervention funded by external support agencies, including for projects in peri-urban areas. Latrines, however, have been shown to have serious limitations in the peri-urban sector. They usually are not feasible at population densities above 250 to 350 persons per hectare, and most peri-urban areas have population densities above 350 persons per hectare. For this reason, technologies appropriate to peri-urban areas are limited. In many high-density informal settlements, there will be little, if any, space available to dig a new pit after the existing one fills up. Often, not enough space exists for even the first pit. Pit latrines also are impractical for multi-story housing. In addition, soil conditions in most peri-urban settlements are often too rocky or too steep, contain too much clay, or have too high a water table to make latrines feasible.

Health, Environmental, and Social Considerations

Improving community excreta sanitation in peri-urban areas is a complex endeavour. Choosing and building the right technology is only one of the areas that must be addressed in this process. Other concerns that must be considered include health, the environment, and social/community organisation.

Sanitation-Related Health Benefits

One of the more compelling justifications for improving community sanitation is improving health, yet the health benefits associated with improved sanitation are difficult to quantify. While this can be said about any location, it is particularly true in peri-urban areas. Part of the problem, is that baseline health information usually does not exist for peri-urban areas. Municipal governments usually do not keep records on peri-urban settlements, including information on current health status, environmental conditions, or existing sanitation coverage.

Another part of the problem is that certain environmental factors, such as intermittent water supply and poor drainage, interfere with accurate predictions of health effects of improved sanitation. The many environmental determinants that can have an impact on health in urban areas. The consequent lack of clear information and conclusions makes it difficult to rank the desirability of improving sanitation on the basis of health benefits. Therefore, if the justification for a peri-urban sanitation project is improved health, it will be complicated and expensive to measure health improvement resulting from a proposed peri-urban sanitation project.

Degree of Health Benefits as a Factor of Sanitation Level

Beyond the question of how improved sanitation improves health is the question of the relationship between the stages of improved sanitation and the degrees of improved health. Peri-urban sanitation improvements tend to evolve in rather large steps: from nothing to pit latrines to pour-flush toilets to full sewerage. Bateman and Smiths 1991 WASH study showed that the proportion of children stunted in Guatemalan urban areas was directly associated with the level of sanitation service . Stunting was lower in children who had access to a flush toilet when compared with those with access to latrines and to those without access to sanitary services.

The same WASH study showed that stunting was also associated with community levels of sanitation. Individual household sanitation improvements did not have a significant health impact if the surrounding households also did not improve their sanitation. The authors found that sanitation coverage of 75 percent or more of a densely populated community is needed before a health impact is apparent. Therefore, the project approach to sanitation improvement in peri-urban areas should focus on community-wide improvements, not on individual households. By contrast, in rural areas, where houses are further apart, the approach to sanitation improvement has largely been toward households.

The study found that children with access to flush toilets in their household but who lived in a community with a low level of sanitation coverage had 1.67 times the risk of stunting compared with those living in a community with high levels of sanitation coverage. More remarkable was the finding that children with no individual access to a toilet and living in a community with a high level of sanitation coverage have no increased risk of stunting compared with children with individual access to a toilet living in a community with a high level of sanitation coverage. These findings indicate that community measures of sanitation are better indicators of health risk than is individual access to improved sanitation.

From a program point of view, in a peri-urban water and sanitation program that expects to improve health, sanitation should receive the same degree of attention and resources as water supply. Further, to increase the health benefits of sanitation improvements, the most important goal and evaluation indicator is not improved individual level of service, but improved community sanitation to the point that at least 75 percent of the community has access to adequate sanitation services and uses them properly.

Transferring Excreta Off-Site

In examining the health effects of sanitation technologies, one must also evaluate threats posed by systems that transfer excreta off-site. Cortege systems and water-borne sewage, for example, result in the transfer of health risks off-site along with the excreta (if the waste is not treated, as it usually is not).

The health risks related to transferring excreta off-site can be reduced or increased depending on the situation. If sewage, for example, is treated and disposed of in a river away from people, health risks probably will be reduced. On the other hand, if untreated sewage is disposed of directly into a river that serves as an untreated drinking water supply, risks will likely be higher than if no sanitation improvements were made. Similarly, if sewage and night soil collected from latrines are discharged in the local environment or used untreated, the health risks are simply transferred and not necessarily reduced. That succeeded in providing improved sanitation to individual households but failed to dispose of the sullage. The result threatened the community with perhaps a more serious health problem than what existed before the project began.

Environmental Issues

The lack of adequate peri-urban sanitation provisions has grave environmental consequences that indirectly jeopardise human health. Peri-urban areas are the largest non-point source of focal contamination in a given city. The inadequate disposal of human waste contaminates surface and ground-water with organic compounds, nutrients, and solids. Organic compounds decompose in receiving waters, depleting oxygen and harming some aquatic life. Nutrients can be toxic to fish and humans and can cause eutrophication (the excessive growth of algae and aquatic plants utilising the nutrients which can lead to decreased oxygen concentrations when the algae and plants die and decay). Solids decay using up oxygen and can harm benthic organisms living at the bottom of water bodies.

Reducing such environmental contamination via improved sanitation technologies can be more compelling to development decision-makers than is improving general health, as can be seen in the following example from Kumasi, Ghana. A year study by the World Bank on sanitation in Kumasi estimated that 24,100 cubic meters of focal waste was generated by Kumasis 600,000 people every month. The types of sanitation technologies used by the Kumasi population included public latrines, bucket latrines, flush toilets (into septic tanks), pit latrines, and nothing (bushes). Independent of the type of sanitation technology or disposal system, the World Bank study showed that 21,600 cubic meters of the total focal waste (90%) eventually flowed untreated into the underground aquifers and streams. The environmental effects of such a quantity certainly would impress upon decision-makers the need to re-examine the sanitation system on hand.

SOCIAL CONSIDERATIONS

Community Organisation and Participation

Citizen involvement has been found to be a key ingredient in the success of peri-urban sanitation projects. Community participation can lead to cost reductions, increased cost recovery, and more effective operation and maintenance of systems. The Working Group on Urbanisation (WG/U) of the Water Supply and Sanitation Collaborative Council, an international organisation, recently reviewed 271 documents describing 67 peri-urban water supply and sanitation (WS&S) projects. Thirty-one of the 67 projects were reported to have been successful; 19 of these attributed a major role in their success to citizen participation.

The lack of a common social composition in peri-urban areas can make organising for community participation difficult, however. The major shared feature of peri-urban inhabitants is their place of residence. People in these areas are likely to come from different ethnic groups, speak different languages, have different religions, and earn a wide range of incomes. Nevertheless, it is imperative to include from the start the users in peri-urban areas because their heterogeneous nature increases the complexity of sanitation improvement approaches. That resulted from effective citizen participation in peri-urban settlements. One occurred in Zambia, the other in Kenya.

Community participation usually does not begin spontaneously and it rarely continues without enormous work and patience, which eventually must be rewarded financially. Often barriers exist that prevent organisation of local institutions in peri-urban communities. Residents may lack the free time to organise, or the knowledge and experience in how to organise n a sustainable way. Most community members cannot survive by working as full-time volunteers. However, communities can still be highly organised. For example, they may have carried out an invasion of the land to form the settlement in the first place.

To organise residents effectively, project planners need to explore opportunities for bridging cultural and other differences within peri-urban settlements early on in the planning of sanitation improvement activities. Residents of peri-urban settlements have shown they are willing to organise around specific issues. Identifying and working through an informal power structure, or through an NGO or other community group, can help overcome cultural or social differences within a settlement.

Organisations that have grown out of other development activities may turn their attention to sanitation projects. For example, community efforts to legalise land rights can lead to organising to get water into the community, followed by organising for a sanitation program. A related institutional issue is that economic rather than social project components often are seen as determining project viability or success. There is widespread belief that peri-urban sanitation projects are essentially technical in nature, with social aspects, including community participation, considered less important for a projects success. Consequently, the technical departments of the implementing agency have much more power and status than those dealing with social aspects, if the latter exist at all.

In most countries, engineers who control the technical departments are mainly senior men, while community development and social workers in the social division tend more to be junior women. Sexual inequalities reinforce the attitude among bureaucrats that the social components of projects are less important. A lack of recognition that community participation requires specialised training also hinders citizen involvement, as does the longer time frame required for implementation of projects based on participatory approaches. The latter implies higher initial up-front costs as well, further discouraging the process.

Behavioural Factors

Other major social considerations to focus on in planning improved peri-urban sanitation services centre around the recipients hygiene behaviour. Hygiene modifications are essentially the changes in peoples behaviour that, over time, improve health. One way behavioural change is demonstrated is by the ways people use improved infrastructure. Usage and sustainability are critical to the success of sanitation projects. Unless facilities are suitable for the people using them and unless the technologies are affordable and efficient, the facilities will remain unaccepted and under used. WASH studies have shown that health benefits associated with peri-urban sanitation projects require that changes in hygiene behaviour accompany infrastructure improvements.

Peri-urban sanitation planners have often given too little scrutiny to the types of technologies acceptable to a given community, or to hygiene education needed to support the chosen option. Behavioural components are often neglected. Because peri-urban areas often lack a common social make-up, however, such information about high-risk sanitation behaviour can be difficult to acquire.

High-risk behaviour can be defined as action by men, women, and children that allows exposure to human excreta. Two sets of information involving high-risk sanitation behaviour are required as a basis for determining the appropriate sanitation intervention: identifying existing high-risk sanitation behaviour and practices in a community, and specifying behavioural changes the community must undertake to improve health. In peri-urban communities, identifying and drawing conclusions about this information are difficult because of the cultural, ethnic, and religious mix typical of these settlements.

In all communities, barriers exist to changing high-risk behaviour. (A barrier as used here signifies a belief, norm, attitude, or condition that either reinforces the high-risk behaviour or limits the modified behaviour.) Barriers may be religious, cultural, social, economic, or technological in nature and may not be readily observable. For example, a crumbling slab or a dark latrine is a condition that may cause people to fear using the latrine, or religious beliefs may dictate that women and men cannot use the same latrine. Similarly, a community norm may allow a certain abandoned field or lot to be considered an acceptable place for children to defecate.

With the cultural, social, and economic diversity common to many peri-urban areas, high-risk sanitation behaviours and barriers to changing them will likely vary widely among inhabitants. This makes surveys and other approaches to information gathering complicated and very difficult, especially compared with a more homogeneous rural community. Because of the great variation in residents, a large sample size is needed for a survey of preferences or behaviours to be useful and truly indicative of a large, diverse community.

Institutional Considerations

In peri-urban areas, various socialite factors may limit the range of acceptable, appropriate sanitation interventions. Chief among these are individual citizens priorities, cost, institutional capabilities, and legal constraints. In addition, the appropriateness of on-site systems in peri-urban areas will be subject to the users perception of land availability, the maturity of the community, income levels, and other perceived priorities. (In peri-urban areas, where so much is needed, the perceived need for sanitation improvements may be low compared with the demand for water, electricity, dispensaries, schools, drainage, roads, or solid waste removal, for example.)

Costs of Improvements

The costs of peri-urban sanitation programs can vary significantly and include labour, material, management, operation, hygiene education, training, legalising land, and community organising. Location, site characteristics, and density also play a major role in cost. Bad soils and steep topography can double the cost of sewerage, for example, and high densities can preclude lower-cost options even where buildings are only one story high. Additionally, off-site connections can cloud estimates of project expenditures because their cost depends on their distance from existing trunk lines. Site variability also leads to difficulty in evaluating feasible options and monitoring project implementation. Ironically, because peri-urban families have settled on the cheapest land, they often require the most expensive sanitation infrastructure by the very nature of the terrains physical condition. As a result of the degree to which the above factors can vary, cost over-runs are common in upgrading programs and range from 50 to 200 percent. Many budgeting difficulties also arise involved in working within an existing social setting. Land tenure issues, rights-of-way problems, inaccurate reference maps, and inadequate soil investigations are common causes of delay and cost overrun.

Cost Recovery

Cost recovery schemes rely on two basic instruments to recover the capital costs of sanitation infrastructure improvements: direct charges to property owners benefiting from the improvements, and indirect charges to users through water or other utility rates.

In general, worldwide experience at full cost recovery for water supply and sanitation projects has not been very successful. In rural areas, recovery of capital costs mostly has not been tried, and even attempts at recovering simple operations and maintenance costs have had mixed results. Recent concern over spiralling public debt in developed and industrialised countries alike, coupled with growing awareness that water is a limited resource and that the majority of institutions responsible for providing water-related services cannot cover their costs, has led most governments and external support agencies (ESAs) to conclude that water and sanitation services should be recognised as an economic good for which it is appropriate to pay. Thus, the cost of WS&S services should be considered chargeable first and foremost to individual users, and not to the public at large. This means that service coverage should be extended on the basis of an assessment of effective demand; that is, the level of service for which potential users are willing to pay. Cost recovery has devoted great attention to the ability of beneficiaries to pay for the improvement provided. Too little attention has been given to willingness to pay and capacity to collect.

Willingness to Pay

To help determine the appropriate level of service for a given peri-urban community, a willingness-pay survey designed specifically for sanitation improvements in peri-urban areas must be devised. Willingness-to-pay surveys have been used successfully with water supply projects, but very few have been applied to peri-urban situations. Peri-urban residents may be less willing to pay for sanitation improvements than for water supply; a survey would reveal whether this is so.

Willingness-to-pay surveys also help identify technologies that are acceptable and affordable to a community. They also can help determine feasible methods of financing. Cost indexing of options, in fact, can be presented to users as questions in willingness-to-pay studies. The results of a willingness-to-pay survey in Kumasi, Ghana, and highlight the important components such a survey contains.

Credit Programs

In some peri-urban sanitation programs, access to credit should be considered as a mechanism for mobilising the economic resources of peri-urban inhabitants. Significant constraints to this access may exist, however, including high transaction costs, lengthy approval processes, high interest rates and loan security requirements, legal land registration, mortgage requirements, and an insufficient number of personnel allocated to serve customers in low-income brackets.

Uncertain Legal Status of Peri-Urban Areas

The underlying legal issue for peri-urban settlements is that they lack official recognition as legal residential areas because the land they occupy usually has not been zoned for housing or is considered dangerous or environmentally protected. Either the residents occupy the site without legal land tenure or they buy it from the landowner, who in turn has not legally urbanised the land (that is, legally registered the land or plots and installed or brought in municipal services such as electricity and water). In both cases, governments are reluctant to provide sanitation infrastructure to a settlement because that would imply that they recognise the settlements legality. In many developing countries, government officials hold biases against squatter areas and providing assistance to them.

In peri-urban settlements, households also may be reluctant to invest time and money in infrastructure improvements that may not benefit them in the long run. Because unstable land tenure means residents can eventually lose the land, they often are less willing make home improvements. Moreover, in these cases, lenders may decline to lend money for such improvements.

Politicians can hardly be blamed for their tough stand against peri-urban settlements. As elected or appointed officials, they are responsible for enforcing codes and laws. Unless project designers can get a political commitment from the mayor or other authorised key decision-maker to agree to sanitation interventions in illegal settlements, it makes little sense to go any further in the project design process.

The challenge to project designers and local authorities, who likely have different though equally legitimate interests, is to find a mutually acceptable resolution of their conflicts. Recognition of these inherent conflicts is important, and facilitated meetings often can help smooth the way for a continuation of the design and implementation process.

Specific legal issues that may need to be assessed when designing a sanitation improvement project include land tenure, plot registration with municipal authorities, and the applicability and appropriateness of building codes, design and construction standards, and environmental regulations. Describes a successful peri-urban infrastructure project that focused on legalisation as one of its first key stages. Indeed, sanitation improvement projects can help to accelerate the natural transformation of peri-urban areas into formally recognised communities. Conversely, when an area obtains legal land tenure, residents have more impetus to demand infrastructure.

Formal Institutions and Peri-Urban Settlements

An insufficient number of formal institutions government and private possess the motivation, mandate, experience, or capability to implement peri-urban sanitation programs. As noted above, governments do not want to condone the existence of informal communities for many reasons. Some municipalities cannot even provide services in more affluent areas; they are overwhelmed in general and do not want to recognise new areas and increase their responsibilities.

Demand-driven urbanisation infrastructure involves a different process than does formal, supply-driven urbanisation. Yet existing institutions have been et up for supply driven urbanisation infrastructure. They are not organisationally structured and prepared to carry out demand-driven urbanisation. These institutions have their own laws and regulations, institutional mission statements, goals, objectives, personnel, and methods. People hired by such institutions are trained at universities that are still supply-oriented in their approach to urban planning. As a result, when it comes to peri-urban areas, institutional staff are often confused about their institutional and personal responsibilities.

Another problem that can surface between formal institutions and the peri-urban community concerns the kind of skills needed to initiate sanitation interventions in peri-urban settlements. Standard technology and approaches as applied in developed countries and in planned urban neighbourhood of developing countries will not work in peri-urban areas because of the latter physical conditions, heterogeneous population, and population density. Consequently, formal institutions, in working with peri-urban settlements, must in the future be prepared to offer creative solutions and alternative technologies. They also must be willing to engage the community in the decision-making process from the beginning. Today, unfortunately, there exists in many places a professional bias among engineers and planners against alternative technologies and community participation. Strong local institutions thus are needed to implement and sustain projects in peri-urban areas, and engineers and planners in these institutions must be able and willing to identify and work with existing community leaders.

Formal institutions also must learn to cooperate with organisations from a variety of different sectors. For example, multiple ministries may require coordination, such as the Ministry of Health, the water and sewerage authority, and the Ministry of Planning. Regulations are needed for health and construction, and a tariff-setting authority is necessary to establish rates and collect fees. Project designers therefore should consult with each of these institutions. In most cases, the institutions have no clear mandates about their role in providing services to peri-urban settlements, given the latter illegal status. A key issue for project designers, then, is to assess whether the government staff members responsible for urban sanitation have the skills, experience, and institutional commitment necessary to change their approach to peri-urban communities.

Intermediary Organisations

NGOs can serve as useful bridges in overcoming the lack of recognition informal settlements suffer from government organisations. For example, it may be easier for NGOs to organise the community at first, followed by out reach to the formal institutions.

NGOs, in working with the community, usually can help find more economical solutions that are acceptable to all residents, ones that involve residents contributions in kind or in labour in building their own infrastructure. Although communities may be limited in resolving their own infrastructure problems, cases of locally built and managed aqueducts are known. With NGO assistance and community labour and pressure, the cost and red tape involved in acquiring infrastructure can generally be reduced, and government support and recognition can be fostered.

Technical Considerations

The decision of which technology or combination of technologies to use for peri-urban sanitation intervention will perhaps be one of the most challenging for project designers to make. Tried and true sanitation technologies for either rural areas or formal urban areas have, for the most part, been found to be inappropriate for peri-urban settlements. In recent years, new and more appropriate technologies for peri-urban sites have been developed by engineers working with social scientists, but actual experience with using these technologies is still relatively minimal.

Perhaps one of the most important points project planners must keep in mind is that the current range of sanitation technologies that might be considered for peri-urban areas is limited. In many peri-urban areas, the combination of harsh physical conditions, high population densities, extreme poverty, and the inability or unwillingness of governments to provide significant subsidies may lead to the conclusion that no existing technology is an appropriate solution. These impossible situations will likely become more common as the explosive rapid urbanisation process continues. Recognising that there very well may be no magic bullet technology will liberate project planners to explore alternative, non-technological approaches to addressing peri-urban sanitation.

Site Limitations

The physical limitations imposed by a peri-urban site can be the predominant constraint to upgrading the area. Cities and towns are often built on land that is unsuitable for productive use, such as farming. As discussed earlier, peri-urban settlements are almost always found on land with the cheapest value, which in turn usually indicates that the land has unattractive physical attributes such as extremely steep slopes or swampy conditions, or that it is subject to frequent flooding.

These types of physical site conditions can increase design and construction costs by 100 percent or more compared with what the same technology would cost on land more suitable for urbanisation. Operations and maintenance costs will also be more expensive on difficult terrain. Many peri-urban areas have soil that is either rocky, sandy, or clayey. Rocky soil makes even pit latrines difficult and expensive to build; sandy soil may require expensive lining of pits to prevent cave-ins or make contamination of underground aquifers very likely; clayey soils make infiltration difficult, resulting in the quick filling of pit latrines. These not uncommon conditions can make even the lowest-cost and simplest technologies either technically infeasible or unaffordable for many poor families living in peri-urban areas.

Institutional and Community Costs of Low-Cost Technologies

The term low-cost technologies usually refers to low capital costs especially the capital required for materials. From an institutional and community perspective, however, low-cost technologies can be far more labour intensive than conventional technologies. Project planners designing a peri-urban sanitation program need also to consider the additional costs of the corresponding labour when comparing technologies. For example, employees of the institutions implementing a peri-urban sanitation project usually must devote a significant number of days or even months to the soft side of appropriate technologies. Depending on the technology and community context, this process can be very labour intensive and may include activities in community organising, attending meetings, construction training, operations and maintenance training, hygiene education, monitoring and evaluation, managing credit programs, and so on. These labour costs can be significant for the implementing institution and need to be recovered if a program is to be sustainable. Nonetheless, they often are not factored into the comparison of costs corresponding to a given technology. Planners need to cost out the level of effort required to meet these tasks and consider these costs when comparing the technologies.

Lower-cost technologies also usually require more labour from community members than do other technologies. Many peri-urban sanitation project designs require communities to provide much of the construction labour, including digging pit latrines, digging trenches for sewage pipes, or building on-site latrine superstructures. Many low-cost technology sanitation schemes also require the community to play a significant role in the operation and maintenance of the systems, including cleaning out latrines, unplugging small-diameter sewer pipes, or emptying septic tanks. Despite this degree of community labour, project planners usually assign it no value or zero cost when comparing technologies.

In reality, labour provided by a community represents real and significant costs to the community and its members. In peri-urban areas, families are by and large in the cash economy and usually need to work very long hours in order to make enough money to meet their basic needs. The axiom time is money is very real to families living in peri-urban settlements. Contrary to the prevailing assumptions on the part of many project planners, labour provided for a peri-urban sanitation project by a community is not free. In many peri-urban sanitation projects, families that are required to contribute labour either lose an opportunity to be earning money or, more often than not, hire a lower-cost labourer to provide their labour contribution. As a result, many peri-urban sanitation projects that have used a low-cost appropriate technology have been stalled or have failed because the beneficiary families living in peri-urban settlements could not afford to donate their labour. Project planners must consider the real cost to a community of a given technology in deciding what is most affordable and appropriate.

They should also be prepared to conclude that even low-cost appropriate technologies may be unaffordable to a given community.

Design Standards and Engineers

In choosing a sanitation technology, project planners should use with caution existing selection and design guidelines. Although peri-urban sanitation needs typically are assessed using selection guidelines developed for rural or formal urban areas, these tools are not always appropriate for peri-urban areas. Rural and formal urban guidelines do not include new, alternative technologies such as con-dominial, shallow, and simplified collection systems, nor do they consider some of the constraints (such as lack of legal tenure) unique to peri-urban areas.

Local engineers, and often their expatriate advisors, prefer to use sanitation systems with which they are familiar. These systems are usually the most modern and are often based on the adoption of engineering design and construction standards for conventional sanitation technologies in developed countries, which in turn are based on the industrialised nations own health standards and institutional capabilities. These systems often turn out to be unsuitable for the difficult topography, soils, lack of water, and other conditions found in peri-urban settlements. In particular, such conditions can make installation of conventional sanitation infrastructure extremely costly.

Two factors that contribute to engineers over reliance on conventional sewage systems is the existing legal framework that has legally codified foreign engineering standards, and the traditional curricula and corresponding textbooks used in developing-country engineering schools that were often founded by expatriate engineering professors or local engineering professors who first received their training overseas. Even in urban areas where more than 50 percent of the city is considered peri-urban, it is very rare to find engineering students who take even one course dealing with peri-urban sanitation.

Another important constraint to servicing peri-urban areas, noted earlier, is that lower-cost technologies usually require a much higher level of user involvement than conventional technology to function properly. Yet engineers, who traditionally play a major role in the formulation of sanitation projects, often have little training or regard for the social mechanics of projects, such as mobilising communities and involving future users, and they have little patience for the sheer time it takes to address them.

Some instructive examples from around the world offer simple and ingenious solutions to providing sanitation under the adverse conditions found in most peri-urban areas. Of particular note are con-dominial or simplified sewers which are described . These options have also turned out to be much cheaper than conventional systems. Nevertheless, for the most part, the world engineering community (in both developed and developing countries) is either unaware of their existence or, because of a lack of hands-on experience, remains distrustful of and reluctant to consider these alternatives.

Finally, it should be pointed out that the conceptualisation, design, and construction of simplified sewerage systems that are appropriate for peri-urban areas pose extremely complicated engineering challenges that require skilled, experienced, innovative engineers working on interdisciplinary teams with social scientists, economists, and others.

Sanitation Technologies

Sanitation technologies can be divided into two general classes: on-site and off-site.

On-Site Technologies

On-site technologies rely on the disposal of excreta at the point of defecation. Material is not removed from the site, although liquids may leach into the ground and eventually be carried off-site. Latrines are an example of on-site systems. The pit of a pit latrine is covered when full, and the excreta stays in place. Composting latrines are emptied, but the composted material is used on-site or nearby.

Peri-urban situations present both advantages and disadvantages for on-site systems. The on-site systems lower cost and minimal institutional requirements match well with the lower incomes and weak institutional capabilities often found in informal settlements. However, peri-urban population densities frequently are too high to accommodate latrines, and site conditions often are inappropriate as well, leading to pit flooding or ground-water contamination.

Latrines

To date, construction of latrines has been the main sanitation intervention funded by external support agencies (ESAs), including for projects in peri-urban areas. Dry, non-flushed latrines can be built with a small initial investment, mainly labour, and require little operating skill. They are also inexpensive to maintain. They are suitable for use in areas where water is in short supply and where land is available to dig new pits when old ones fill up. If no land is available, provision for cartilage and treatment must be made. If piped water is provided to an area, provisions must be made for proper drainage away from the latrine, and care must be taken to prevent ground-water contamination from latrine leachate.

Experience to date has shown that latrines have serious limitations in peri-urban areas. For one, they usually are not technically feasible at population densities above 350 persons per hectare, and most peri-urban areas have population densities that significantly exceed that rate. In many high-density peri-urban settlements, little, if any, space exists to dig a new pit after the existing one fills up. Space may not even be available to build the first pit.

Additionally, latrines are impractical for multi-story housing. Settlements with many high buildings may have insufficient circulation of air streams normally required to blow over the tops of the vent pipes of ventilated improved pit (VIP) latrines. Finally, latrines used in high-density areas run a high risk of contaminating nearby wells and underground aquifers.

Double pit latrines may be an appropriate solution for many settlements until off-site technologies become feasible. Double pit latrines share many of the advantages of single pit latrines, but in addition, they last longer. These advantages, however, are countered by higher initial costs, the need for more user education, and more complex construction requirements.

Compost latrines: One current alternative that is currently in vogue as an appropriate technology for many ESAs is the dual vault composting (DVC) latrine. Unlike pit latrines, composting latrines have their contents composted and emptied. As with pit latrines, actual experience with the

DVC latrine in peri-urban areas has been generally unsatisfactory. The DVC only makes sense if there exists a market for the compost and a community tradition for human waste reuse.

Composting toilets require significant and conscientious user care and operation, which peri-urban inhabitants are unlikely to maintain unless the implementing agency provides significant and continuous extension work. The more typical scenario, in which implementing agencies do some up-front promotion of compost latrines, provide materials for their construction, and then move on to another site without providing ongoing education to reinforce proper maintenance of the latrines has consistently resulted in 50 to 80 percent of the latrines either being misused or not used at all.

Communal latrines: Communal sanitation facilities can be an appropriate interim solution for peri-urban areas. In general, communal latrines address the major constraints commonly found in peri-urban areas:

1. Low water availability
2. Site conditions inappropriate for latrines
3. Unwillingness to pay by users who have no legal land tenure or have very low incomes
4. Population densities too great for individual household latrines
5. Institutional capabilities insufficient to support off-site systems
6. Social factors that make the reuse of excreta implausible

Communal latrines address this combination of constraints by reducing the land area required for sanitation facilities, minimising cost, and requiring little water. However, project planners should use caution when considering this option because examples abound of such facilities that are not maintained because of ambiguity as to who owns the latrine (the community or the government) and who is responsible for its maintenance. In these situations, communal latrines fall into disrepair or become unsanitary and therefore are not used.

Pay-per-use communal latrines have been successful in some cases for those people who can afford it, but even when most users can pay, subsidies may still be necessary for those who cannot pay, to ensure more complete coverage of the entire population.

Septic Tanks

Septic tanks are another on-site sanitation system, although partially treated solids must be disposed of and further treated off-site. Septic tanks offer two particular advantages. They provide better treatment of waste than pit latrines and can be used to dispose of gray water, and they are simple enough to include the participation of the users, the community, and the local or regional governments.

The disadvantages of septic tanks versus latrines are the larger investment they require, their higher operating costs, the need to clean them, their land usage, and the higher level of water supply they require. In high-density areas, the same space constraints that affect pit latrines also affect technologies such as pour-flush toilets, which require soak pits or septic tanks. Water to flush the toilet may also be too costly, too cumbersome to carry from the public tap, or only intermittently available.

Dual soak-away pits, which are shared by several households, are a variation of the above. In this scheme, several households pour-flush toilets are connected to a common pair of soak-away pits. Cooperation must be assured among users to prevent blockage and ensure the cycling and the cleaning of the pits.

Off-Site Technologies

Off-site systems dispose of waste away from the user. A simple bucket latrine is one example of an off-site system. The more complex water-borne sewage collection system is another example.

Off-site sanitation interventions often solve sanitation-related health problems by isolating the excreta from the user, only to fail ultimately by contaminating ground-water or by exposing downstream population to disease. In the long term, cities must develop environmentally sustainable methods to treat and dispose of waste.

Conventional Sewage Collection Systems

Conventional sewage collection systems have a high initial construction cost (including a high foreign exchange requirement for certain materials and equipment) and require skilled labour for installation. These systems often include pump stations and screening equipment, which need trained maintenance personnel and moderate operation and maintenance expenditures. Maintenance of the sewer lines consists of the periodic cleaning and removal of obstructions. Rights of way are required for the initial construction of and maintenance access to conventional sewerage systems. They also require a significant water supply to minimise plugging of sewage lines. The overwhelming majority of peri-urban settlements around the world do not have the required amount and reliability of water supply for the proper operation of conventional sanitation systems. The most significant constraint, however, is the inability of the majority of peri-urban areas to afford conventional sewage systems.

Alternatives to Conventional Sewerage

Alternatives to conventional sewerage include simplified, con-dominial, and small bore systems.

Simplified sewerage: Design standards for conventional sewerage are altered; sewers can be built with smaller pipes, shallower trenches, and fewer appurtenances.

Con-dominial sewers: Simplified sewerage can be built and maintained by users and located between houses, rather than in streets or other rights of way.

Small bore sewers: Septic tanks can be connected to small-diameter pipes that carry the solids-free effluent.

All of these alternatives have significantly lower initial and operating costs and a lower requirement for amount and reliability of piped water supply than do conventional systems. However, project planners should recognise that even though these alternatives are much lower in cost, they may still be unaffordable to many peri-urban communities. Similarly, peri-urban areas may not have the required minimum piped water system to accommodate these technologies. In addition, project planners must realise that these alternative sewerage systems require more labour-intensive installation and increased maintenance. Unlike conventional sewerage, with its large pipes, the small pipes used in alternative systems frequently clog up. The increased maintenance needed to unclog the pipes is the responsibility of individual households and the community, and requires ongoing community organisation and extension work by the implementing agency.

A clogged pipe at a household in unconventional sewers affects a significant portion of the community, since these systems are more interdependent in their piping. Clogging at one household blocks up the pipe for everyone else using the system. As discussed earlier, these systems are not as common as conventional sewerage; therefore, there is relatively little operational data for engineers to use as a basis for rational design and planning.

Pit Latrines with Cartilage Systems

Under certain conditions, single pit latrines can work as a short-term intervention even in densely populated peri-urban areas to create a physical barrier between residents and excreta. As discussed above, in high-density areas, latrines must be emptied periodically because land is not available to dig another pit. Unfortunately, technologies for latrine emptying and excreta treatment that are appropriate for peri-urban areas are not yet widely known or available. However, presents one approach to overcoming the latrine emptying and collection problem that is proving successful in Nairobi.

Waste water Treatment

As discussed above, Con-dominial and small bore sewers offer significant initial cost savings over conventional sewage collection while still providing the advantages of water-borne sewage systems. These alternatives, however, must include waste water treatment to increase health and environmental benefits, and they require cartilage capabilities to empty septic or interceptor tanks, if used. Septic tanks have been used as a treatment receptacle for block sewers. However, innovative on-site treatment technologies, such as anaerobic filters, need to be tested on peri-urban applications. Decentralised treatment technologies have not yet been applied to peri-urban areas.

Conventional high-technology waste water treatment systems are usually too expensive to build and operate for peri-urban areas. Some of the small-scale, low-technology waste water alternatives worth considering are the following:

1. Stabilisation ponds
2. Constructed wet lands
3. Duckweed ponds
4. Up-flow anaerobic sludge blanket reactors

5. Communal septic tanks/anaerobic filters
6. Oxidation ditches

An important disadvantage of many of these alternatives is their requirement for a large area of land, which can be expensive, especially in urban areas.

Key Principles

This section summarises the key principles identified in this chapter, the key questions to ask and information to gather in planning and designing peri-urban sanitation projects, and the basic approaches that should be considered when devising project strategies for improving community excreta sanitation in peri-urban areas.

1. Improving the health of the rapidly growing number of families living in peri-urban areas and protecting the urban environment are urgent needs and compelling program objectives that host country governments, as well as external support agencies such as the Agency for International Development, must address. In reaching these objectives, improving community sanitation should be accorded the same (if not higher) priority as water supply.
2. To improve health in densely populated peri-urban areas, sanitation programs must target the community rather than individual households. Individual households with improved sanitation will not experience improved health if their neighbours are still disposing of focal matter in ways that contaminate the general environment of a peri-urban settlement. In addition, improved community excreta sanitation may not improve health if other environmental factors such as solid waste disposal and drainage are not also considered.

3. The current planning paradigm for formal urbanisation, which begins with the installation of basic urban services, does not coincide with the actual peri-urbanisation process, which begins with the informal and/or illegal settlement by poor urban families on land that has not been urbanised. The peri-urbanisation process is a reality for 50 to 80 percent of most cities in developing countries. Therefore, authorities must recognise that providing sanitation services to existing densely populated peri-urban settlements must follow a different paradigm than that of traditional urbanisation. Additionally, officials must acknowledge the need to reform existing service provision agencies to coincide with the particular needs of the peri-urban sector.

4. The economic, social, legal, and physical conditions generally found in peri-urban areas present unique challenges to WS&S sector specialists attempting to improve community sanitation. In large measure, conventional engineering approaches and standard technical solutions used for formal urban and rural sewerage systems must be significantly modified or even rejected for peri-urban areas.

5. Installing a sanitation technology can be done relatively rapidly. Setting up and implementing a long-term sustainable peri-urban sanitation program that successfully improves community health and protects the environment takes significantly more time.

6. To improve health, changing individual and community behaviours that cause focal-oral contamination is at least as important as constructing new sanitation facilities. For efforts to change behaviour to succeed, projects must be designed around a thorough and correct understanding of existing knowledge and hygiene practices in the community and a thorough knowledge of the social, cultural, and religious context

in which high-risk behaviour takes place. Moreover, efforts to change behaviour must be institutionalised and enjoy strong support from donors, governments, and other key actors.

7. Recognising that improving peri-urban community sanitation is a complex process, project planning should involve the many institutional actors that influence or have responsibility for peri-urban sanitation, including the respective agencies that handle sanitation, the agencies responsible for hygiene education, and non-health agencies such as municipalities, urban planning agencies, and credit institutions. The most effective way to ensure that cooperation is elicited from the widest possible range of agencies and institutions is to take an inclusive, participatory approach to the planning process.

8. Peri-urban sanitation projects should not be solely technology driven. Successful sanitation interventions should also consider health, economics, social, legal, and institutional factors.

9. The conceptualisation, design, and construction of peri-urban sanitation systems pose extremely complicated engineering challenges that require skilled, experienced, and innovative engineers working on interdisciplinary teams along with planners, social scientists, environmentalists, lawyers, economists, and others.

10. Citizen involvement and community participation are critical to successful peri-urban sanitation programs. Community participation can lead to initial cost reductions, increased acceptance of program interventions, increased cost recovery, and more effective operation and maintenance.

11. Institutions providing peri-urban sanitation services should seek to recover as much of their costs as

possible in order to reach some level of financial sustainability and be able to expand services to other peri-urban areas. Individual households should be expected to pay for the real value of the sanitation services. Providing access to credit can greatly facilitate peoples ability to pay for the services. If subsidies are necessary to reach the extremely poor, they should be clearly accounted for. Successful cost recovery results from providing services that families are able and willing to pay for and from developing effective institutional capacities to collect tariffs, loan payments, and other fees.

A comprehensive approach that recognises the interrelationships between various socialite sectors is needed to increase the effectiveness of a peri-urban sanitation project. Projects should be able to depend on cooperation between and among community, municipal, regional, or national organisations and involve both the formal and informal sectors. Complementary projects in water supply, solid waste collection, drainage, and health education may be needed to ensure the effectiveness of sanitation projects. Furthermore, implementation of a sanitation solution may be a multi-step process, starting with simple interventions to address the large problems and becoming more complex as finances and institutional capabilities allow. To promote a comprehensive approach, project design and implementation teams should be interdisciplinary. NGOs can also play an effective role because they can organise illegal/informal peri-urban settlements and serve as an intermediary with formal legal institutions such as banks, municipalities, and utilities.

Much was learned during the International Drinking Water Supply and Sanitation Decade (1981-90), especially about developing affordable, durable, and simple technologies, and about the equally important human elements of water and sanitation. Much of what was learned during the decade came from rural experiences, which may not be relevant to peri-urban situations. Similarly, the engineering sector in formal urban areas is strongly biased toward the use of conventional sewage technology that is clearly out of reach of the overwhelming majority of families living in peri-urban areas. This bias is reinforced by existing engineering and health regulations and standards. Consequently, the ?lessons learned from the rural WS&S experience, as well as the conventional wisdom of established engineering professions in urban areas, must be re-focused and altered dramatically to have meaning in a peri-urban context.

The greatest need is for action, comprising the following steps:

1. Making existing knowledge on peri-urban sanitation more accessible
2. Maintaining statistics that describe the residents of peri-urban areas and their needs
3. Sharing the practical implications of applied research within and among countries
4. Designing and implementing activities and projects that bring sanitation to the urban poor, and perhaps most importantly
5. Documenting and learning from the experiences of those carrying out sanitation activities in peri-urban areas of developing countries.

Everyone involved or interested in peri-urban upgrading projects must recognise the uniqueness of the sanitation challenges presented by peri-urban areas. Interested parties must also confront head-on the difficulties in providing appropriate excreta disposal systems in these areas and recognise that many impossible situations prevail for which no feasible technical solution exists. WS&S professionals must also challenge the status quo the reluctance of municipal and national governments to act and respond to the demands of peri-urban people who lack water and sanitation infrastructure. By necessity or choice, government institutions, bilateral and multilateral aid organisations, and NGOs in the foreseeable future will be compelled to shift more of their attention and resources to the sanitation needs of peri-urban population.

3

Challenges of Urban Sanitation

India is a nation of ancient and firmly entrenched tradition and culture. For thousands of years, religion, geography and the necessities of a rural agrarian society have sculpted a complex caste system based on status, hierarchy, and, above all, a strict division of labour. As India is becoming increasingly urbanised, and her people are leaving their traditional rural communities and entering into an environment marked by fluidity, change and drastically different technological and physical conditions, traditional divisions of labour and living habits forged in rural settings are increasingly out of step with contemporary conditions. Yet, Indians continue to cling to traditional cultural mores, often causing great problems, especially for the poor.

Bombay is India's largest and fastest growing city and exemplifies many of these problems as traditional, rural culture clashes with the reality of conditions in the modern mega city. Over half of Bombay's residents live in poorly serviced slums marked by overcrowding, pollution, poor sanitation and a host of other problems shared by the urban poor the world over. Of particular concern in Bombay is the problem of human waste. The lack of clean and adequate toilet facilities, the lingering rural custom of relieving oneself outdoors, and deeply entrenched attitudes and taboos preventing most slum dwellers from cleaning up human waste, have all resulted in slums littered with faces and reeking of urine. Despite the construction of public toilets by municipal agencies, the problem has persisted. The mere presence of toilets is not enough; they need to be maintained, kept clean, and widely used. This implies more than just the construction of new facilities, but a widespread change in the attitudes and traditions of all city residents, one that would promote sanitary practices, an appreciation of the importance of hygiene and the urban environment, and the reform of a cultural system that only allows a small minority to clean toilets or deal directly with human waste.

The Community of Resource Organisations (CORO), in response to a request from the Indian Department of Science and Technology (DST), has undertaken the management of several municipal pay-and-use toilet complexes in the slums of Bombay. CORO has reformed the toilets' management and maintenance structures, using local labour and introducing incentives which have resulted in cleaner toilets, less corruption and more community participation. By combining toilet maintenance and administration with their already existing work in literacy and book distribution, CORO has increased their reach into the slums, increased education about the importance of sanitation and the urban environment, and laid the groundwork for more effective community organisation around other issues. Through a two-pronged approach stressing literacy and hygiene, CORO has begun to create a whole new culture of urban sanitation, waste management and environmental education.

Over the last ninety years, India has seen phenomenal urban growth, concentrating more and more people in larger and larger towns. Between 1901 and 1991, the number of cities and large towns in India doubled, and their total population increased eight fold. In 1991 26% of Indians lived in cities and large towns, and the Registrar General projects that by 2001, 29.4% of the country, or 278 million people, will be urban dwellers. One of the most striking examples of this urban population explosion is Bombay, and as the largest and fastest growing city in India, it continues to struggle with many of the problems such drastic change entails.

Case of Bombay

Bombay was a group of seven swampy islands inhabited by fishermen when it caught the attention of European explorers and traders. As early as 1529 the Portuguese established a naval provisioning base there, and under the British East India Company, it became the most important port and trading centre in India, especially with the opening of the Suez Canal and the development of railroad in the Indian interior in the 19th century. Bombay continues to be the commercial and financial capital of India, as well as the centre of the largest film industry in the world, and an important transportation centre with an airport that handles 60% of the country's international flights and 40% of its domestic ones. Bombay provides 10% of the India's industrial jobs and pays one third of its income tax, one fifth of its excise tax, and 43% of its corporate tax.

Greater Bombay had a population of 9.9 million in 1991 and is one of the fastest growing cities in the world. An estimated 300 families, or about 1,500 people, move into the city every day, and the city is expected to grow to 15 million by the year 2000. With the expansion of industrial and commercial activities over the last few decades, land in the central island city has been converted to commercial use, and with no more space available in the core city, housing colonies and slums have developed in the eastern and western suburbs (Table 1). Most of Bombay's new residents live in slums far from the city centre and without many basic civic amenities; the city's recent growth has taken place far away from the traditional service networks and places of employment.

Table 1. Population of Bombay (in thousands)

Year	City	Suburbs	Extended Suburbs	Percent Total Increase
1951	510	155	2,924	—
1961	1,037	343	4,152	42
1971	2,167	733	5,970	43
1981	2,799	2,169	8,226	38
1991	3,986	2,762	9,907	20

Obviously, such a quickly growing population places extraordinary stresses on traditional service delivery systems and limited municipal resources. These stresses are exacerbated by economic and political factors. Despite higher revenues from an expanding tax base, Bombay has gotten little in return for its increased contributions to the state and national exchequer. Even more problematic has been the stagnation and recent decline of industrial growth and employment during the 1980s. From 1981 to 1988 only ninety additional factories were built in the Bombay Metropolitan Region, and actual industrial employment fell sharply from 604,000 to 474,000.

Because of the loss of industrial jobs many Bombay residents have had to look for work in an informal sector marked by low-skill, low paying jobs without any benefits or job security. This informal sector is accounting for a growing share of a stagnant labour market and is unable to fulfil the city's employment needs. Bombay's population growth has not been accompanied by an expanding job market, leaving many of Bombay's residents unable to pay for basic necessities and the city as a whole unable to provide for its ever-growing number of poor. Many of the city's basic services are inadequate, and the poor suffer especially. There is a lack of recreational space and educational opportunity. Although Bombay has more doctors and hospital beds per person than the national average, many of the medical services are inaccessible and unaffordable for the poor. There is an extensive public transportation system serving Bombay and its suburbs, but it is unable to alleviate the huge congestion caused by the large number of commuters to the city, and Bombay is plagued by traffic problems and air pollution from cars and buses.

Bombay produces 4,000 tons of rubbish a day and 1,500 tons of silt and debris. The city is hard-pressed to remove it all, though the department of solid waste management employs a work-force of 22,000 and has an annual budget of Rs. 12.6 million (US$ 400,000). Slums are especially cluttered with trash.

Bombay is unable to meet the high demand for water. The recommended daily use is 254 litres per capita per day (lpcd); yet in Greater Bombay, domestic supply of water on an average is not more than 130 lpcd. In the outer sections of the Bombay Metropolitan Region it is even less than 70 lpcd. In addition, most people have access to running water for just a few hours each day and must collect and store water for the day's use, often carrying it from public standpipes to their homes.

Despite the existence of a relatively modern sewage network installed in 1935, and even with a vast new system financed by the World Bank and scheduled to open in 2005, Bombay is simply unable to treat the vast amount of waste-water and human waste the city generates. Most of the city's sewage flows into local creeks and coastal waters inadequately treated.

Air pollution is also a major problem in Bombay, the result of factories, the vast numbers of motorised vehicles, cooking fires, and the nation's largest chemical industry (Bombay is home to about 50% of the nation's chemical production). 1,700 tons of pollutants, mostly sulfurdioxides, suspended particles, hydrocarbons, carbon monoxide, and oxides of nitrogen bensyprine, are discharged into the air every day. Not surprisingly, Bombay's residents suffer from unusually high and constantly rising rates of emphysema, asthma, bronchitis, coughs, colds and headaches. 25-30% of the city's children have emphysema or asthma as a result of sulphur and nitrogen oxide in the air.

The most obvious problem caused by exploding growth has been the incredible population density and an acute shortage of suitable and affordable housing. Government agencies and private developers are only able to build a third of the estimated 60,000 new housing units needed every year, and those that are built lie beyond the means of the vast majority of residents. By 1982, 82% of Bombay's households lived in one-room units and the city wide average of 3.99 persons per room made Bombay the mostly densely populated city in India.

Because of the great shortage of housing and the city's inability to expand infrastructure and services to its exploding population, an estimated 5 million people, or nearly one half of all Bombay, live in slums marked by overcrowding, poor living conditions, pollution and a lack of basic services and amenities.

Services in the slums vary, according to the slum's size, age, population, and residents' ability to establish links with municipal officers and elected officials. Nonetheless, conditions in the slums are generally awful. Lack of paved roads and improper drainage leads to widespread flooding and water logging in slums during the rainy season, and access to huts is often limited because of excessively muddy conditions. During the dry season, access is often blocked by accumulated garbage, as solid waste collection is often inadequate or simply nonexistent. The incredible overcrowding in the slums exacerbates all of these problems. With so many people living in such small areas without many basic services, life in the slums is marked by pollution, disease and squalor.

Obviously, the municipal government cannot begin to solve all of the problems of the slums on its own; however, it is widely seen as responsible for providing services and infrastructure and residents are extremely reluctant to assume the responsibility for conditions in their own neighbourhoods. In the absence of concerted community action and initiative, the government is left to itself to perform tasks way beyond its resources.

Lack of Toilet Facilities

The proper disposal of human waste is a huge problem in the slums of Bombay because of a great shortage of latrines and suitable sewage systems. Unfortunately, traditional technologies have been unable to solve Bombay's human waste problem and have proved impractical given Bombay's large slum population and scarce resources.

1. *Conventional Sewerage System.* Traditional sewer systems are very effective, but they require a large and continuous supply of water and sizable financial resources. Although they are convenient, their average per capita cost, including house connection, is more than Rs.5,000. Operation and maintenance costs, as well as necessary adjustments to house plumbing prior to connection, makes these systems even more expensive. The system often takes up to ten years to plan and install. They also require high levels of energy and a large quantity of water. At least 100 litters of water per capita per day is needed to maintain the minimum flow in the pipe without deposition. Lastly, although the number of microorganisms is substantially

reduced during treatment, the effluent from a conventional treatment plant is still highly charged with pathogens which are capable of polluting a river and spreading disease. This can hardly be considered an optimal solution for households in the slums.

2. *Septic Tank.* A septic tank with a soil absorption system is a method for excreta disposal in answered areas, but this is not an appropriate option in Bombay for a number of reasons. Septic tanks require extravagant use of water for flushing faces from the pan into the tank, and Bombay already suffers from inadequate supplies of water. Moreover, after partial treatment of sewage in the septic tank, the effluent has to be discharged in a drainage field having permeable soil. This, too, is impractical for Bombay, where the water table is very high and where there is a shortage of available land for drainage fields. Lastly, the capital cost is high, and it requires periodic dislodging necessitating expensive outside help.

In the face of these inadequate solutions, some alternatives have been designed to solve the problems of human waste in Bombay's slums.

1. *Mobile Toilets.* Mobile toilets have been introduced in Bombay to provide service for slum dwellers. Mobile toilets are made of easy-to-clean fibreglass and have a collecting tank at the bottom which can be emptied remotely by a valve at the site of disposal. Unfortunately, poor scheduling, inadequate maintenance and a lack of access to nearby sewer lines have undermined their effectiveness. However, if the operational problems were solved, this system could yield good results in urban slums.

2. *Sulabh Shauchalaya.* Sulabh Shauchalaya is a low cost pour flush water-seal sanitary latrine. It is an improved version of the designs already available in the country

based on research conducted by different organisations and institutions on pour flush water-seal latrines. The designers of Sulabh Shauchalaya sought to provide an appropriate, efficient, cost effective and affordable excreta disposal system and to free scavengers from having to collect night soil and carry it on their heads.

Sulabh Shauchayala is very popular in India because it has the following advantages:

1. It is odourless as it provides a water-seal between the pan and the pit.
2. It can be constructed inside the house. The cover slab of the pit may be used for various household uses like peeling vegetables, washing utensils, etc.
3. The excreta can be flushed with a small quantity (1-2 litters) of water per use.
4. It is a permanent structure requiring only a small space (1.80m x 1.20m).
5. It can be constructed in nearly all subsoil conditions.
6. After a period of 2 years, the digested sludge in the pit becomes odourless and free from pathogens, at which point it may be used as manure.
7. It is acceptable both from the aesthetic and health points of view, as the excreta is removed from sight and the smell is trapped under ground.
8. It is cost-effective and affordable for the majority of Indian households.
9. Its maintenance is very easy and hardly requires outside help.
10. It can be upgraded to the water-borne sewerage system without any alterations.

Even with the advent of such promising new technologies, people in the slums of Bombay suffer from a terrible lack of suitable latrines. Over 90% of slum dwellers depend on public latrines, and the Bombay Municipal Corporation has built 1,400 public toilets. However, there is widespread dissatisfaction with the city's public toilets, they cannot begin to meet the great demand and they are woefully overused. Long lines and inconvenience mark them.

In addition, existing latrines are very unhygienic and dirty. The municipal workers responsible for maintaining the toilets are often undependable, and there is rarely enough water to clean the latrines sufficiently. Indeed, they are often so filthy that they become a problem in and of themselves, breeding disease and discouraging the use of toilets, especially for small children who are too small to use toilets designed for adults.

As a result of all of these problems, many slum residents must relieve themselves in open spaces near their homes. This results in extremely dirty and unhealthy conditions, with streets and alleys dotted with human excrement.

Excreting in the open creates particular problems for women. In a culture which demands modesty for women, they suffer a humiliating lack of privacy when forced to use open spaces in lieu of a latrine. Most women feel forced to wait for darkness to maintain a minimum of privacy, and their effort to control themselves often has adverse effects on their health. Also, using open spaces in the dark can be unsafe for women, and there have been instances of women being molested while going to defecate at night or in the early morning. In addition to the present problems with Bombay's latrines, there are many substantial barriers to positive change.

1. *Cultural.* A vast majority of rural Indians still do not use confined space for toilets and generally relieve themselves in open spaces away from their homes. In Bombay, most slum dwellers belong to this rural

culture and are not yet fully urbanised in their habits. They do not understand that a toilet can be clean and hygienic, and do not attach toilets to their living spaces, perpetuating a dependence on public latrines. Furthermore, they often continue to use open spaces even when latrines are available, even though this practice is inappropriate and unhealthy in an urban setting.

2. *Spatial.* In a city like Bombay, as slums grow, people do not reserve space for toilets or baths, so there is often no place to put new public latrines. This lack of space contributes to the small number of toilets typically available to slum dwellers; a slum community of about 300 households may commonly have only about six to twelve common toilets. Also, as long as a community is not officially declared a slum, the Municipal Corporation of Greater Bombay does not provide toilet and water facilities. When it provides them, people are expected to pay for water while the corporation provides for toilet upkeep and maintenance. Unfortunately, there is often not enough water, either for individual use or for cleaning the toilets. Further, municipal maintenance is often unsatisfactory. Toilets are overused, filthy, and poorly maintained.
3. *Social and Historical.* In a city like Bombay it is also evident that an overwhelming majority of residents do not set high standards of cleanliness and sanitation for their toilets and urinals. Hence public toilets, including those in offices, hotels, restaurants, railway stations and streets, are filthy and unclean.

In India, over the last two thousand years, the caste system has dominated society, sharply separating intellectual work from physical work, productive work from services, and clean work from that associated with filth. Thus most people would be forbidden to clean up human waste, and there would always be a particular group who would be responsible for cleaning and removing it. Even today, most urban dwellers do not clean their own toilets. They usually engage someone else from the appropriate caste to do it, usually someone who is uneducated, culturally backward and without a sophisticated sense of sanitation. However, with growing urbanisation and industrialisation, even members of these castes have discontinued doing this particular work. Because of accelerating development, the caste system is beginning to break down, but Indian society has not found new ways to solve the problems of sanitation and related services.

Against this background, urban India needs not only clean toilets but also a whole new culture of urban sanitation and waste management. The construction of toilets must take place within the context of an overall effort to educate people about the need for sanitation and hygiene and to break down entrenched social attitudes which prevent urban dwellers from adopting healthier, more sanitary lifestyles.

Innovative Approach to Urban Sanitation

As an innovative approach to the problems of human waste disposal in the slums of Bombay, Community of Resource Organisations (CORO) combines literacy efforts with a new system of maintaining toilet complexes under a locally run pay for use plan. Using its experience with slum residents gained through its literacy program, CORO has set up a new administrative structure which uses local labour to clean and oversee public latrines. These administrative teams are able to provide residents with clean and effective toilets, encourage latrine use, and help create a new culture of cleanliness and responsibility among the poor of Bombay. With this well-run system, residents have proved willing to pay to use clean latrines with sufficient water, and have begun to move away from their traditional role as passive recipients of free government services which often proved to be inefficient or unusable.

Objectives

In combining its literacy campaign with efforts to run pay-for-use toilets CORO seeks to achieve the following objectives:

1. Promote literacy among uneducated slum dwellers and provide them with reading materials;
2. Provide clean, efficient and affordable toilet facilities for slum dwellers and promote their widespread use, especially among women and children;
3. Reduce defecation and urination in open, public spaces, providing a cleaner environment in the slums and reducing the health risks associated with large amounts of human waste;
4. Provide jobs for slum dwellers;
5. Make public toilets economically self-sufficient;
6. Use literacy and latrine use to educate slum dwellers about environmental issues and the importance of local sanitation;
7. Provide a structure for community activism;
8. Create a new culture of cleanliness and responsibility in which residents expect to pay for reliable service and in which they begin to take responsibility for conditions in their neighbourhood.

Moreover, through the toilet blocks, CORO hopes to promote reading habits among the users. For instance, it proposes to built libraries at D.N. Nagar, Chamber and Dharavi toilet complexes from where latrine users can borrow literacy kits and other reading material. The idea is to promote environmental education through literacy work and developing reading habits.

History of CORO

CORO began as a loosely formed group of different activists from several voluntary agencies in Bombay. These original members were concerned about increasing illiteracy levels among Bombay's slum residents. Despite a relative lack of experience in literacy training, they started a Mass Program of Functional Literacy in the Dharavi-BARC belt in Greater Bombay in 1989. At first, while visiting schools and trying to gain support for their efforts, the group was viewed with suspicion as outsiders from different backgrounds. It took some time for CORO to break down these barriers of mistrust. By establishing links with local community workers who were experienced political organisers, CORO was gradually able to generate community enthusiasm for literacy and reading.

Young community workers were especially helpful in this process of mobilising residents, and they became enthusiastic about the idea of promoting literacy. Contrary to their previous political experiences, which often involved frustrating encounters with passive residents or unresponsive bureaucracies, literacy training involved personal contact and visible, concrete, positive results.

Through CORO's initiatives, communities supported efforts to abolish illiteracy. With funding from the National Literacy Mission, teachers were trained, and materials were purchased and distributed. Famous celebrities were invited to distribute literacy kits in selected communities, creating interest and stimulating participation in the program.

In spite of their ability to mobilise slum residents, CORO had difficulties. The teachers were not highly qualified and the training programs were poorly designed.

CORO's survey indicated that 90 percent of the illiterates were women who were willing to learn but were often discouraged from learning to read by their husbands. The illiterate men were not willing to admit to illiteracy and were more difficult to contact since they had to commute long hours to work and often did not return until late in the evenings. Moreover, many men preferred to spend their free time drinking and gambling rather than learning to read. Lastly, CORO workers often found themselves over-extended, unable to take enough time away from their jobs to work on the literacy program. However, 12 CORO members were able to negotiate with their employers and voluntary organisations and began to work full-time for CORO. Gradually, the literacy program began to succeed.

Roving Libraries

The concept of libraries ('Savitri Vachanalaya') grew out of a need for a literacy network and in response to a lack of reading material in the slums. To form a library, a CORO activist consults with local contacts and recruits librarians, usually school children, adolescent school dropouts, or unemployed youths, but occasionally newly literate adults. First, the librarians count and number houses in the slum and organise the houses into clusters of four libraries, 100-150 households per library. Every librarian then goes house to house to enrol members. Membership is free, one member per household. There is no charge for torn or lost books since this is a part of learning to use books and happens very infrequently. Each librarian begins with about 25 books worth Rs.200 (US$ 6.67) and every month books worth Rs.100 (US$ 3.33) are added. Four libraries in a cluster receive different books and the stacks of books are rotated among the four libraries every week. Hence, members get to see new books all the time. The librarian gives books to about 25 households one day and collects them after one day to give them to the next 25. In this manner, 150 houses are served in a week. As the number of books grows, members can either keep a book for a longer period or can borrow more books.

The entire project costs about Rs.1.50 (US$ .05) per household per month. The cost has been kept deliberately low so that the members can run the libraries through monthly contributions after their first year. Most members who use the library free of cost are willing to pay membership fees after three months of operation, and about fifteen percent of the members are willing to participate in running the libraries.

Today, 80 libraries have became operational and provide at least one book every week to each one of the 10,000 households covered by them. A recent sample survey indicated that on average two to three people per household, especially girls and semi-educated women, read the books regularly and want more titles.

In addition to providing slum residents with reading materials, each library provides an organisational infrastructure for local slum people to come together free of so-called political or other petty rivalries.

Public Toilets

In 1984 the Government of India undertook several projects designed to apply science and technology in a manner more responsive to the needs of communities. One of these projects, over-seen by the secretary of the Department of Science and Technology (DST), was the Integrated Waste Management Pilot Project to be implemented in Bombay and then expanded to all major Indian cities. The pilot was to include a city wide project to provide clean, supervised, pay-and-use toilets for the entire city and to manufacture fuel pellets from 4,000 tons of daily municipal garbage.

The project began in late 1990 with the planning and construction of public toilets in several Bombay slums and the planning of a Refuse Derived Fuel (RDF) plant. By February, 1992, 12 toilet blocks had been constructed at Malwani, a large slum made up of displaced residents relocated from communities throughout Greater Bombay.

The toilet design has following features:

1. An attractive external appearance unlike a stereotypical Indian toilet facility;
2. Use of ferro-cement technology to produce pre-fabricated construction elements;
3. Excellent ventilation and lighting due to circular design with a central space open to sky;
4. Water storage tanks to store 20,000 litters of water;
5. Twenty-four to twenty-six toilets in two circles of a block.

While prefabricated materials were meant to facilitate on-site construction within one month or less, in reality, several problems related to drainage, sewerage, water, and electrical connections, all requiring interfacing with the municipal and other authorities, meant a minimum construction period of 3-4 months. Nonetheless, users have been happy with the design.

Until August, 1992, the toilets were managed and maintained on a pay-for-use basis by a small private contractor. The contractor was paid on a monthly basis to run, guard and maintain the toilet blocks. The toilets were to be open daily from 5 A.M. To 9 P.M. And continually manned by teams of one supervisor and two sweepers working in eight hour shifts. At night a watchman would guard the complex. Total expenditure was expected to be around Rs.5,800 (US$ 193) per block each month, with Rs.4,800 (US$160) going towards salaries and Rs.1000 (US

$33) for cleaning supplies and other maintenance costs. Thus to attain basic self-sufficiency, a block would have to collect Rs.200 (US$6.67) per day in fees.

The block-staff was to collect Rs.0.25 (25 praise) per use from the users above the age of eight and turn over these fees to CMC Ltd., a public sector undertaking entrusted with construction and maintenance of the toilet complexes. Water and electricity was provided free of cost.

By June, 1992 it was obvious that this maintenance system had some serious problems. The staff, especially the supervisors, were of questionable character. Their accounts and those of their employers could not be verified and considerable cheating was suspected. Assurance of monthly salaries regardless of how much was collected from latrine users eliminated any incentive to keep track of all the collected fees and to turn all of them over to CMC Ltd.

In addition, there was a resistance to the pay-and-use scheme. The Malwani toilets were constructed after demolishing existing public toilets that were filthy but free. Thus local people had no choice but to pay and use the new toilets. Daily payment of 0.25 praise per use was expensive, as the entire family would spend anywhere from Rs.30 to Rs.50 per month.

In comparison, monthly room rents in slums are generally Rs.15 and are hardly ever paid. Local elected representatives encouraged people to use the toilets without paying, even though these same officials had participated in the implementation of the scheme. The contractor who constructed the toilet blocks failed to complete planned improvements in areas surrounding the toilets, and construction faults interfered with the toilets' proper functioning. At 5 toilet blocks municipal corporation supply of water was insufficient. Finally, residents resented the profits made by the toilets' administrators. Residents felt forced to pay for a service that was inefficient in order to contribute to the profits of allegedly corrupt contractors.

In July of 1992 the private contractor was dismissed and CORO took over the management of the public toilets at Malwani. CORO had developed an interest in hygiene in the slums through their observation of conditions in the settlements where they were doing literacy work. In addition, the beginning of toilet construction in the Chamber, Govandi area, where CORO is promoting literacy further aroused their interest, and they went to Malwani to inspect the toilets being run under private management. Under CORO's direction, the management scheme was redesigned in response to the problems mentioned above. A family pass system for local users was instituted. At Rs. 10 a month, it represented an affordable alternative to the .25 praise charge for each use and encouraged families to use the latrine regularly. Non-pass holders continue to pay a .25 praise charge per use. CORO pays for a night watchman, cleaning materials and minor repairs as well as small stipend of Rs. 250 for substitute staff in case of illness or absence. The expenses incurred by CORO are reimbursed by the DST through CMC Ltd.

Staff members are in charge of keeping the latrines clean and collecting the fees, and their salary comes from an even division of the money collected. At Malwani, CORO hoped that community residents would take an active interest in managing and supervising the latrines. This has happened at two of the toilet blocks, and there is substantial community input and participation. However, the unsatisfactory initial experience with the pay-for-use toilets and Malwani's status as a relocated slum with little strong community feeling has limited community participation in the rest of the blocks to the presence of a community representative who monitors the work of the staff and keeps accounts of the daily records.

The improved model of management has resulted in the following:

a) The community has realised that this is not a commercial venture since their money goes towards salaries of those who serve.

b) The staff have less reason to cheat. If they cheat at all, it is at the expanse of their colleagues.

c) The blocks are staffed by only 3-4 persons who can be sustained by the block earnings.

d) The staff strives to keep the toilets clean since collection is also related to the standard of cleanliness.

As toilet blocks were completed in other slums, including Chamber, Govandi, where CORO had begun literacy work, CORO took over their management and operation. Having learned from mistakes made at Malwani, the new toilets were constructed in open space, and the old free toilets were left standing, giving residents a choice between free toilets that were dirty and poorly maintained, or pay toilets that were clean and well maintained.

With more time and experience, CORO was able to make improvements on its management scheme. As a first step, CORO created a cooperative comprised of its most active members, mostly literacy volunteers with experience working in the slums and community organisers from organisations like Stree Mukti Sanghatana, Granthali Readers' Movement, Yuvashakti Pratishthan and All India Women's Conference. As latrine maintenance staff were recruited from the communities themselves, they became cooperative members as well.

The cooperative (called the SUVIDHA cooperative) is committed to self-sufficiency; all salaries, materials and repairs would be paid for with money collected at the toilet block. DST continued to guarantee reimbursement for materials and repairs if necessary but the SUVIDHA units tried to avoid the use of any external funding. Finally, the entire cooperative general body meets once every month to discuss problems and progress. This reformed management structure has resulted in a more flexible, accountable and responsible staff and greater financial independence and allows for community input and democratic decision making as well as providing community residents with employment.

With introduction of this new concept, CORO started to tackle the main problem of sanitation faced by most of the slum dwellers in Greater Bombay. While implementing the scheme, CORO also tapped the need to promote reading habits among slum dwellers, which they thought would be useful in developing a new outlook towards sanitation and to create a clean and hygienic environment in Bombay.

Resource Utilisation

Ideally, public toilet blocks run by CORO would be clean and accessible for twenty-four hours a day; members of families that owned monthly passes would all use the toilets every day; and toilets would be affordable and completely self-sustaining. These goals have come to depend on two main factors – the availability of water and the ratio of users with passes to 25 p. Users. The relationship between these factors.

The factor which ultimately controls cleanliness and the number of users is water. Without enough water, the toilets cannot be cleaned, and users will not be willing to pay to use the latrines. Water has to be stored since it is supplied only for about 3-4 hours in the morning or evening. Toilet blocks that get their water in the mornings are better off than blocks that get their water in the evenings, since usage is heaviest in the morning. Where water is supplied in the evening, only the 15-20 thousand litters of available stored up water can be utilised. This often causes shortages, and water has to be used sparingly.

Demonstrates the balance that needs to be struck between users, self sufficiency and cleanliness. Obviously, larger numbers of users are needed to make the toilets self-sufficient, and the optimum number of users goes higher as the relative percentage of pass-holder users increases. This in turn puts pressure on available water. Also, although 3,600 pass-holder users can, in principle, make a block self-sufficient, it means each toilet will be used by more than 100 users, an unrealistic number.

At the moment, the toilets are managed with a large number of daily 25 p. Users. Now several systems are self-sufficient but they cannot be said to be fully successful because a 25 p. User often does not use the toilets every day. In spite of CORO's desire to give more family passes, to do so would cause a serious financial imbalance, since the toilets depend on 25 p. Users to be self sufficient; monthly passes will not pay for the toilets.

In order to achieve CORO's social goal of as extensive use of latrines as possible, the system must be based on family passes. This will mean that either the water storage capacity needs to be doubled to 40,000 litters or economic self sufficiency will have to be sacrificed and external financial sources sought. As the use of family passes rises, CORO will probably depend on a combination of these two strategies.

The self-sufficiency achieved in the CORO model is based on a monthly salary of Rs.1500/US $50 for the core Group members and the lower salary of Rs.600/US $20 for the sweeper. If people with much higher salaries are accommodated, self-sufficiency is lost. Furthermore, fees collected do not presently cover the cost of major repairs costing more than Rs. 2,000. It is estimated that every toilet block will need at least Rs.10,000 by way of external support per annum.

It is clear that ideal self-sufficiency coupled with high standards of cleanliness are unlikely with the present per use charges and limited water storage capacity. In the long run, with more and more community toilets being built, the percentage of 25 p. Users will come down and the system will not be self-sufficient unless salary requirements are reduced. In order for that to happen, users will have to be better educated about the environment, and the toilets will need to require less maintenance. Even so, CORO may need to depend on partial outside funding to keep public toilets running efficiently.

Through its literacy program, roving libraries and management of pay-and-use toilets, CORO has provided essential services to previously underserved communities and begun to lay the foundation for improved awareness of health and sanitation issues and a new culture of cleanliness and responsibility. By maintaining clean public toilets honestly and efficiently, CORO has provided a viable and affordable alternative to filthy, unhygienic free latrines or open spaces near homes. CORO-run toilets have been well received and are heavily used, demonstrating that slum residents are willing to pay for suitable service. Widely used latrines have also resulted in a noticeably cleaner and healthier environment in the slums, with less human waste in streets, fields and other open spaces.

Table 2. Characteristics of CORO-run toilets

Area	*Blocks*	*Toilets*	*Users*	*Self-sustaining*
Malwani	12 380	About	15,000	No
Jogeshwari	126	About	1,240	No
Andheri	126	About	1,800	Yes
Dharavi	126	About	1,400	Yes
Chembur	2 52	About	3,000	Yes
Govandi	4 120	About	6,000	Yes
TOTAL	21 600	About	28,440	No

For women, clean public latrines have provided a way to relieve themselves in privacy, avoiding the humiliation of using public, open spaces and the danger to their health and their personal safety resulting from waiting until dark to relieve themselves.

By enlisting local residents to serve as maintenance workers and SUVIDHA cooperative members, CORO provides employment and income in an area marked by unemployment and poverty. Maintenance workers and cooperative members gain valuable work and organisational experience. Use of local labour also ensures greater accountability and community participation; as community members, the maintenance workers are trusted, can raise community concerns during cooperative meetings and cater service to community needs.

Community workers also gain valuable experience in CORO's literacy campaign and working as librarians for the roving libraries. They have been able to enlist the support of slum residents and to recruit library members. There are now 80 functioning libraries providing over 10,000 households with reading materials in the slums of Bombay.

Taken together, CORO's literacy campaign and its management of pay-and-use municipal toilets have helped to lay the groundwork for more substantial changes in the attitude and culture of Bombay's poor. Through literacy classes, reading, and the efforts of local latrine workers, residents are learning about the importance of sanitation, hygiene, and the environment. Latrine workers have begun to provide an alternative to the increasingly unworkable system of cleaning and maintenance based on the caste system, and have begun to demonstrate that individuals and communities can take care of their own human waste problems. Maintenance workers, literacy advocates, and librarians have ceased to be passive recipients and are taking an active role in improving conditions in their neighbourhoods. Residents have shown a willingness to pay for service instead of demanding service for free and placing an even greater strain on an already over-extended municipal government. By combining libraries with latrines, CORO can serve communities, create a springboard for community efforts centered on other important issues, and extend their network's reach into more homes.

Obstacles

CORO has had to overcome several obstacles in order to achieve success in literacy training, distributing reading material, and running pay-and-use toilets. Attitudes take a long time to change, and there is still a considerable amount of resistance to the kind of change CORO envisions in Bombay's slums, as well as continuing problems of a more mundane and technical nature.

CORO has had difficulty getting children to use the public toilets, despite not charging them and even going into the neighbourhood in order to bring children accustomed to defecating outdoors to the toilets. A major problem lies in the toilet design, which is too large for small children. CORO is working on possible new designs to be used in new toilet complexes.

In spite of the generally cooperative nature of CORO's relationship with the municipal government, there have been problems. Toilet construction is often delayed because of difficulties with municipal agencies in charge of electricity, drainage, water and sewage. Despite prefabricated elements that should allow construction to be completed in one month, toilets usually take three to four months to be built. In addition, CMC Ltd. was initially skeptical of CORO's ability to run the toilets. A meeting had to be arranged with satisfied users to convince CMC that CORO was indeed able to manage toilets competently and efficiently.

There is continued resistance to pay-and-use toilets among many residents, especially at Malwani where the destruction of a free alternative, the actions of local politicians, and the initial experience with unsatisfactory service and inefficient, sometimes corrupt management created resentment among some residents. CORO's effective management and the cleanliness of the latrines themselves are gradually eroding this resistance, and residents are becoming more willing to pay in order to use clean toilets.

Initially, CORO had difficulties within the management units. Staff members felt that cleaning toilets was degrading work, beneath their station as educated citizens. Their ancestors had been discriminated against within the caste system for doing precisely this kind of work. After discussion and experience managing the toilets, workers began to feel that they were not engaged in demeaning work, but in cooperative self-development. They were beginning to make a difference in their communities and were fulfilling an essential role in a collective undertaking in which they had an important say.

Groups had problems with inefficient workers and dishonesty. They set up internal vigilance groups and even fired some workers who were cheating or not working. This was extremely difficult for the units to do, but it was essential in order to maintain standards. It represented a change in attitudes, one in which labour and honesty were rewarded and workers were held accountable for their behaviour.

Groups also had trouble with expensive repairs to the toilets, especially when they had to depend on outside repairmen. They were able to cut down on this expense by finding their own repair people from among CORO community literacy activists.

CORO also had troubles at the beginning of their literacy campaign. CORO activists had little experience with literacy training, and the program suffered from ineffective teachers and poor training courses. Men were especially difficult to teach, as they were unwilling to admit to illiteracy, and had little free time to learn because of long commutes to work. They also often discouraged their wives and daughters from learning how to read, further undermining CORO's efforts.

In all of CORO's efforts entrenched attitudes and cultural mores continue to cause problems. Most Indian slum dwellers retain rural customs and are unused to using toilets or reserving space for them when planning homes or communities. Such habits are difficult to change. Also, centuries of a rigid caste system has trained people to leave much essential work to others; they are forbidden by caste rules and custom to engage in a host of necessary activities. This has produced a culture of resignation and robbed many people of initiative; they do not see it as their responsibility to improve their lot, clean their toilet or any number of other things. CORO faces a constant challenge in motivating residents to fulfil roles and do jobs to which they are not accustomed and which they might find objectionable.

Diffusion

Because of the success of their programs CORO has been able to expand their management of public pay-and-use toilets as well as their roving libraries into new slums. DST has asked CORO to run new toilet blocks in five new slums since their successful administration of the Malwani toilet block in 1992. (The five slums are Jogeshwari, Andheri, Dharavi, Chembur and Govandi.) CORO is now forming new libraries, recruiting new librarians and signing up new library members.

In addition, the innovation has been documented and publicised in the press, on video-tape and on television.

Many voluntary agencies, community groups, and individuals within Bombay and throughout the country have learned about CORO in this way. Also, CORO workers have attended training programs, seminars, and workshops to make presentations and share their experiences.

Key Elements

When faced with the challenge of promoting literacy and managing public toilets in the slums of Bombay, CORO devised several strategies which were innovative and essential to the project's success.

Integrating Literacy and Sanitation

By combining the running of municipal toilets with pre-existing efforts to combat illiteracy, CORO was able to capitalise on community knowledge and contacts they already had.

As an organisation that was already working in the slums, CORO already had some understanding of the problems in the community and credibility with the residents. They were able to build on their pre-existing organisational strength and to call on the resources of their activists to motivate residents to utilise pay and use toilets and join roving libraries. As an organisation dedicated to promoting literacy and distributing reading material, CORO was already involved in education efforts. When CORO began to manage community toilets, they found themselves equipped to address the cultural and educational issues involved in promoting new norms of cleanliness and sanitation.

Using Local Volunteers and Labour

With local staff members running latrines, CORO was able to gain residents' trust and be responsive to community needs. CORO was able to provide jobs to slum residents, generate income for poor workers and give them organisational and job experience. As community-run enterprises, CORO managed toilets demonstrated that communities could work to solve their own problems, including problems of human waste. This is an important lesson for communities bound by habits of passive receivership and centuries of caste-determined labour and sanitary practices.

In their literacy work, the enthusiasm of local activists was essential in motivating residents to learn to read and to join the roving libraries. Local librarians distribute books, sign up families, and recruit other librarians. Such participation gives residents a stake in the project and a sense of being able to create positive change in their neighbourhoods.

Forming a Cooperative

By forming a cooperative and including local community members, CORO opened up the decision making process and involved the community in identifying problems, devising strategies and sharing responsibility. CORO became a community organisation run for and by the community.

Instituting Monthly Family Passes

By selling monthly family passes at a fixed price, CORO was able to encourage daily toilet use, while making it more affordable. With a pass, family members were more likely to use the toilets often, as each use did not cost any more.

Tying Salaries to Fees

By tying staff members' pay to the amount of fees collected, CORO devised a built-in incentive for workers to work efficiently and to encourage community members to use the toilets. Staff salaries are a result of staff efforts; the cleaner the toilets and the more effectively they can convince residents of the need to use latrines, the more people will use the toilets and the more money the staff will make. This system also minimises corruption. The staff monitor each other and are less likely to cheat since it would be depriving their co-workers, who often are also their neighbours, of money. The residents also appreciate this system and prefer that their fees go towards staff salaries rather than a corrupt private contractor.

Partnerships

CORO benefited from the efforts of the following important partners:

1. *Indian Government Department of Science and Technology (DST).* DST oversees the Integrated Waste Management Pilot Project, including the construction and maintenance of the public toilet blocks. DST was the agency which first approached CORO to take over the administration and maintenance of the toilet blocks and is the source of funds for construction, major maintenance projects and, when needed, materials.
2. *CMC Limited.* This is a public sector corporation which has been charged with the construction and maintenance of the public toilets in Bombay. CMC Ltd. distributes DST funds to CORO and works with them to construct and maintain toilet facilities.
3. *National Literacy Mission.* This organisation provided funding for teacher training and literacy materials.
4. *Famous celebrities.* Celebrities distributed literacy kits in the slums and helped raise interest and enthusiasm for CORO and literacy.
5. *Community organisers.* At the beginning of their literacy efforts and throughout the ensuing literacy

project and toilet maintenance scheme, community organisers lent enthusiastic and valuable support. They helped mobilise residents to participate in libraries, take literacy classes and use public pay-and-use latrines.

6. *Slum Residents.* Residents have shown a willingness to pay for clean latrines and to join local roving libraries. Without their participation, none of CORO's efforts would have been successful.

Despite its inexperience in sanitation and toilet management, CORO was able to maintain latrines, gain acceptance of a previously unpopular pay-for-use scheme, institute participatory management and increase latrine use in the slums of Bombay. The key to CORO's success was its fundamental redefinition of the basic problem; latrine maintenance and use was not a problem of service delivery, but one of organisation, education, and legitimacy in the eyes of the community. By creating a structure more open to community accountability and with built-in incentives for maintenance workers, and by combining toilet maintenance with education and literacy efforts, CORO was able to integrate latrine maintenance and promotion into an overall framework of community development and change.

The project itself is fairly specific, applicable only where people are forced to depend on public toilets for their sanitary needs and unaccustomed to using toilets in the first place. Given this, the following preconditions must be satisfied in order to implement a program based on CORO's New Culture of Urban Sanitation.

1. *Governmental Role.* When looking to solve toilet maintenance and usage problems, governments need to redefine the problem as one of organisation and awareness. They need to be open to the possibility of solving what seems like a straightforward service delivery problem by calling upon the services of

community organisations or NGO's with little experience in service delivery but organisational capacity, credibility and experience in the intended beneficiary community. Governments must also be willing to invest resources in sanitary improvements for the poor. The construction and maintenance of toilets is expensive, and CORO's experience shows that planning for them to be economically self-sustaining is unrealistic; an outside funding source will almost always be necessary.

2. *Implementing Agency.* There must be an organisation well-positioned to implement a new organisational structure for the maintenance of public toilets and able to integrate toilet maintenance into a broader program of community development and education. The implementing agency should have experience in the beneficiary community, be responsive to community concerns, and have effective mechanisms to ensure community input and participation in decision-making and action.

Beyond the issue of latrine use and maintenance, CORO's New Culture of Urban Sanitation has wider implications for municipal governments faced with what appear to be traditional service delivery problems. CORO has shown that those problems may be organisational or cultural ones, and the solution may be found by organisations with little experience in the specific problem area. Governments looking for solutions to such problems might find success in partnerships with community development organisations and NGO's.

4

Urban Ecological Problems

The science of ecology was born from the expansive curiosity of the biologists of the late 19th century, who wished to understand the distribution, abundance and interactions of the earth's organisms. Why do we have so many species, and why not more, they asked—and what causes them to be distributed as they are? What are the characteristics of a biological community that cause it to recover in a particular way after a disturbance?

Such questions took Charles Darwin and other naturalists on journeys far from human civilisation. And more than a century later, ecologists still tend to search for answers to these questions in "pristine" environments—the tropical rain forest, the coral reef. From the perspective of a field ecologist examining a natural ecosystem, people are an exogenous, perturbing force. Human beings—and especially their cities, seemingly so "artificial"—fail to fit neatly into ecological theory.

But people mobilise nutrients and pollutants, drive species extinct, promote the survival of others, change the composition of the atmosphere and alter landscapes. Thanks to advances in technology and to humanity's growing population and penchant for consumption, we are today a global ecological force capable of affecting every species and ecosystem on the planet. Over the past several decades, moreover, we have rushed to the cities. Soon more people worldwide will live in cities than in rural areas. In cities people mobilise some nutrients and deplete others, create habitats that never before existed, divert water, increase temperatures and, by intent or by accident, manipulate the communities of other species found within city boundaries and beyond. Cities are some of the most profoundly altered ecosystems on the planet; within their boundaries are also found some of the most diverse ecological conditions. If there is a laboratory where ecological change can be viewed at close hand, it is the city.

Ecologists, however, have hardly rushed to the city. A mere 0.4 percent—25 of 6,157—of the papers published in nine leading ecological journals in the past five years dealt with cities or urban species. Whatever the reasons for ecologists' persistent tendency to focus on pristine environments, human-dominated ecosystems represent a problem for the field.

Dependent Ecosystem

Urban-ecology research at this stage consists of vastly more questions than answers. If ecologists are to study urban ecosystems, for instance, they must decide two questions first: what an urban ecosystem is, and what measures appropriately describe its interactions with other ecosystems? In some respects these are the same question—and a good place to begin.

Among the traditional ways to look at an ecosystem is by examining how it balances primary production (photosynthesis, or solar-energy conversion by plants) with respiration, by which energy is converted to unusable form. Although the calculations that make up a system's internal energy budget are far more complicated than this simple ratio suggests, for most ecosystems the overall calculation is fairly well balanced between inputs and outputs. An urban ecosystem, a concentration of people and human activity, is an energy-intensive ecosystem, and viewed in traditional ecological terms it is more unbalanced than most other ecosystems. Its unique energy signature, then, is one way of distinguishing an urban ecosystem.

Howard T. Odum of the University of Florida noted that a typical city daily transforms into heat about 70 times more usable energy per square meter than a close non-human equivalent to a city—an oyster reef. A natural ecosystem is likely to be self-powered by photosynthesis or chemosynthesis. By contrast a city is a heterotrophic ecosystem, one that depends primarily on external sources of energy. Take Chicago's famed pizza: It may be made with wheat from Kansas, tomatoes from California, anchovies from the Mediterranean and cheese from a Wisconsin dairy farm. The pizza oven may be fired with fuel from the Middle East and made of steel forged in Pennsylvania or perhaps Japan. Pizza-making thus borrows, in one form or another, energy that originated with photosynthetic activity in other ecosystems. Heterotrophic ecosystems are rare on earth, including some marshes, the deep ocean and streams, but even among such systems cities are extreme.

There are a variety of ways of describing flows between urban areas and other ecosystems. One is an input-output model. People import to cities foodstuffs, fuels, building materials and other products that can be described in the energy currency of ecology. Land conversion or degradation, agricultural production and the harvesting of plant-derived building materials can be seen as ways in which the urban ecosystem appropriates the primary production of other ecosystems. In addition, we can consider how energy flows: Imports and exports are mediated by meteorologic, hydrologic and biologic vectors. A city along a river, for instance, imports energy via hydrologic vectors from an entire watershed and typically returns to the downstream environment water containing heat and nutrients such as phosphorus and nitrogen.

Urban energy budgets, dominated as they are by deliberate human energy imports and by losses via fossil-fuel burning, or "industrial respiration," do not resemble the energy budgets of any other ecosystem on earth, as the work of Eugene P. Odum of the University of Georgia has shown. Although calculating these budgets can be complex, energy use is a common currency that can be measured for all ecosystems, providing a basis for comparing systems that are human dominated with those that are not. Ecology has been called "nature's economy," and such calculations potentially afford a means for linking ecological theory with social-science theories using resource-economics concepts.

Urban Footprint

The different characteristics of urban ecosystems may call for some non-traditional ways of assessing how dependent they are on other ecosystems. Stuart Fisher and Gene Likens, both then at Dartmouth College, working in the Hubbard Brook Experimental Forest of New Hampshire, examined the heterotrophic ecosystem of Bear Brook. Primary production was negligible in the stream itself, and all of the ecosystem's respiration (2,935 kilocalories per square meter annually) was supported by material imported from the surrounding forest, which had an annual net primary production of 4,680 kilocalories per square meter. Yet the amount of material required could be supplied by an area of forest equivalent to a strip of vegetation about two feet wide (0.31 meters on each bank) along the stream's length, much narrower than the stream itself.

By contrast, William Rees of the University of British Columbia estimated that the city of Vancouver consumes an amount of material equivalent to that produced by a productive land area 180 times its size, assuming that area is not dominated by people.

Rees employs in his analysis an instructive measure of urban energy dependence called an "ecological footprint." The footprint of a city is the total area of productive land required to support its activities in a sustainable way. In other words, that land must produce an amount of resources equivalent to the sum of all resources consumed by the city—and assimilate an amount of waste equivalent to that produced by the city. Cities' footprints can be impressive—tens or hundreds of times larger than their actual area—because in addition to the plant, microbial and animal metabolisms that characterise all ecosystems, cities have an "industrial metabolism"—a metaphorical hunger whose satisfaction requires mining of non-renewable resources as well as exploitation of renewable ones.

The footprint concept is a new (and somewhat controversial) way of assessing ecosystem dependence. Matthew Luck and other LTER scientists at ASU are exploring, among other questions, how the concept of a footprint could be used to consider the impact of a city within its particular geology and climate. Many of the earth's fastest-growing cities are, like Phoenix, located in low-productivity arid or semi-arid lands. In terms of land area, these cities' footprints are huge, if this local context is taken into account.

Local conditions are just one of several independent variables that would be expected to influence the magnitude of an urban ecosystem's dependence on its surroundings. Others are the fertility of the surrounding land, the average income of the city's inhabitants, cultural variables, a city's size and age, and its political context. And this general dependence measure could be partitioned into separate measures for different ecological variables such as water, elements, food, waste assimilation and energy.

City In Space And Time

Since the characteristics of any ecosystem vary from one part to another, ecologists conceive of ecosystems as consisting of habitat "patches." A city—with its concrete-and-glass downtown, its golf courses, industrial parks and tree-lined residential streets—is quite a patchy ecosystem, and together with all its patches it is part of a larger landscape full of other patches. A landscape ecologist tackling an urban ecosystem would look at the pattern of patches within a city, and the variations in the way the land is used from one patch to the next, and ask how these patterns and this variability influence bio-geo-chemical processes and affect how organisms and resources are distributed, and how species interact.

As the pioneering ecologist C. C. Adams observed early in the 20th century, ecology will need to incorporate the social sciences to answer such questions when human beings are taken into account. Models to explain how people as a species affect the composition of habitat patches and their patterns will have to integrate historical, political, cultural and economic factors with traditional variables such as competition, predation and nutrient availability, which also control the distribution, abundance and relations of organisms.

But we can begin by looking for spatial patterns. Traditionally these include the species composition of patches and how the patches are arranged in space. These variables affect ecological processes by regulating competition among species and energy flows within the ecosystem. The scale of the pattern also affects the scale at which these processes operate. Such patterns have practical use: Once they are known, they can provide indicators for ecological monitoring.

The predictions one might make based on landscapeecology concepts. If you consider a city in a semi-arid or arid region where water limits natural biotic productivity, you might predict that soil respiration would be more variable in the undisturbed natural ecosystem than in the fringes of an urban area, where water and nutrients are more uniformly supplied for agriculture and suburban residential development. As you move toward the urban core, the fine scale pattern of land use changes, and you would expect more variability in irrigation from one patch to the next. Therefore in the city's centre there is more point-to-point variation than in the natural ecosystem, although along the fringe there is less. Similarly, the natural temporal variation in hydrological conditions might be "smoothed out" by agricultural and horticultural activities along the fringe but might vary more in the centre because of extensive modification of hydrology.

One of the issues we face is defining what an urban ecosystem is. Having introduced the urban core, the urban fringe and the energy intensity and heterotrophic nature of the city, we can begin to sketch out an emerging view of what an urban ecosystem is. First, we have the advice of the U.S. Census Bureau, which defines an area with a population density over 620 individuals per square kilometre as "urban." These individuals exhibit a high per capita energy consumption and that their habitat is characterised by large-scale environmental modification. But these characteristics are variable. One useful paradigm for viewing them is that of the environmental gradient. Mark McDonnell (then at the Institute for Ecosystem Studies in New York) and colleagues in 1997 showed that urban-rural environmental gradients measuring change in these characteristics can be used to capture the indefinite boundaries of many urban ecosystems. But many other characteristics could be used to do so.

Strange Changes

Like any ecosystem, an urban ecosystem is dynamic and changing. Are the forces that drive change similar to those in a non-urban system? Some clearly are: Disturbances such as fire, flood and earthquake are inevitable in cities. Yet people constantly struggle to control and manage the frequency and magnitude of disturbance. Therefore—although we're not likely to be able to control earthquakes—disturbance regimes are often altered by human action. Separated from the Mississippi River by dikes, New Orleans is protected from much of the flooding that would be its natural disturbance regime.

Likewise, the way an urban ecosystem recovers from a disturbing event may be altered dramatically by human intervention. In non-urban ecosystems a fire or flood is typically followed by a gradual and somewhat predictable series of changes called ecological succession . Human intervention may suppress such patterns altogether. An abandoned home site may begin to fill with plant growth—vegetative succession, to an ecologist—but redevelopment typically truncates the process that might otherwise fill the patch with trees and animals. Such redevelopment is an example of the single most important force of landscape change in urban areas: land conversion, driven by institutional decisions, population growth and economic forces.

We generally think of climate change and biological evolution as occurring on much longer time scales than fire and flood—and far longer than the frame of reference for urban ecology. Yet evolutionary and climatic change are likely accelerated or enhanced in urban ecosystems. Recent studies have shown that fruit flies and egg-laying butterflies have rapidly adapted to prefer new human-introduced host plants. And in recent decades many organisms placed under strong selection pressure by human action have evolved resistance mechanisms—bacteria to antibiotics, rats to poison, weeds to herbicides. The extreme selective pressures exerted by human environmental changes suggest that evolution in urban ecosystems will likely be evolution under the non-equilibrium conditions of rapidly changing environments. Surviving species in urban ecosystems will be those, such as cockroaches, rats and cats, that cope with anthropogenic selection pressures by rapid evolution or phenotypes plasticity.

The possible effects of urban ecosystems on climate regimes have hardly been investigated, but a few observations suggest they should be. Consider the well-known "urban heat island" effect—the fact that temperatures within cities can exceed those in surrounding areas by several degrees on average. Current research in Phoenix shows that carbon dioxide concentrations within the city centre are elevated to several times the global average, a change that has likely taken place on a decade time scale. How such rapid change within an urban micro-climate affects plant, animal and microbial species has hardly been investigated.

In fact, there are findings that suggest that human activity may be capable of altering regional climate patterns in striking ways. In 1998 Randall S. Cerveny and Robert C. Balling, Jr. of Arizona State University demonstrated that the five-day work-week and accompanying commute affected precipitation patterns on the East Coast of the U.S. By making rainfall more likely on weekends than weekdays. In this case the patterns of human activity, unlike those of most animals, did not follow natural rhythms but seemed to alter them. In other cases human activity, of course, has tended to follow natural cycles: We are active by day and sleep by night; throughout human time our festivals have tracked harvests or grown out of the need to fill winter nights. Natural reliability in weather and climate can dictate temporal patterns in the organisation of society, but it is unclear whether people living in modern urban ecosystems are as likely to develop social rhythms responding to natural cycles as are rural human societies that depend vitally on a local resource hunter-gatherer societies or subsistence-agriculture villages, for example.

Can ecological theory be extended to study these new forms of change and disturbance? One way to do so is to analogise human disturbance regimes to known ecological regimes. Home construction may be viewed as an ecological disturbance, framing a new question: How does an urban ecosystem recover from such disturbance? Patricia Gober, an ASU geographer participating in the LTER study, and her colleagues viewed the zone of rapid land conversion at the Phoenix urban fringe as a wave of disturbance spreading outward from several urban nodes in the desert alluvial plain. They have calculated land consumption rates and are seeking indicators of incipient urban expansion at the fringe.

And the Cerveny and Balling result is provocative. In ecosystems not dominated by people, individual plants, dispersal distances and the scale of disturbance can define the spatial scales over which processes are influenced and patterns emerge. Both the temporal and spatial scales of patterns in human-dominated ecosystems are likely to emerge from social forces far removed from foraging and dispersal strategies. There are many clear examples of human-imposed spatial scales in our history. The opening of the American West and the Homestead Act enforced a pattern of 160-acre plots on the landscape. Urban ecosystems are usually developed within a grid of blocks each 100 or 200 meters long. Thus we should not be surprised to find new spatial scales emerging for ecological processes within urban systems. However unusual it seems to a landscape ecologist, we are likely to be studying processes on the scales determined by the human-built infrastructure: perhaps the individual home site, or a city block.

Toward Synthesis

Is there a possibility of simply stretching current ecological theory to encompass urban ecosystems? It can be argued that our understanding of dynamics and processes for population and soils can be extended to homeowners' associations and pavement. Perhaps the tools already developed for understanding the emergence of different life-history strategies can be extended, without conceptual changes, to people. Human beings, we might argue, are like other organisms. Selective pressures and evolved strategies lead to certain population dynamics and patterns, to certain impacts on surrounding regions and species and finally to certain changes in the allocation or flow of nutrients and resources. It could be that the differences in the ways in which people and other organisms evolve, interact with, and influence their surroundings are merely quantitative, not qualitative.

Or one can take the position that current ecological theory is insufficient to capture the key patterns and processes in these human-dominated or urban ecosystems. Human beings, that is to say, are qualitatively unlike other organisms. The emergence and influence of culture, the constraints and opportunities afforded by our institutions, and our ability to create strategies in response to anticipated (rather than realised) selection pressures mean that standard ecological and evolutionary theories and principles apply only imperfectly to human population. This view would obligate would-be urban ecologists to seek out a great deal of interaction with, or "borrowing from," the social sciences to advance ecology in general to a point where it can explain patterns and processes in human-dominated systems.

Either approach implies hard philosophical truths. If a person can be treated as any other organism, the distinction between "natural" and "unnatural" systems disappears, and with it the idea of a "pristine" ecosystem. The whole notion of environmental stewardship may suffer as well. If people act as other organisms do, guided by individual self-interest, there are no grounds for a moral or aesthetic call to stewardship. In the second case, we are forced to face the question of why people are not like other organisms: Is there, for instance, a spiritual or moral dimension that defies explanations offered by evolution or natural selection?

Philosophy aside, it is not clear that any ecologist has to make a hard choice. Standard ecological theories can be and have been applied to human systems; they can be used, for instance, to understand the "dispersal" or "successional dynamics" of urban systems. We can then determine which patterns or details, if any, are impervious to explanations emerging from these standard theories. At the same time, we should examine whether inter- or multi-disciplinary approaches between the biological and social sciences provide more elegant theories or explanatory power.

Consider some of the leading conceptual questions mentioned above. How do we study the change in the position or shape of the "urban fringe"—the dynamics of the edge of the city and its expansion? Borrowing tools strictly from ecology, we could begin by employing plant-dispersal and competition models. Thus expansion of the urban fringe could be understood in terms of the density of surrounding neighbourhoods, with residences "produced" from nearby "occupied" cells and dispersed to nearby empty cells. One can imagine density-dependent processes controlling neighbourhood changes. Another tool is the contact-process model, wherein the probability of a lot undergoing a transition from empty to occupied (with a house) could depend on the "state" of the neighbouring lots—whether they are devoted to residential, commercial, agricultural or recreational purposes. Empty cells could be assigned probabilities for colonisation based on their own properties, which could vary across the landscape: Is there good drainage, a good view, an adequate ground-water supply?

The processes of urban-fringe expansion also can be described in the ecologists' language of disturbance, as Patricia Gober has. Urbanisation at the outer edges of a sprawling metropolis involves both the spatial expansion of human disturbance and the alteration of ecological processes. For any given patch, we can assign a probability of transition (or new disturbance). We might hypothesise that this probability is low in the non-urban matrix, increases steeply at the urban fringe and returns to an intermediate level of disturbance in the centre of the city. As urbanisation of the surrounding matrix proceeds, the probability for patch transition increases in areas that were previously non-urban while decreasing in the former urban-fringe areas, now incorporated into the metropolis. A simple hypothesis derived from these patch-transition probabilities is that a wave of high disturbance radiates through time outward from the initial city edge.

These approaches could help us capture some of the patterns and dynamics of urban-fringe expansion. But what would they be missing? To start with, a dose of economics is surely necessary to explain year-to-year patterns in housing starts. What are the variations in interest rates? In unemployment? In inflation? Economic modelling might predict the number of new houses produced and sold each year, and we could return to ecological theory to examine their dispersal. But there are still more factors to consider. How are decisions for locating roads, establishing sewer lines, or extending emergency services made? How does the power and the approach of state or city institutions change as cities grow? Does the proximity of other municipal organisations affect decisions for developing city boundaries? To capture these effects, we would need to know much more about political theory and the evolution of government institutions.

At this point we would still lack insight into why people value certain spaces over others, or how those values vary by socioeconomic class, family situation and age. For this we may need to turn to sociology to improve our predictions about "dispersal" of houses, and how dispersal patterns might change with economic development, a changing age structure of inhabitants or with new cultural traditions introduced by new arrivals. A return to ecological theory would be required to understand how housing starts affect the landscape, including its bio-diversity, and thus potentially alter people's preferences for these sites.

We are still missing information, finally, on how individual and socialite preferences vary over time. To take an obvious example of changing preferences, consider the role of the city centre in medieval versus modern times. In medieval times, citizens returned to the city centre at night for protection. In modern times, we find many inhabitants avoiding the city centre at night, again for protection. Similarly, our desires for privacy or large yards or suburban/ rural surroundings have changed over the course of this century with changing socialite values. Both social sciences and evolutionary biology might provide tools for understanding this "evolution" of culture.

Evolutionary biology could be invoked to examine variations in selection pressures along urban to rural gradients. But social-science tools are required to explain the preferential cultivation or destruction of some species by the human inhabitants of the city, and how these preferences vary as a function of socioeconomic class, age or place of birth. The presence of exotic species and the increased opportunities for dispersal or invasion caused by habitat disruption and fragmentation would force us to return to the tools of ecology to understand the effects of introduced species on native population.

Ecological theory might benefit from the use of analogies to accelerate the development of new concepts that can be applied to urban human-ecological systems. Gregg Mitman has discussed how this approach was used in the 1920s and 1930s by University of Chicago sociologists Robert Park and Earnest Burgess and their colleagues and ecologists such as W. C. Allee, Alfred Emersion and Thomas Park to develop ideas of "human socialite." These were the early urban ecologists who attempted to understand human actions by analogy with ecological systems. Although we recognise the danger inherent in its indiscriminate use, comparison of succession and urbanisation reveals the heuristic utility of this kind of analogy. In a city with spreading growth, the perimeter or "urban fringe" can be viewed as an active disturbance area, and locations farther removed from the fringe (inward) as earlier in succession (space-for-time substitution).

William Cronon, an environmental historian, argued that the disciplines of ecology, history, geography, anthropology and others could "learn from one another if only we can scale the walls that separate us to start working together on the problems we all find fascinating." The challenge of understanding urban ecosystems will require disciplinary specialists, but it will also require at least some individuals willing to think in interdisciplinary and multi-disciplinary ways—a task that can be difficult to accomplish. These investigators will have to knock down the walls, rather than scale them, to integrate diverse disciplines into a synthetic research area and a novel perspective that will advance ecological theory.

5

Urban Population Dynamics

Rapid urbanisation in the poorest countries is straining the capacity of cities to provide basic amenities, degrading the quality of life, and impoverishing the environment. Although the same strains on quality of life, health, and the environment were evident in the earlier urban transition in the industrialised world, there are significant differences between the two transitions. Firstly, the sheer numbers of people taking part in it are of a dramatically different scale. Secondly, owing to complex changes in the global economy, the prospects for economic development among the poorest countries are not nearly as bright as the situation faced 150 years ago by today's industrialised countries. Lastly, the global environmental context has changed dramatically, and today there is real concern about the impacts of further industrial development in the face of climate change and the rapid loss of ecosystems. Unfortunately, instead of bringing economic dynamism, improved health, environmental standards, education and democratisation, urbanisation in many least developed countries is accompanied by economic stagnation, negligible health gains, lax environmental standards, low education levels, crime and social instability.

Urban Growth

At the present time, some 3.2 billion people already live in towns and cities; this is expected to rise to almost 5 billion by 2030. In comparison, the world's rural population is expected to decrease by some 28 million between 2005 and 2030. Ergo, at the global level, all population growth in the future will be in towns and cities. No less than 97 per cent of this huge absolute increase in urban population will accrue to developing regions. Asia will be, far and away, the primary site of all future growth, followed by Africa and then Latin America.

Urban growth is increasingly being recognised as one of the critical development issues of the 21st century. Yet discussions in the media and even among policy-makers persistently make three erroneous assumptions about ongoing trends. It is generally assumed that:

a) current trends are due to an unprecedented rapid rate of urban growth;

b) most urban growth is occurring in megacities;

c) most urban growth is due to migration from rural to urban areas.

All of these assertions are in fact misleading and can lead to erroneous policy decisions.

As observed in a seminal study by the US National Academy of Sciences, the main difference between the current urban transition in developing countries and the past experience of Europe and the United States lies in the *unprecedented scale of change*. The real story ere is no longer the rapid rates of city growth but *the absolute size of the increments* in the urban population of less developed regions. Between 2000 and 2030, according to the latest UN estimates, the urban population of the developed world is expected to grow only from 870 million to 1.01 billion. That of Latin America and the Caribbean will increase from 394 to 609 million, while Asia's will grow from 1.36 billion to 2.64 billion, and Africa's from 294 to 742 million. By 2030,

Africa, Asia and Latin America will include 8 out of every ten urban inhabitants in the world. And this unprecedented scale of urban growth is occurring despite a significant decline in actual *rates* of growth of the urban population.

As concerns the evolution of megacities, it is true that they have obviously grown in size and number in the last few decades. As countries urbanise, they inevitably develop one or more large agglomeration, often incorporating two or more large urban cores. In 1950, the world knew of only one behemoth (New York) having more than 10 million inhabitants: by 2005, there were 20 such megacities, 15 of which were located in less-developed regions and, by 2015, there will be 22 of them. However, the growth in the number and size of such cities has been much slower than predicted in earlier decades. Today, megacities account for 4 per cent of the world's population and 9 per cent of all urban inhabitants; this is undoubtedly an important slice, but not one that is expected to expand quickly in the foreseeable future as the growth of the major megacities has slowed down and will continue to do so, both in more and less developed regions.

A fact that has garnered much less attention but which is actually more important for the planning of our urban future is that small and intermediate cities are where most urbanities live. At the present time, 52 per cent of the urban population still lives in "small and intermediate cities". Moreover, contrary to popular opinion, this ascendancy of smaller cities will persist in the foreseeable future. Thus, it is expected that, in the future, most urban growth will actually take place in urban locations having less than 500,000 people. This observation concerning the prevalence of smaller towns and cities in the urban future of less developed regions is of the utmost significance in any effort aimed at improving the lives of urban dwellers in the future.

As regards the sources of urban growth, most people assume that rural to urban migration is the main demographic cause. Thus, policy-makers have increasingly tried to reduce urban problems by deviating migratory movements from cities to other rural destinations and/or dissuading migrants from coming to cities. The latest comprehensive effort to separate out the components of urban growth put the contribution of natural increase at about 60 per cent in the median country. The remainder is the result of a combination of migration and reclassification. The important point is that, over time, the ascendancy of natural increase in urban growth will inevitably grow as urbanisation (i.e. the rise in the proportion of the total population living in urban areas) progresses.

In short, urban administrators wishing to reduce urban growth thus need to give greater attention to the factors that affect fertility decline rather than to migration. At any rate, attempts to prevent rural-urban migration have generally met with failure.

Case Studies

Each of the five PRIPODE case study cities is experiencing rapid growth in excess of 3 percent per annum. Here we present the population and economic profiles of each city, with particular reference to their growth trends, starting with Ho Chi Minh City and then moving to Africa.

Ho Chi Minh City is the largest city in Vietnam and is located near the Mekong River delta. The city centre is situated on the banks of the Saigon River, 60 km from the South China Sea. It is the most important economic centre in Vietnam. Some 300,000 businesses, including many large enterprises, are involved in high-tech, electronic, processing and light industries, also in construction, building materials and agro-products. The economy is growing at an astounding 11% per annum.

In the study, the researchers found that the city grew from roughly 5 million people in 1997 to more than 6.2 million in 2005, or a 2.8% annual rate of growth. Recent rates are in excess of 3 percent. Natural increase was almost twice as important as migration in 1997, but between 2003 and 2005, this trend was reversed, with migration contributing roughly 63% of the total growth.

Moving over to Africa, where the remaining PRIPODE urban studies are located, four cities were studied (from east to west): Kampala, Brazzaville, Lagos, and Accra. Kampala is typical of many primate cities in Africa, insofar as it grew from the seat of a tribal kingdom (the Buganda) to become a colonial outpost of the British Empire, to eventually becoming the nation's capital, replacing Entebbe at independence. Since that time its population has grown at an annual rate of more than 5.5 percent, effectively doubling every 12 years. Kampala has grown in part by engulfing former satellite towns, which has yielded a metropolitan area spanning approximately 386 square kilometres. As a classic primate city, it houses 1.2 million people, which is 12 times larger than the next largest city, Jinja, and 40% of Uganda's urban population. What little industrial activity the country has is largely concentrated in the capital, and being the seat of national government, this is where most civil service jobs are also located.

Brazzaville is the capital and largest city of the Republic of the Congo and is located on the Congo River, across from Kinshasa, the capital of the Democratic Republic of Congo. More than a third of the population of the Republic of Congo lives in the capital, and it is home to 40% of the country's non-agricultural employment. Like Kampala, it serves as the financial and administrative capital, and many of the nation's small industries (e.g., drink and tobacco packaging, wood and metal working, food processing, construction, and chemical plants) are concentrated there. According to the PRIPODE study, based on 2005 census data, Brazzaville had a population of 1.2 million, having grown at a rate of 3.3% per year from 856,400 in 1996. Although the precise proportions attributed to natural growth and migration are not known, large population displacements from rural areas, owing to civil strive and the effects of structural adjustment programs, have contributed to the city's rapid growth.

At more than 12 million people, Lagos is the largest of the cities considered by the PRIPODE teams. The 2006 Census has reported national level results, but disaggregated results by city have yet to be released. The UN, however, projects a population of 20 million people by 2010, with an annual growth rate of more than 4 percent.

Unlike the other three African cities considered here, Lagos is not the capital, but it is the economic hub of the country, concentrating financial services, industry, and port facilities for the whole country. Rural-urban migration rates are assumed to be quite high due to "loss of prime rural land and weakening of traditional land management systems, lack of local multiplier effects needed to stimulate agro-industry and non-agricultural job creation in the region as well as disintegration of local cultural relations and institutions".

Finally, Accra has a population 1.97 million in 2005, playing host to one-fifth of Ghana's total population. The population growth rate is estimated at 3.4 % per annum in the city itself but up to 10% in its peri-urban districts. It is Ghana's largest city and its administrative, communications, and economic centre. Like Lagos, the primary economic activities are financial and government services, communications, construction, transportation and agriculture (including fishing). More than 70% of Ghana's manufacturing capacity is located within the capital area.

Economic Development

Population dynamics are intimately connected to economic development in developing country urban areas. On the one hand, the economically active population forms the labour pool for urban areas. Because of the shortage of formal employment opportunities in the public and private sectors (owing to the effects of structural adjustment programs and competition stemming from economic globalisation), many developing country cities have burgeoning informal sectors. On the other hand, economic development, and particularly changes in urban land markets, when coupled with population trends, has tended to lead to a process of urban spatial expansion into peri-urban areas.

Public and Private Sector

Inurah *et al.* point out that many medium sised cities find themselves unable to attract the external investment that would lead to job creation or that would provide the tax revenues necessary to create supportive infrastructures. According to their analysis, cities in low and medium-income countries suffer from two disadvantages. First, in terms of business opportunities, their markets are weak due to high levels of unemployment, low skill levels, low incomes and a weak infrastructure base. Second, weak governance, unstable political environments, the prevalence of corruption, high levels of crime and threats to property rights are viewed as major threats and risks to investment.

The results are high establishment and transaction costs that make these cities unattractive to global capital. This contributes to a vicious circle in which there is no or little economic growth, high unemployment and poverty, a weak revenue base, declining competitiveness and attractiveness, and thus further economic stagnation. That Inurah *et al.* find this dynamic operating in two reasonably prosperous African cities—Johannesburg, South Africa, and Gaberone, Botswana—bodes ill for the many less advantaged cities of that continent and elsewhere. Furthermore, lack of education and training for industry or service sector jobs means that many city dwellers or recent migrants do not stand a chance of employment in these sectors—in fact, even well-educated workers find a paucity of decent jobs.

In recent years there have been ominous predictions of the impacts of the "youth bulge" the large number of un and under-employed men under on social and political stability. Whether or not these dire predictions are borne out the presence of high fertility and continued in-migration, despite economic stagnation, paints a somewhat worrisome scenario in which far from being engines of growth, the cities may easily concentrate some of the worst socialite problems.

The problem of economic stagnation in the face of rapid population growth is characteristic of most African cities. By contrast, many cities in low income Asia–including many in India, China, and Vietnam–are experiencing unprecedented economic booms. As noted earlier, Ho Chi Minh City has experienced very rapid growth between 2002-2005. In the context of such an astounding growth rate, employment represents less of a problem than provision of services and infrastructure to new homes and enterprises. In fact, the unemployment rate has declined from 10.3 to 8.8% since 1997, despite a population growth rate in excess of 3%.

Urban Informal Sector

According to Hinrichson, most urban poverty does not result from a lack of jobs, but from a lack of well-paying, steady jobs. Unemployment rates are generally below 15% in most developing country cities, but wage rates are depressed in the formal sector, and many are self-employed in the informal sector. Although often maligned, the informal sector is not just a chaotic jumble of unproductive activities. On the contrary, it is an increasingly critical part of national and local productive structures. The very nature of poor countries' participation in globalised economic competition dictates the reduction of socially protected formal sector activities and increases their dependence on less stable but more flexible production structures.

The Kampala study which, as previously mentioned, is growing at more than 5% per year, found that migrants "cannot be absorbed by the narrow formal sector as most of them are untrained, un-trainable and illiterate." Owing to land shortages and economic stagnation, a return to the rural areas is inconceivable for most. So, migrants find jobs in the informal sector cottage industries (woodworking, auto repair, metal working, transport services) or are self-employed in street hawking and trade, urban agriculture, or waste recycling and reuse. Some fall into illegal activities such as drug trafficking, robbery, pick-pocketing, and prostitution.

The Accra study confirms the high rates of informal sector employment of 50% or more found by others in African cities. In one slum area, Nima, 54% were self-employed, and in another, Maamobi, the rate was 50%. Roughly 30% of the economically active adults in both neighbourhoods were employed by the public sector, but no one was employed by the private sector. In Accra as a whole, 65% of the population works in the informal sector.

One of the difficulties for city administrations is that many informal enterprises do not pay taxes and are difficult to regulate. Despite these concerns, it would be wrong to paint too bleak a picture of the informal sector. Studies reviewed by Montgomery et al. show that the boundary between the informal and formal sectors is fairly fluid, with many workers participating in both, and some formal workers using their savings to launch into self-employment. Indeed, were it not for the informal sector, there would be little if any economic vitality in most least developed country urban areas. Even rapidly developing economies such as that in Hô Chi Minh City, Vietnam, have significant levels of informal sector employment of around 12% of the work-force.

Peri-urban Development and Land Speculation

The growth of cities in the developing world is dynamic, diverse and disordered and increasingly space-intensive. A recent study commissioned by the World Bank shows that average urban densities (that is, the number of inhabitants per square kilometre of built-up area) have been declining at an annual rate of 1.7 per cent over the last decade in developing countries. This disordered and leapfrog process of urban expansion, which takes place largely in non-contiguous transitional zones between countryside and city, is increasingly being referred to as "peri-urbanisation". It defies easy characterisation or quantification.

Peri-urban areas put agricultural land to mixed economic uses. This ranges from farming and animal husbandry to the installation of globalised firms that are looking for large tracts of land in order to install production processes that benefit from economies of scale. Improved communications and transportation networks make these outlying areas increasingly accessible to such concerns. Cheaper infrastructure, land and labour also encourage the de-concentration of more traditional firms who can no longer find space in city centres.

Peri urban areas are also a critical site for settlement of the poor. Because of high rents in the centrally located urban core, the urban poor, low income residents and new migrants are by default pushed to the peripheries. For example, most newcomers to the city settle in peri-urban areas where land and jobs are more plentiful. Peri-urbanisation also transforms rural dwellers into urbanities without changing their place of residence. For example, villages on the fringes of Kampala have increasingly been incorporated into the urban agglomeration and integrated into the urban economy through provision of goods and services to the core. Such settlements generally lack infrastructure and services and their residents can be easily displaced by other economic or residential uses.

Peri-urban areas fulfil many other functions for cities, ranging from the supply of energy, water and building materials to the provision of ecological services such as wildlife corridors, micro-climates, buffer areas against flooding and sinks for waste disposal. Social and ecological systems are often incapable of the rapid and complex readjustment that this requires.

Population and the Environment

The relationship between population and the environment in developing country cities ranges from local environmental health concerns to issues of regional or global concern such as habitat loss, changes to the hydrological cycle, urban consumption "footprints" on distant areas, and greenhouse emissions from transportation and industry. Although the latter are undeniably important, we will focus only on health issues here, since they are a more frequent focus of the PRIPODE studies.

A worrying sign in recent years is that urban areas, which since the early 20th century have been characterised by improved public health relative to rural areas, increasingly have pockets of poverty so deep that the health metrics in those areas are sometimes worse than those in poor rural areas. The primary environmental challenges facing developing country urban areas are provision of adequate water and sanitation; adequate waste removal; slum and informal settlements in environmentally sensitive or risk-prone areas; and air pollution.

Water and Sanitation

Lack of access to adequate water and sanitation is, first and foremost, a public health concern. MDG 7, Target 10, aims to "halve by 2015 the proportion of people without sustainable access to safe drinking water and Sanitation." Infant mortality rates in urban areas are significantly lower in homes with piped water.

The PRIPODE studies confirm the severity of the situation. In a study of child (aged 0-5) diarrhoea prevalence in two medium-sized Cameroonian cities, Ebolowa in the south and Maroua in the north, researchers found prevalence rates of 13% in the former and 24% in the latter, compared to a national rate of 16%. In Maroua, only 6.5% of households had modern toilets, versus 18.4% in Ebolowa, though a slightly higher proportion had access to improved latrines (68.3% vs. 58.7%). The proportion of children with diarrhoea increased in direct relationship to the quality of toilet facilities. Perhaps reflecting source water quality, the semi-arid Maroua diarrhea had prevalence rates of 19% for internal tap water and 24-25% for public taps and wells, whereas in Ebolowa it was roughly half these levels. Treatment of water reduced prevalence by 62%. Demographic factors—such as the education level of the parents—are intimately associated with diarrhoea prevalence, presumably reflecting an income/amenity effect as well as a personal hygiene effect.

In the Brazzaville study, the researchers found that 85% of households report have access to tap water, but because of the unreliability of the public water supply, households also depend on rainwater, wells, water services, and the river (in descending order from 30 to 10%). The study found that 35% of respondents reported a case of typhoid in the household in the past 12 months. The researchers attribute this to the poor state of the public water service, which employs neither water testing nor treatment before delivering water to households. Malaria was the most widespread illness, with 96% of households reporting a case; this very high rate is attributable in part to poor drainage and environmental sanitation.

The study finds that industrial and agricultural wastes and runoff, especially heavy metals and agro-chemicals, are polluting streams and aquifers. Contamination is particularly acute near industrial facilities. Because of regular flooding (56% of households in the districts studied had experience flooding), contaminants mix with flood waters to produce severe environmental health problems. The study of Kampala finds that inadequate evacuation of solid wastes from disposal areas create lactates that are washed into water sources. As a result, 90% of protected springs have been declared unfit for human consumption, yet the population continues to drink the water for lack of alternatives.

Waste Disposal

Functioning solid waste disposal systems are generally lacking in low income country cities, which contributes to the spread of infectious diseases. The lack of adequate waste removal can be attributed to rapid growth of new settlements, reductions in public sector spending associated with SAPs, and budgetary constraints.

The Brazzaville study found that 38% of households reported some kind of trash collection (either public or private), whereas 36% threw their trash out in "natural areas" and 24% burned or buried their trash. The Cameroon PRIPODE study found a high proportion of residents disposed of waste by depositing them in pits outside their compounds or by burning. They found little relationship between the type of trash removal and diarrhea prevalence.

In a survey conducted for the Accra study, residents of the two slums, Nima and Maamobi, reported the lack of proper solid waste disposal as the biggest environmental risk. Poor drainage and clogged gutters ran a close second, which is also the result of improper waste disposal. A high percentage of residents in these slums favoured the provision of rubbish containers and regular trash collection.

In the Lagos study, a survey of residents in four Local Government Areas (LGAs) representing different income and population density levels found that about 8% of the respondents' claimed that the dump sites in their areas of abode were never evacuated, and almost 46% said that they made private arrangements to evacuate the dumps in their areas. Interviews with local government chairmen suggested that they understood that it was their responsibility to evacuate refuse, but that it required the assistance of the federal government and also local cooperation. Particularly they cited a need for behavioural changes by new migrants who, either because of poverty or practices brought with them from their places of origin, were used to dumping wastes at their backyards.

Slum and Informal Settlements

The increasing social segregation of housing in low-income countries has resulted in the dramatic growth of slums, the entrenchment of poverty, the concentration of violence and social problems, and growing environmental health problems . Given high rents in city centres and rapidly developing peri-urban areas, the resident poor and new migrants to the city have little alternative but to rent rooms in slum neighbourhoods or to construct shanties in hazard-prone areas: i.e., on steep slopes (such as in Rio de Janeiro and Caracas), flood prone areas (such as parts of Kampala and Lagos), in low elevation coastal zones (such as Mumbai), and in industrial zones handling hazardous materials (such as Bhopal).

The Accra study examined health levels across the city, with a focus on two poor neighbourhoods: Nima and Maamobi. Through a survey the researchers ascertained that 14% and 80% of respondents complained of flooding, and 88% and 91% complained of environmental health pollution. When it comes to city-wide assessment of slums, the results are somewhat ambiguous: according to the authors, many of the worst slums in Accra also have the poorest health levels, but some do not. Weeks *et al.* in related research, found that infant mortality rates vary significantly by ethnic group in Accra, with people of the Ga tribe having highest mortality rates because they tend to live in the most impoverished parts of the city, places where one-room dwellings and poor infrastructure predominate. As Utzinger and Keiser point out, such heterogeneity in urban contexts is quite common, and is illustrated by the prevalence of malaria.

The Kampala study found that informal settlements are rapidly encroaching on wet lands, which has significant public health consequences owing to flooding and reduces the overall capacity of the city to absorb and purify runoff from hill areas. Between 1991 and 2002, swamps were reduced from 20.6% to 1.9% of the land cover of the Kampala administrative area, and lowland forests also changed form 7.6% to 0.4%. This change implies loss of swamp forests to land uses including industrial and residential developments.

Air Pollution

Urban air pollution is a function of a number of factors, most notably transport-related emissions from the growing fleets of cars, trucks and buses, as well as industrial emissions and waste burning. In a 2003 PERN cyber seminar, 5 Cohen reported that considerable uncertainties exist in the estimates of the portion of the global burden of disease attributable to air pollution. Cohen estimates that outdoor air pollution (fine particulate matter smaller than 2.5

microns, PM2.5) is currently responsible for about 0.80 million (1.2% of world total) premature deaths and 6.4 million (0.5% of world total) years of life lost (YLL) in the population of the world's cities with more than 100,000 people. The estimates were subject to considerable uncertainty, due largely to the lack of air pollution measurements and information about the shape of concentration-response functions in developing countries.

Other health impacts include contamination of food, either due to lead uptake in urban agricultural plots or food preparation in polluted areas. The Lagos study found that street food prepared in the poorest slum areas had far higher contaminant levels of lead, cadmium, and zinc owing in part to air pollution contamination than street food prepared in more affluent neighbourhoods.

Air pollution can have regional impacts, especially through the transport of ground-level photochemical smog or ozone. This can reduce crop yields and affect forest growth. Air pollution may also be a factor in migration decisions. It was cited in a study of migrants who left Mexico City for secondary cities in Mexico as an important factor in their decisions to leave the capital.

Policy Implications

Here we look at policy implications of the research described in previous sections.

Population-environment linkages have received an enormous amount of attention from scholars, policy-makers and the general public over the last few decades. Most of this has focused on whether, and to what extent, population growth is responsible for the aggravation of environmental problems.The unprecedented scale of ongoing urbanisation is linked to large and rapidly growing population. Typically, such discussions have prompted out cries that the population bomb needs to be defused through aggressive fertility control. Such simplistic solutions overlook the inertia of demographic processes, overstate the ability of family planning programs to reduce fertility rapidly, and neglect the role of development in population environment interactions. Moreover, they detract attention from the other important ways in which population dynamics influence environmental change.

Population has grown rapidly in developing countries, especially over the last half century. But this is due to mortality decline, not to fertility conditions. Moreover, fertility has recently declined significantly in most regions of the world. The practical ability to "deal with the population problem" through population control and/or "family planning" programs is largely overestimated. Without some significant form of social transformation, modernisation or "development", it is highly unlikely that fertility can be forcefully reduced. Secondly, even with a drastic reduction in the current fertility rate, population size will continue to grow rapidly for some time in countries that have recently experienced high fertility levels. At the present time, almost 60% of all population growth at the world level is attributable to inertial factors (i.e. due to population composition stemming from patterns of growth in previous eras, rather than to current fertility and mortality patterns).

Both population and environmental outcomes are linked to development trajectories that need to be understood within their particular historical contexts. The critical framework which enfolds them all at this time is economic globalisation, wherein all countries are feverishly trying to emulate the production and consumption patterns of the world's main polluters. Ultimately, population control in the absence of some measure of development or social transformation is not likely to work from a demographic standpoint. Without drastic changes in the production and consumption patterns of both developed and developing countries–a sustainability transition–even rapid population stabilisation will not avert major environmental problems.

Sustainable Use of Space

As the focus on population growth per se diminishes in importance, spatial distribution, and within that, unprecedented urban spatial growth, assumes increasing significance in the environmental agenda of the 21st century. Indeed, it can be argued that, today, the most pertinent PDE relations are space specific. Where the resident population of a given territorial area actually lives, on what type of land, with what forms of occupation, in what ecological conditions, whether it is concentrated or dispersed, all this makes a great difference in terms of sustainability. Nevertheless, these aspects have received relatively little attention to this moment.

For much of the last century environmentalists took a dim view of urbanisation and city growth. But the recent turnaround among environmental scholars concerning the value of urban areas for global and local environmental outcomes is rather remarkable. It is increasingly recognised that urban localities actually offer better chances for long-term sustainability, starting with the fact that they concentrate half the Earth's population on less than three per cent of its land area.

The dispersion of population and economic activities would likely make the problems worse rather than better. Adopting the right approaches in anticipation of urban growth can also prevent many of the environmental problems linked to urbanisation. Density is potentially useful.

With world population at 6.6 billion people in 2007 and growing at over 75 million a year, demographic concentration gives sustainability a better chance. The protection of rural ecosystems ultimately requires that population be concentrated in non-primary sector activities and densely populated areas.

In this light, it has been suggested that instead of trying to figure out the theoretical carrying capacity of the Earth, we could profitably focus on a more practical issue, namely, how can an existing population make the most sustainable use of a given territory, in light of available resources, population, economic potential and the current development context? What is the best way that this concrete population can be distributed over its territory, currently and into the future, so that it will cause the least possible environmental damage and best promote sustainability, while also making the best possible use of its comparative advantages (and thus attaining the highest tolerable levels of economic growth and social development)? These arenot easy questions to answer, yet they open up an area that holds much promise and that is ripe for policy intervention.

Planning for the Needs of the Poor

A crucial fact that is often overlooked in discussions of the ongoing urban transformation is that the up coming massive growth of urban population will be largely composed of poor people. Urban growth stems largely from natural increase and rural to urban migration. In developing countries, the poor generally constitute the largest proportion of migrants. Poor people also tend to make the greatest contribution to natural increase in the cities because of the relative size of this population group and because they have higher fertility levels.

Hence, planning realistically for future urban growth means, first and foremost, planning for the needs of the poor. The current size of New York, Los Angeles, and Ottawa, may be comparable to that of Mumbai, Manila and Kampala, respectively. Yet, planning for the future of the latter three developing country cities requires a totally different paradigm, one that has an over arching concern with the needs of the poor at its core. It will also require more creative approaches, given the low level of resources available to local governments in most developing countries.

Improved governance—responding effectively to local needs in a participatory, transparent and accountable manner —will require an adequate understanding of the nature of the problems and good local information. The above discussion has highlighted some of the main problems and also some of the key misconceptions that have plagued planning efforts. Improved governance will also require that, while responding to current needs, those in charge turn a prospective eye to inevitable future growth. The trends towards massive increases in urban population, particularly in smaller and intermediate cities, will continue. The short-term mandate of most policy-makers favours attempts to resolve short-term problems without concern for the medium and longer-term future. Such an approach explains why so many master plans in developing country cities are outdated by the time their implementation begins.

The Millennium Project Slums Task Force lists a number of proposals to target the problem of urban poverty. They suggest community participation, including working with local communities to upgrade slum areas. They also describe processes that would decrease socioeconomic segregation by acknowledging poor people's "right to the city." A key issue is security of tenure and bringing an end to evictions, as well as providing adequate water and sanitation services, and access to public transportation. Although the task seems daunting, the financial resources required to provide basic services is surprisingly little–on the order of $294 billion by 2020.

PLANNING FOR INEVITABLE URBAN GROWTH

Theoretically, urban areas present considerable advantages in economic, social, demographic and environmental terms. In a globalised economy, cities are better able to take advantage of emerging opportunities and thus better able than rural areas to improve the social or health situation for large numbers of people. Urbanisation may help to retard rural environmental degradation, by serving as an outlet for rural migration. Urbanisation also promotes the empowerment of women, while changing aspirations and lifestyles that accelerate fertility decline.

Despite these real advantages, poverty and environmental degradation are growing faster in urban areas and many least developed countries are struggling mightily to cope with rapid urban growth. The disparity between principle and practice can be attributed, to an important extent, to the difficulties being encountered by developing countries, and especially in Sub-Saharan Africa, to participate effectively in global markets. However, many of the difficulties faced by cities in developing countries can be traced to urban mismanagement.

A more effective approach would require, at the outset, a more pro-active and positive attitude towards urban growth. Urban policy-makers are increasingly set against urban growth and also fail to anticipate inevitable future growth. In this scenario, one can only expect a deterioration of existing conditions. Politicians and planners have to accept the reality of inevitable growth and learn to work with local community organisations and other Organisations of the Urban Poor (OUPs) to plan ahead for their social and environmental future.

Providing land and shelter for the poor ahead of the curve is critical; trying to help them after they have invaded inadequate lands is socially, economically and environmentally costly. Helping to orient future urban growth in directions that will be least harmful to the environment, and planning infrastructure needs ahead of time can save thousand of lives and billions of dollars.

Bringing together the different politico-administrative units that are affected by peri-urbanisation into some sort of regional entity and convoking the different social actors to participate in deliberations regarding the future of this area can help to head off some of its most negative outcomes. All this requires looking ahead.

6

Transportation Planning in Cities

Given the widely accepted and imminent peaking of world oil demand or the "big rollover", it is imperative that cities tackle the issue of transport energy use. Urban transport systems are the most dependent and vulnerable of all sectors to rises in the price of oil and potential shortages. This chapter examines a set of data on an international sample of 84 cities, 58 in developed countries and 26 in developing countries in order to better understand the range of urban transport and land use patterns that exist in the world today, the resulting energy consumption patterns in transport and some of the key factors that underpin these transport and energy use patterns.

Highlighting the critical importance of urban form, primarily the density factor, and the role of transport infrastructure provision and policies towards congestion in determining transport patterns and energy use, it suggests how to reconstruct an automobile dependent city around a set of centres bound together by high quality transit. Such centres would form a series of transit cities within the metropolitan region, each one with greatly enhanced opportunities for walking, cycling and transit, allowing more people to maintain there daily travel time budget or Marchetti Constant of 1 hour without resorting to excessive car use and significantly reducing their dependence on oil.

It is suggested that in order for cities to adapt to the post-petroleum age, relying purely on technological fixes will not provide the needed changes. Rather it is argued that a combination of changes are needed to provide the essential paradigm shift for cities to fundamentally reduce car use:

1. Curtailing or scrapping high capacity road construction;
2. Dumping congestion relief programmes and recognising that congestion can help cities move in a
3. Positive direction with respect to reducing car use and energy consumption;
4. Priorities the construction of speed competitive transit systems;
5. Integrating development around those transit systems, and;
6. Creating attractive conditions for walking and cycling through good urban design in and around centres, in effect making all centres small, contemporary "walking cities".

Technological changes in vehicles and fuels can occur in parallel with such broader urban systems changes and will be much more effective in the context of greatly reduced travel demand for private transport. It is argued that technological innovation is not a panacea to the energy problem in transport and that the time required to restructure cities for less car and energy use can be at least equal to or even less than the time required for significant technological changes in vehicles and fuels.

The data in this chapter are drawn from the *Millennium Cities Database for Sustainable Transport* compiled over three years by Kenworthy and Laube for the International Union (Association) of Public Transport (UITP) in Brussels. The database provides data on 100 cities on all continents, though 16 cities provide only partial data. Data summarised here represent averages from 84 of the fully completed cities in the USA, Australia and New Zealand, Canada, Western Europe, Asia (high and low income areas), Eastern Europe, the Middle East, Latin America, Africa and China.

The database contains data on 69 primary variables. The methodology of data collection for all variables was strictly controlled by agreed upon definitions contained in a technical booklet of over 100 pages and data were carefully checked and verified by three parties before being accepted into the database.

From these primary variables, some 230 standardised variables were calculated. Cities can thus be compared on urban form, private and public transport performance, overall mobility and modal split, private and public transport infrastructure, the economics of urban transport (operating and investment costs, revenues), passenger transport energy use and environmental factors. For this overview, which is focused on transport energy use in cities, only a selection of the most relevant features was chosen for comment.

Peaking of Global Oil Production

Urban automobile dependence, insights into which can be gained from the data, has large implications for energy use. In this new century, the world is going to have to face the reality that the assumption of cheap and easily available oil will no longer be valid. This change will affect every industry and aspect of life, e.g. food production and consumption, the automotive industries, land development patterns and how much private transport requirements are built into them, rising and unsustainable household expenses for transport and even perhaps the very survival of highly auto dependent cities or parts of cities. World oil production is predicted to peak by 2010 ("the big rollover") and then to enter a phase of irreversible decline, leading to shortage and supply interruptions, rapidly rising prices and a greater concentration of oil power in the Middle East. Some senior commentators in the field believe that world oil production may have already peaked, but this will probably not be known for sure for another 5 years, as was the case when US oil production peaked in 1970.

The peak in world oil production will have profound implications for transport, which is utterly dependent upon conventional oil and cannot restructure or alter its technologies overnight. The relative certainty of peaking oil can be seen historically in the accuracy of M. King Hubbert's original prediction of the US oil production peak in 1970 (Hubbert's bubble). He predicted in the 1950s and 60s that world oil production would peak shortly after the year 2000, which is now being confirmed by many people, based on much more comprehensive data, though there is still some dispute over the seriousness or immediacy of the problem.

Comparative Urban Transport Patterns

Car Usage

The critical factor that underpins transport energy use is car use. US cities 'require' over 18,000 car passenger kms per capita to meet the access needs and discretionary travel of their inhabitants. By contrast, their high-income counterparts in Europe and Asia have only between 20% and 63% of that level of use. In the lower income regions, car passenger kms per capita range from a mere 814 (4% of the US figure) in Chinese cities, up to 3,300 in Middle Eastern cities (18% of the US figure).

In order to gain some insight into the degree of motorisation in cities around the world relative to their wealth or "capacity to pay", we can express the above car use figures as per dollar of their GDP. Average metropolitan

GDP figures are shown for the respective regions. Amongst the wealthier cities, the US and ANZ cities are the leaders in car use relative to wealth with 578 and 576 car passenger kms per $1000 of GDP, with Canadian cities some way behind at 415. The Western European and prosperous Asian cities distinguish themselves in their significantly lower levels of private car mobility.

In lower income cities the rates of private car mobility per unit of wealth are comparatively high. African cities have some 940 car passenger kms per $1000 of GDP, which is close to double the US and ANZ level. This effect seems to come from the South African cities where two clearly distinct transport systems exist side-by-side (the sizeable automobile-based system for prosperous people and the informal, public transport and walking-based systems for the vast majority of poorer residents). Latin American and Middle Eastern cities are virtually identical to the US and ANZ cities in this factor (580 and 595 respectively). In 1995, low-income Asian cities and Chinese cities (494 and 344 car passenger km per $1000) had already far exceeded their wealthy Asian neighbours (193) and even Western European cities in this factor (114).

It is clear that less wealthy cities, although far lower in their per capita car use than most higher income cities (except those in Asia), are experiencing comparatively high levels of car use in relation to their modest wealth as motorisation proceeds, in most cases, unrestrained.

Motor Cycle Usage

Usage of motor cycles is comparatively small in high-income cities. Motor cycle use, as a percentage of total private passenger kms, ranges from 0.25% in the US cities up to 9% in the high-income Asian cities. By contrast, in low income Asian cities and Chinese cities, motor cycle mobility represents 26% of private passenger kilometres, while in the other lower income regions it again is small, at between 0.7% and 3.8%. Again, if we normalise this by wealth, the huge commitment to motor cycles in low income Asian cities and Chinese cities is apparent (averaging 152 motor cycle passenger km per $1000 of GDP, while all the other regions average a meagre 10).

Why motor cycles have burgeoned to this extent in most Asian cities and in no other parts of the world (nor in Manila where motor cycle ownership is actually about half the US level), is an interesting policy question. The low penetration of motor cycles in Manila is possibly a result of the extensive and effective jeepney system and paratransit-like motorised tricycles.

The role of motor cycles in urban transport, their potential to facilitate urban sprawl by providing low cost private transport to large numbers of people, and their environmental and human impacts, are important issues to understand. This is especially so in cities like Taipei where ownership is some 200 per 1000 people and usage represents 35% of private mobility. Notwithstanding this, they are the most energy-efficient form of private motorised mobility available.

Private Motorised Transport Modal Split

The final variable that provides insight into private transport patterns is the percentage of all daily trips (all purposes) that are catered for by private transport . Not surprisingly, US (89%), ANZ (79%) and Canadian cities (81%) head the list. By contrast, their wealthier counterparts in Europe and Asia have only 50% and 42% respectively of all trips by private transport. In the lower income cities private transport caters for only between 16% (Chinese cities) and 36% (Asian cities) of all trips. The exception is the Middle Eastern cities where the proportion rises to 56%.

Despite the overwhelming visual and sensory impacts of traffic and its capacity to rapidly saturate the public space of a city, private transport is a minority player, relative to public transport and non-motorised modes, in 7 out of the 11 areas in the study. Because of their size, cars and other private transport vehicles have a huge impact, even at relatively low ownership levels, in urban environments not designed for them. This is true in most dense, rapidly developing cities in the world and, of course, it has enormous social justice and equity implications. If urban transport priorities are primarily directed towards facilitating car and motor cycle travel through new freeways, parking facilities and so on, then this can threaten public and non-motorised mobility, which operate at high energy efficiency and provide effective transport services to a high proportion of people.

Public Transport Usage Levels

There are two clear extremes in public transport use. The US cities stand out globally with only 3% of daily trips, while Eastern European city residents use transit for 47% of all trips. The other high public transport modal split cities are high and low income Asian cities and Latin American cities. ANZ, Canadian and Middle Eastern cities are comparatively low public transport modal share cities. Western European cities have only 19% of daily trips on average by public transport, which is neither very low nor very high in this sample of cities.

Although some low-income cities enjoy comparatively healthy public transport use for their very low level of service (e.g. in China), this will not last. The crowded, unreliable and poor safety of public transport is something that people in such cities will try to escape at their first opportunity, given access to a car or motor cycle. Many low income cities may be unable to resist further rapid motorisation unless they improve the quality and speed-competitiveness of their public transport systems. This will generally mean developing more extensive rail systems, or fully segregated bus ways. If not, transport energy use is likely to rise rapidly.

Non-motorised Modal Split

The most egalitarian and sustainable modes of urban transport are foot and bicycle. These modes have few fossil fuel implications outside of the embodied energy in human food, bicycles and pedestrian and bicycle infrastructure. There is an extraordinary range in the use of these energy efficient modes. In US cities, only 8% of all trips are made by foot and bicycle.

Other auto cities are a little higher. Eastern and Western European, high and low income Asian, Middle Eastern and Latin American cities, all have very similar levels of non-motorised mode use, ranging from 26% to 32% of all trips. The African cities have 41% walking and cycling, due to the majority low-income population who rely heavily on walking, while the world leader in 1995 was still the Chinese city with 65%.

It would appear very sensible for social, environmental and economic reasons, and certainly from an energy perspective, to priorities the use of non-motorised modes by ensuring that facilities for them are actively promoted and not eroded by motorisation. This is especially urgent in rapidly developing cities, especially in China where their pedestrian and cycling advantage appears to be under increasing threat from policies against bicycles and the sheer scale of motorisation.

Private Passenger Transport Energy Use

What are the transport energy use implications of these broad transport patterns in cities? A very large range in transport energy consumption, with US cities leading the world at over 60,000 MJ per person per year of energy used for cars and motor cycles. This is twice as high as their nearest rivals, the Canadian and Australian cities, and four to six times more than their biggest competitors in the global economy, the western European and wealthy Asian cities, such as in Japan. Even cities in the oil-rich Middle East only use 10,600 MJ per person, despite some relatively conspicuous consumption in cities such as Riyadh. The three Chinese cities consume an average 2,500 MJ per person in private passenger transport, which means that an average US city of 400,000 people consumes in one year, the same amount as a Chinese mega-city of 10 million people.

Three groups of cities stand out as being the most intensive in passenger transport energy use relative to their wealth. These are the US and the Middle Eastern cities, and the African cities, again highlighting the high consumption and private transport orientation of a wealthy minority against a backdrop of widespread poverty in African cities. The outstanding cities are again the Western European cities and wealthy Asian cities who consume only 489 and 303 MJ/$1,000 respectively, showing comparatively modest demand for transport energy relative to their level of economic development and their economic capacity to sustain considerably higher private transport orientation. All the other regions fall between these extremes with an average of 1,364 MJ/$1,000.

As countries stake out their claims on ever diminishing and more costly conventional oil, especially those who so far have not yet significantly shared the benefits that flow from this valuable non-renewable resource, oil is likely to become a major destabilising geopolitical and economic issue. Oil is also likely to become a significant force in shaping urban development patterns, as it will no longer be economically or socially sustainable to create land use patterns that build in automobile dependence.

Public Transport Energy Use

The use of energy in urban public transport systems is small compared to private transport, regardless of the significance of the transport task undertaken by public transport, which varies widely, as already discussed. In the US, ANZ, Canadian, Western European and Middle Eastern cities, public transport energy use per capita does not exceed 7% of the combined private and public passenger transport energy use (average of 4%). The biggest contribution is in Latin American cities (23%), with the other five regions averaging 17%. Also, it should be noted that where rail is extensively used, electricity is a major energy source for public transport, which is often generated without oil (gas, hydroelectric, nuclear), and of course can also come from renewable sources. Public transport operations can thus more easily weather the coming peak in oil production because their demand for energy is numerically very much lower and also in many cities, not as reliant on petroleum-based fuels.

Modal Energy Consumption Differences Between Private and Public Transport. Relatively energy-inefficient private transport is compared to public transport. Energy consumed per passenger km in public transport in all cities is between one-fifth and one-third that of private transport, the only exception being in the US cities where large buses dominate public transport and attempt to pick up thinly spread passengers in suburbs designed principally around the car. In US cities, public transport energy use per passenger kilometre stands at 65% that of cars. Part of the reason for this is that in US cities the public transport vehicles have the highest use of energy per vehicle kilometre of all cities (26 MJ/km, with most other regions under about 16 to 17 MJ/km, or as low as 10 MJ/km in African cities).

Examining the overall modal energy consumption of motorised transport in cities (private and public transport combined), Canadian cities are the least efficient at 3.5 MJ per passenger km, followed closely by US cities at 3.2 MJ per passenger km. This reflects the large vehicles in use in North American cities, especially 4WD sports utility vehicles, their low use of motor cycles and their high levels of private versus public mobility. The private vehicles in US and Canadian cities consume about 5 MJ/km, whereas most other regions are under 4 or even 3 MJ/km, despite generally worse levels of congestion in these latter areas. By contrast to North America, ANZ cities average 2.4 MJ per passenger km for their total motorised passenger transport system, while all the lower income regions range between 0.9 (China) and 2.0 MJ per passenger km. All these lower income cities have a more significant role for energy-efficient public transport, some have high use of energy-efficient motor cycles and many operate fleets of minibuses, which are relatively energy-efficient (especially with high lodgings).

Energy Consumption by Different Public Transport Modes Modal energy use can be examined on a per vehicle km or per passenger km basis. The former is an indication of the inherent energy use of the particular vehicle, the technology it exploits and the environment in which it operates (congestion etc.). In the case of rail modes, the data are reported on a per wagon km basis, not train km. Energy use per passenger km is an indication of the mode's efficiency in carrying people, based on the kind of lodgings that the mode achieves in different cities.

Transport Energy Use Patterns in Cities

The first and most important is the urban density data, which are very important in explaining transport patterns, especially car use. If we correlate urban density data for the

58 wealthier cities with passenger car passenger kms per capita from Kenworthy and Laube, urban density explains 84% of the variance (Figure 1) and in the more heterogeneous low income sample it explains 47%.

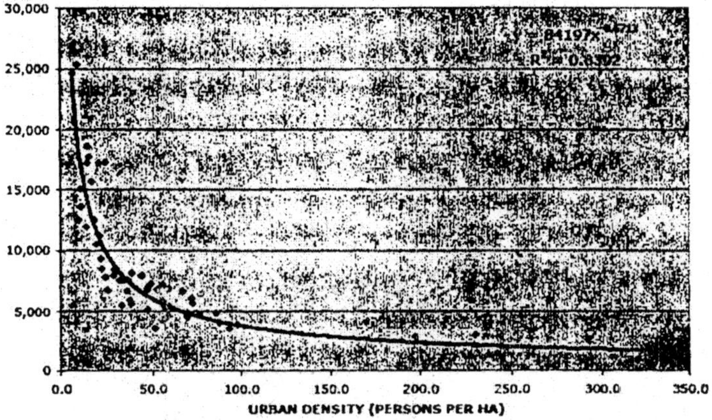

Figure 1. Urban density versus per capita car use in 58 higher income cities, 1995.

Similar correlations occur with private transport energy use per capita, all showing that as density increases, car use and energy use decline very significantly. The auto cities in North America and Australia/New Zealand are clearly the lowest density in the world and have the highest car use and energy use. Globally, the lower income cities are clearly denser than their wealthier counterparts (the clusters average 109 per ha, compared to the wealthier five clusters averaging 52 per ha). They contain the densest cities in the global sample, although Hong Kong at 320 per ha, which in the high income Asian group, is also exceptional. Cities throughout Asia, whether wealthy or not, are universally high density.

Transport Infrastructure

Urban freeways: It has been understood since the 1970s, how urban freeway provision is directly associated with higher car and energy use in cities. The mechanism for this, in terms of longer travel distances rather than savings in time, has been explained elsewhere. US cities, without any surprise, have the highest availability of freeway per person in the world, followed by ANZ and Canadian cities with 83% and 78% as much respectively. Outside of these three regions freeway provision falls away rapidly, especially in Latin American and Chinese cities (only 2% of the US level). The other 8 regions altogether average only 0.028 metres of freeway per capita, compared to 0.156 in US cities (18% of the US level).

It is not surprising that cities with the highest freeway provision also have the highest average speed of general traffic. The other cities with considerably lower freeway provision achieve only 29 km/h average road system speed. Lower income cities have marginally higher provision of freeways per $1000 of GDP than highincome cities (4.5 km compared to 4.1 km). In fact, Eastern European, Middle Eastern and African cities exceed the US figure in kilometres of freeway per $1000 of GDP. Poorer cities appear to be giving priority to freeway construction and are reaching higher levels of motorisation than one would expect based purely on wealth.

Public transport infrastructure: Western European, high income Asian and Eastern European cities, and to a lesser extent the ANZ cities, are the only regions that have significant reserved alignments for public transport. This consists mainly of railways, but also a few physically segregated bus ways. All of the lower income city groups, apart from Eastern Europe, have comparatively scarce reserved public transport right-of-way. Chinese cities stand out as being particularly low in this factor and in the wealthier auto-dependent groups, US cities are clearly the lowest in segregated public transport right-of-way, though Canadian cities are not far behind.

Congestion: Freeways and congestion issues are often linked together in discussions, especially in relation to efforts to save energy. Increasing urban traffic congestion is frequently cited as being responsible for huge wastage of energy in cities. The results in the study run directly counter to this assertion. They suggest that as congestion increases, there is less car use, more motor cycle use, more public transport use and more use of non-motorised modes. Conversely, lower congestion reflected in higher average speed of traffic, is associated with the direct opposite of this. Figures 2 and 3 demonstrate these points showing how car use per capita in cities around the world increases as the average speed of traffic increases (i.e. as congestion is reduced) and how public transport use is higher the more congested is the city.

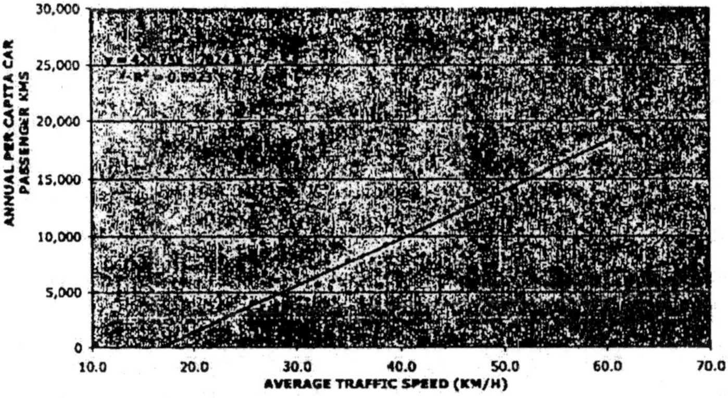

Figure 2. Average road traffic speed versus per capita car use in 58 higher income cities, 1995.

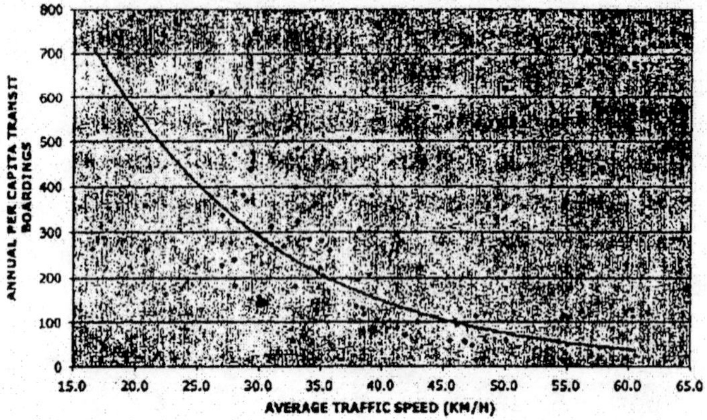

Figure 3. Average road traffic speed versus per capita public transport use in 58 higher income cities, 1995.

The results suggest that congestion acts as a brake on car use. Congestion encourages greater motorcycle use, and works in favour of public transport, but only where these options offer speed advantages over cars in congested conditions, and where parking is limited. This is often the case in more congested high-income cities, since they commonly have urban rail systems, or less frequently, bus ways. Such speed advantages to public transport occur on specific corridors and especially with urban rail systems where in every group except African cities, suburban rail system speed exceeds that of road traffic, often by a big margin (some metro systems also exceed traffic speed). However, it is only in the high income Asian cities that system-wide public transport speed exceeds that of road traffic. In all other groups of cities overall public transport system speed is significantly below that of general road traffic. This highlights in particular the need to improve operating speeds of buses, which are all always well below general road traffic speed. This means developing more dedicated rights-of-way for this mode and giving less priority to major new road construction.

Overall, the results suggest that rather than saving energy, reduced congestion, reflected in higher traffic speeds, increases energy use. Higher traffic speeds favour cars, increase urban sprawl and travel distances, and reduce the viability of other modes. Speed is not used to save time, it is used to travel further. Cities should not be in any rush to reduce congestion in order to decrease energy use. Rather they should be strategically improving the public transport and non-motorised mode alternatives to help travellers avoid congestion.

Importance of rail and comparative modal speeds: Not only are they the most energy-efficient modes, but they are the most effective at capturing modal share from private transport. In the high income cities, only the European and Asian cities have public transport systems that capture a healthy share of the overall transport market and these are the cities where urban rail systems are most developed, especially in relation to their private transport equivalent, the urban freeway. The ratio of fully segregated public transport right-of-way to urban freeways in these rail-oriented cities is over 3 compared, to 0.4 and 0.5 in US and Canadian cities and 2 in ANZ cities. In the lower income sample, by far the healthiest public transport use is in the Eastern European cities where segregated public transport right-of-way is some 9 times greater than urban freeways.

Whilst there are cities in Latin America, Africa and China that achieve significant public transport use with little or no rail systems, they rely mostly on poor 'captive' riders. As already suggested, as incomes rise and car ownership levels grow, the public transport systems of these low-income, bus based cities will tend to lose market share, because they cannot compete in speed or comfort with private transport. Motor cycles in particular tend to compete heavily with bus systems that are engulfed in traffic.This is seen in the comparative modal operating speeds. There are no regions where the average speed of bus systems exceeds 26 km/h and the overall average across the 11 regions is only 19 km/h. In Chinese cities buses operate at an average 12.5 km/h, or about the same speed as cycling. On the other hand, metro systems operate between 30 and 37 km/h (average 34 km/h). Suburban rail systems across the regions average 42.9 km/h. When these speeds are compared to general road traffic speed, which averages 34 km/h across all regions, it can be seen that only rail systems can compete.

Cities wishing to protect, rebuild and grow their public transport base, save energy (and reduce CO_2 emissions) as incomes rise and competition from motor cycles and automobiles escalates, need to seriously consider some form of segregated rail system. At the very least, cities need effective bus ways or Bus Rapid Transit (BRT) systems as demonstrated in Curitiba and São Paulo, and more recently, the Transmilenio BRT system in Bogota.

Parking: Parking in the central business districts (CBD) of cities is another indicator of private transport infrastructure, which varies dramatically across regions. Parking supply in the CBD is an important factor in determining modal split for trips to these space-constrained areas of cities. The availability of parking, much more than price, tends to determine the attractiveness of car commuting to the central city. High levels of parking will encourage the most energy consuming trips to work, while well-loaded, radial rail systems will use the least energy.

The highest providers of parking are the US, ANZ and, perhaps surprisingly, the Middle Eastern cities, all having over 1 parking space for every 2 jobs in the CBD. By contrast, Chinese, Eastern European and Latin American cities average 17, 75 and 90 spaces per 1000 jobs respectively, with Canadian cities at 390.

Reconstructing City for Post-petroleum Age

The previous discussion has highlighted, amongst other things, the importance of urban density and transport infrastructure in influencing private transport use and energy consumption in transport. In particular, the role of urban density and the provision of speed-competitive public transport systems as opposed to freeways, have been highlighted. The link between urban intensity and automobile dependence has been confirmed both between cities and it has also been demonstrated within cities. The vertical axis can be car use or it can be transport energy use and the horizontal axis can be population per urban hectare or jobs per urban hectare or both together – called activity intensity.

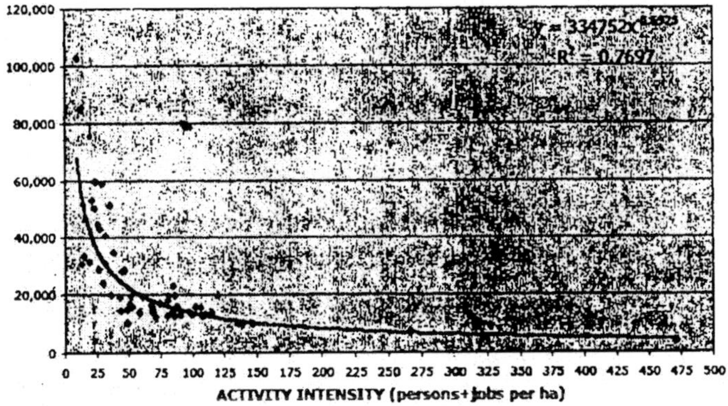

Figure 4. Activity intensity versus private passenger transport energy use in 58 higher income cities, 1995

The point on the graph where rapid acceleration in car usage appears to occur seems to be around 35 people and jobs per hectare; the error band is around 30 to 40 per ha.1 This same critical density figure, below which automobile dependence increases dramatically, has been noted in many studies.

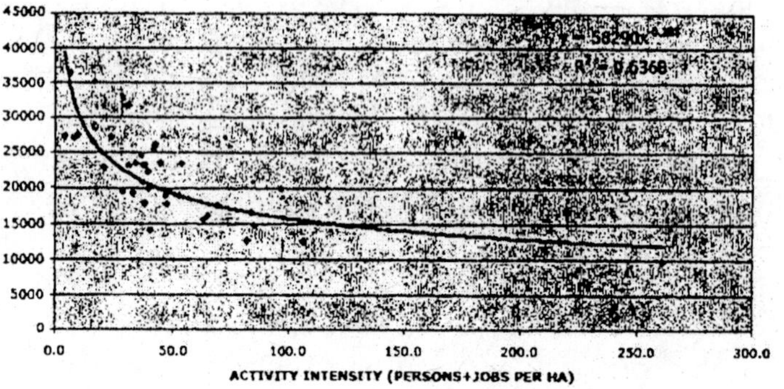

Figure 5. Per capita passenger transport energy use versus activity intensity in Sydney Local Government Areas in 1981.

Cities across North America and Australia that built in car dependence over the past 50 years are now trying to transform their urban environments into places where more transport options are available for the future. This usually involves developing new or refurbished transit systems, generally rail, and a set of centres to focus urban activity. However, one new rail line and a few centres are unlikely to significantly change a city because they lack sufficient coverage. However, based on the Marchetti idea, it is possible to restructure the expanses of an automobile city into a series of transit cities that are linked together with high quality speed-competitive rail transit. Transit cities are 20 to 30 kilometres across (based on typical overall transit operating speeds of 20 to 30 km/h), with a rail and bus service that feeds into a Town Centre lying at their heart. Along the lines feeding in to the Town Centre, which might be buses running on dedicated rights-of-way or LRT, would be a series of Local Centres. The whole region would be made up of a series of these transit cities joined together and linked by a fast rail service. Most people in the city could then live within the framework of local services in their Local Centre, or have easy access to an adjoining local centre. Main services, including work, would generally be located in the Town Centre. Some higher level services will always be in other Town Centres, especially the historic Central Business District, and these would typically be easily accessible by rail. However, the key to sustainability is to generate these Local Centres and Town Centres as genuinely viable, attractive and more people oriented places in each of the transit city sections comprising the majority of the city-region. Walking and cycling within such centres would be priority modes and the urban design of centres would be to maximise their use.

This has recently been applied to the development of the Metropolitan Plan for the Sydney Region where it is possible to see six distinct transit cities, each around 20 to 30 kilometres across and each having a major Town Centre and a series of Local Centres. By focusing the plan on these six areas and knowing the kind of intensity of activity that could make them viable, it becomes feasible to determine where to direct growth and where new transit infrastructure will assist the development of a more sustainable, energy-efficient city.

In many ways, the evolution of the city into the kind of polycentric structure described here is a natural urban systems response to the need to maintain the Marchetti Constant and is happening in many cities such as Vancouver, Sydney, Portland and even Perth. In this sense it is a response to the problem of traffic congestion where most cities find it simply impossible or downright self destructive to be trying to maintain this constant by building more and more high capacity roads to keep acceptable access time to work and other urban amenities. Rather, the city tends to "morph" into a new form to ensure that it remains functional and liveable.

Solving The Energy Problem

There are very large differences in the energy consumption levels between private and public transport, with public transport systems and especially urban rail systems offering dramatically greater energy efficiency than any private transport fleet in any city today. Clearly, the substitution of private transport passenger kilometres for public transport passenger kilometres has very large potential to save energy. This is enhanced by the fact that it has also been shown that there is a "transit leverage" effect at work in cities whereby one 1 kilometre of travel by public transport replaces between 9 and 12 kilometres of car travel in US cities. Globally "this appears to be more like between 5 and 7 to 1, based on the relative decline in vehicle kilometres travelled per capita for every passenger kilometre travelled per capita on transit.". Of course, the substitution of car travel for walking and cycling has enormous energy conservation potential as well. More compact, mixed use urban form that creates much shorter travel distances would make such substitution more feasible.

Of course, there is a view that the energy problem in transport can be solved primarily by technological means. This can involve the development of smaller, more fuel-efficient conventional internal combustion engine cars, new fuels to substitute for conventional oil, new energy systems for cars such as electric, hybrid or fuel cell vehicles or the development of radical new car designs such as Amory Lovins' "Hypercar". Such a single-sighted approach is not supported for a number of reasons:

1. From a more holistic urban viewpoint, the less car use in a city, the more manageable and liveable is the city,

regardless of the type of car or how it is fuelled. This is because energy and emissions are only two of the car's many problems. The most intractable problem is its space demands for movement and storage and the resulting impacts on the public realm of cities, especially the quality of the environment for pedestrians and cyclists. Car-based cities are not on a human scale and cannot deliver the quality public environments characteristic of, for example, many European cities.

2. More efficient cars or ones that run on new sources of potentially cheaper energy can actually encourage extra car use. As stated by Newman and Kenworthy, "The problem with technological solutions is that they invariably forget the Jevons Principle. This principle was first enunciated in 1865 by the economist Jevons, who predicted that making coal burning more efficient would lead to more coal use as the efficiency would lead to more economic uses of coal." Extra car ownership and use can exacerbate a whole range of other problems such as safety, sprawl-related social isolation and lack of community, the proliferation of non-human scale environments unsuitable for non-motorised modes, further marginalisaton of public transport systems and of course destruction of natural areas and productive food growing land. The energy problem must be tackled in a way that recognises and helps to address the many other problems of the car in cities.

3. Technological change is by no means instantaneous. The infrastructure systems that cities have built around internal combustion engine cars running on conventional oil are immense, as are the fleets of vehicles that need to be replaced. The penetration rate of new technologies is invariably slow and requires

multiple hundreds of billions of dollars to achieve the changes to factories producing the new cars, fuel distribution systems, support industries, retraining programmes etc. So far such changes have been very minimal.

4. One of the arguments used against land use change as a way of mitigating dependence on cars and tackling the energy problem is that the time required to effect significant change is very long, because urban systems change very slowly, whereas technological change can be introduced more rapidly. However, the time required for significant land use change and development of extensive new public transport systems can, in reality, be even less than that of technological change.

For example, in the space of 20 years the Vancouver metropolitan region has constructed a large new automated rail system that has led to very substantial high density, mixed use sub-centre development, which in turn has helped it to begin to change the region into a more sustainable form. Massive redevelopment of central and inner city land uses such as at False Creek and Coal Harbour have occurred over a slightly longer period allowing tens of thousands of people to lead a less car-dependent existence. During the same period from 1986 to 2006, the changes in vehicle technology and fuels has had a virtually negligible effect on fleet fuel consumption, notwithstanding the fact that much larger vehicles today are achieving similar rates of fuel use as much smaller vehicles decades ago.

From the initial vision in the mid-1970s Portland, Oregon scrapped a major planned freeway and instead has progressively constructed an extensive LRT system and separate inner city tram system. It has at the same time radically transformed its central area into a highly livable, people-oriented place, pulling down an elevated freeway, transforming car parks into public squares and focusing the majority of new development in the last 20 years around urban rail, thus helping to contain sprawl. The technologies for cars and fuels over the same period, although having improved, have not been able to have any real effect on fuel use because people are driving further, thus overriding any enhanced technological efficiency.

Perth, Australia since 1988 has electrified its entire train system, constructed a new 36 km line to the northern suburbs and will open a 74 km southern extension in July 2007. Urban rail use has more than quadrupled and is set to more than double again. Many examples of new transit-oriented developments have taken shape over the same period and many more are planned, These are helping to contain urban sprawl and beginning tc create a more transit-oriented urban form for the city, allowing more and more people, even in distant outer areas to be less dependent on cars. Though the major policy response in Australia over the last 30 years to the need to save fuel in transport has been to improve the technology of vehicles, the average fleet fuel consumption of cars in Perth and Australia-wide has remained virtually unchanged from what it was in the 1960s. In 1963 it was 11.4 litres per 100 km and in 1995 it was 11.5 litres per 100 km. Relative gains in fuel efficiency through better technology have been eaten up by more power consuming items such as power steering and air conditioning and increased weight.

There are many other examples of significant and rapid trends in land use change, such as the revitalisation of downtown areas across the United States and Canada bringing hundreds of thousands of people closer to work and other destinations available as short walking trips. At the same time it is difficult to find any significant progress in the overall fuel-efficiency of vehicle fleets, notwithstanding improved technologies in cars and the gradual appearance of small numbers of electric and hybrid vehicles in cities.

Reconstructing cities to be more sustainable from a transport and energy perspective is clearly a long term project but can proceed at a significant rate when priority is given to it. Technological changes to improve vehicles and fuels should proceed in parallel with such changes but should not be seen as a panacea to the transport energy problem or as a soft option that avoids the need to address the structure of the city and the modes of transport available to people.

Cities around the world vary enormously in their transport patterns, energy use, infrastructure systems and urban form. Low density land use patterns, priority to freeway provision over speed competitive transit systems and policies that treat congestion always as a negative to be removed, are significant factors in understanding transport and energy use patterns. Many cities today are responding to the imperative to reduce automobile dependence through changes in transport policies that are generating attractive and well-utilised public transport systems and significant changes in land use and urban form in the form of central and inner area revitalisation and TOD around transit stations.

Such large scale changes to the structure of cities occur and have been occurring over relatively short time periods (10 to 20 years), allowing cities to reduce the growth in automobile dependence and energy use, whereas the long term policy in many cities to save energy or expand fuel options through technological fixes has produced almost no tangible changes to date. If cities are to achieve paradigm shifts to confront the post-petroleum era they are going to need to recognise that technology is not a panacea but only one factor in the bigger venture of fundamentally restructuring cities to reduce automobile dependence and creating overall more sustainable and liveable cities.

7

Regulatory Design of Basic Services

In the past, regulatory advisers often focused on the need to introduce international best practice— generally in the form of an independent regulatory organisation—to solve a wide range of performance problems. However, this approach was seldom straightforward, nor was it always successful. There is no one-size-fits-all regulatory design that can be reliably applied to resolve performance problems. Rather, regulation is best developed on a country-by-country basis through answering questions such as the following:

1. What are the real sector problems, and which of these can regulation solve?
2. What specific objectives is regulation aiming to achieve?
3. What combination of organisations and instruments is most suitable and would work best for achieving these regulatory objectives?

By carefully delimiting what the regulatory system is to achieve, and objectively determining how it can be structured to achieve these objectives, governments can design a system that is coherent, predictable, and legitimate. Identifying the key decisions to be made is just one element of design. The hard part can be actually making these decisions.

Water and Sanitation Services

Good water and sanitation services are essential for health, well-being, and economic development. However, in many developing countries the way these services are delivered can be less than ideal. Service quality may be low, service providers' financial capacity to deliver may be under threat, and large segments of the population may not receive service at all.

To improve urban water and sanitation services, a government first needs to identify the sector's underlying problems. Such problems become especially clear when the water services that people actually get are compared with the services people would like to get, and the conditions under which most stockholders would like the services to be provided. As the table shows, the gap between the actual and the ideal is often considerable.

Having identified the principal sector problems, the government then needs to define a path of reform that can move the sector from the actual (the services people get) toward the ideal (the services people want). This reform path needs to be well planned. It will involve a number of important decisions, including who should make policy decisions, who should own and manage the entities providing water services, who should invest and finance the investments, and how services should be paid for.

Regulation of Private and Public Providers

Water and sanitation is an essential service, and its provision—in particular, through piped supply and collection—has strong (natural) monopoly characteristics. This makes it important to control providers and make them accountable in some way, *regardless* of whether the provider is publicly or privately owned and operated. Private providers are generally regulated by autonomous agencies contracts, or both. Regulation is often considered necessary, because without it private providers might make unreasonable profits by overcharging and under-delivering.

Whether publicly owned providers can or should be regulated by an autonomous regulator is less clear. Among the questions to be considered are the following:

1. Whether certainty and predictability in the regulatory environment can strongly and positively influence the performance of government-owned water operators.
2. Whether transparency in political and policy interventions is also important for good policy making, and for stronger government and service provider accountability when the service provider is government-owned.
3. Whether potential benefits are outweighed by the costs and resource constraints—especially for small municipal service providers.

Public providers can be controlled and made accountable through ownership and governance. However, the line separating ownership and governance from regulation is not a bright one. Some analysts recommend making the separation between these forms of control more formal by turning the publicly owned and operated utility into a corporatised, regulated entity that mimics a privately owned company. This highlights the range of operating models that exist for government-owned water service providers.

A variety of regulatory approaches can be used across the range of operating models. In some cases, "autonomous" regulators try to control publicly owned providers as if they were privately owned. In other cases, mayors or ministers approve prices through informal, non-transparent processes. At present, there is little quantitative information on the linkage between regulation, governance structures, and performance outcomes. Some analysts highlight the success of some governments—such as national governments in Botswana and Burkina Faso, and municipalities in the Netherlands, New Zealand, and Scandinavia—in owning, operating, and controlling public utilities successfully without separate regulatory agencies. In other jurisdictions with public utilities—such as in Scotland and New South Wales (Australia)—regulatory agencies have been established to provide greater transparency and facilitate performance improvements and price reform, with some apparent success.

Approach to Regulatory Design

Governments embarking on water and sanitation sector reforms need to decide how providers will be given better incentives to deliver the services that people want at a reasonable price. This is where regulatory design becomes important. The regulatory system (a combination of rules and organisations) needs to be able to help solve the country's key regulatory problems, and to work well with existing sector institutions.

These may seem like simple objectives, but regulatory systems have often failed to resolve problems effectively. Many newly minted regulators have fit poorly with other sector institutions. Governments can reduce the risk of failures and poor fit by thinking carefully about regulatory design and by following a logical decision making process.

The process of regulatory design needs to assess where and how regulation is needed, before setting out to put regulatory systems in place. A good way to design effective regulation involves four basic steps:

1. Defining the underlying problems and objectives in the sector.
2. Assessing whether existing regulatory systems are well suited to achieving the objectives.

3. Identifying the specific regulatory functions needed to achieve those objectives.
4. Deciding, in light of existing institutions, which legal instruments are best suited to embody the regulatory rules, and which organisations are best suited to perform the regulatory functions.

These steps are illustrated in figure 1.

Defining the Problems and Sector Objectives

The provision of water supply and sanitation services in developing countries often faces a number of performance problems. On one level, these problems can easily be identified: leaking pipes, inadequate water pressure, poor water quality, and low service coverage. A one-off cash injection could feasibly solve many of these issues in the short term, but sector reform needs to focus on realising improvements that can be sustained in the long term. To achieve such improvements, the *underlying* causes of poor performance need to be identified and remedied. For many countries, the underlying causes of poor sector performance include the following:

1. Inadequate investment in, and maintenance of, system assets. This may be caused by
   a) Inadequate cash flow, due to tariffs being set below cost-recovery level, or costs being inefficiently high.
   b) Poor planning or disagreement between the government and provider over investment plans.
   c) Lack of confidence in the regulatory arrangements or, more generally, broad political risk.
2. Poor maintenance and operating practices.
3. Poorly defined or enforced service standards.

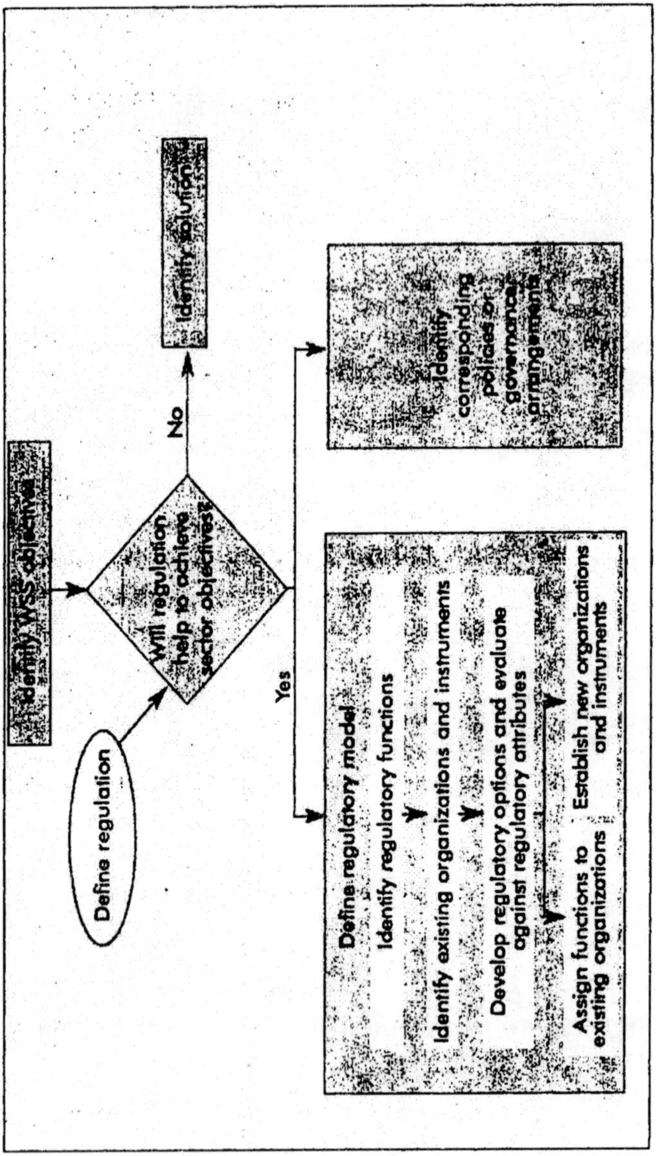

Figure 1. Framework for Thinking about Regulation

4. Lack of clear policies on service coverage expansion.
5. Barriers to entry for small private providers.

By examining existing sector policies and consulting with providers, consumers, and other sector participants, governments can build a clear picture of what the real problems are and thus what the reform objectives should be.

Assessing Whether Regulation Can Solve the Problems

Some of the underlying problems identified in the first stage can be effectively solved by a good regulatory system; other problems need a policy or structural solution. It is important to clearly identify which problems regulation can solve. This requires understanding what economic regulation is and does, and what it cannot do.

Defining Economic Regulation and the Problems It Can Solve

Economic regulation is best thought of as the legal controls placed on water and sanitation providers in order to overcome the problems inherent in an essential, monopoly service. This points to a core definition of economic regulation as the rules and organisations that set, change, monitor, and enforce allowed tariffs and allowed service standards for water providers.

Water is an essential service, and is generally worth a lot more to people than it costs to supply. Private providers could take advantage of this by overcharging and making high profits at the expense of consumers. In some cases, this opportunity for profiteering may be limited by competition. In the case of large-scale piped provision, however, competition is not feasible. Economic regulation can usefully be thought of as mimicking the pressures that competition provides in other markets. In other words, it can help to stop tariffs from increasing above the level required to recover reasonable costs and make the service provider bear costs that are considered excessive.

Regulation can also set and enforce service standards to ensure that utilit:es are providing the services that people want. However, tariffs and service standards are inevitably related—if tariffs are too low to recover costs, the provider may not be able to meet the required service standards, or the government may bear the fiscal burden of providing (implicit or explicit) subsides. Thus, regulation also has a role to play in ensuring that tariffs are not "too low."

Beyond this narrow role of setting, monitoring, and enforcing rules on tariffs and service quality, economic regulation begins to overlap with other areas of regulation and policy. This overlap is illustrated in figure 2. The darkest area in the middle represents the core of economic regulation—addressing the monopoly problem. In the "gray area" around the core, a choice is needed as to whether a particular regulatory function should be considered part of economic regulation or dealt with in another way.

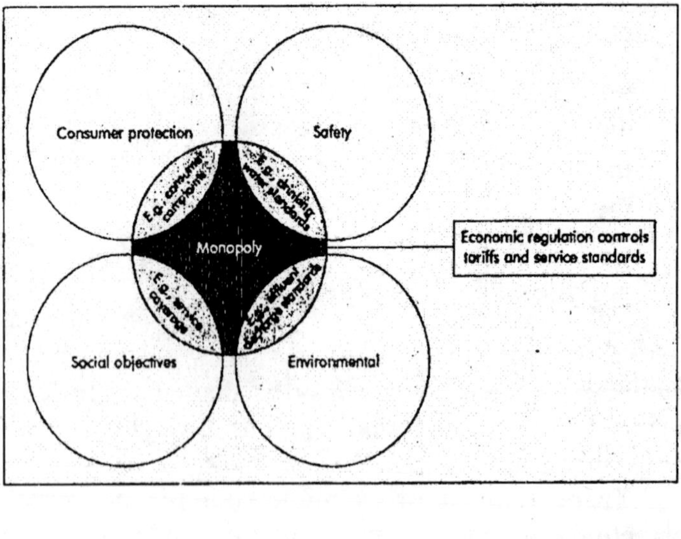

Figure 2. Economic Regulation—Addressing the Monopoly Problem

For example, setting drinking water standards may be considered part of economic regulation, or it may be dealt with as an aspect of health or food safety regulation. Service coverage may be governed by regulatory requirements on the provider to connect more customers, or by subsidies for service expansion, or both. Another way could mean a different form of regulation— governments can use the power of the law to instruct providers to do certain things, and to enforce these instructions through penalties and other forms of compulsion (such as providing incentives or withdrawing privileges). Another way could mean a different form of control altogether. Governments have a range of tools they can use to achieve social, environmental, safety, and consumer protection objectives. For example, governments may aim to achieve social objectives by influencing providers through subsidies and tax incentives.

There are also problems that economic regulation cannot solve—or at least cannot solve alone. For example, integrated policy approaches are often necessary for the following:

1. Ensuring that services remain affordable to low-income households.
2. Increasing provider efficiency.
3. Improving capital expenditure planning.
4. Improving poor payment records by government departments and agencies.

Thus, even when governments choose to expand the role of regulation beyond simply setting, monitoring, and enforcing rules on tariffs and service quality, supporting regulation with other policy initiatives is generally necessary.

There are vital government roles in water supply and sanitation services that support regulation, but which are distinct from it:

1. Policy making. Policy defines sector objectives and principles and sets out who should do what to achieve those objectives. The extent to which consumers or taxpayers should pay for water services and infrastructure is a policy decision, as is the ownership of the providers and the general strategy for controlling tariffs and service standards.
2. Ownership, service provision, and governance. Provider performance is greatly influenced by who owns the water assets, who is responsible for service provision, and how the owner exercises control over the utility's management (governance). The government needs to ensure that these factors and regulatory design are aligned with each other.
3. Coordination. Governments must coordinate water supply and sanitation services by ensuring that policy decisions and implementation plans are consistent, managing input from the various bodies involved in water sector activities, and coordinating public expenditure priorities.

Defining Specific Regulatory Functions

In developed countries with private providers, the core regulatory goals may be to keep tariffs down and to keep service standards up. In developing countries, it cannot be assumed that the regulatory functions are the same. Before putting a regulatory system in place, governments should be clear on the following issues:

1. Will the regulatory system be designed with the aim of keeping tariffs "down" and service standards "up," through regular and in-depth scrutiny of the provider's financial and technical performance?
2. Or is it more important to move tariffs up through rules that require cost-recovery tariffs?

3. Is there a need for neutral, fair adjudication between the government and a private provider ?
4. Or is the provider owned and managed by the government in a way that makes third-party adjudication less necessary or acceptable?

Clarity on sector objectives and priorities is essential for choosing effective regulatory instruments and organisations.

Choosing Legal Instruments and Organisations

Regulatory systems can take a number of forms. In the past, some regulatory advisors have advocated that some of these forms are better at achieving good regulation. In particular, advisors have viewed an "independent regulator" as the best-practice model. This view was based on the model's perceived success in other infrastructure sectors, and in such countries as the United States, the United Kingdom, and Australia. In practice, which models work best depends on a country's objectives and circumstances. Regulatory systems that seem structurally different may carry out the same regulatory functions to solve similar problems. As figure 3 illustrates, a number of different legal instruments and organisations can be combined to create a variety of regulatory architecture. For example, regulation in Florida is based on a combination of statute, a regulatory office, and a government ministry or department. The Public Services Commission (PSC) was established by statute, and it has broad discretion to set, change, monitor, and enforce limits on tariffs. However, the regulatory function of setting standards for water pressure is the job of the Department for Environmental Protection. This department also controls drinking water quality and effluent discharge standards.

A different regulatory architecture can be seen in Colombia. The Regulatory Commission for Water and Basic Sanitation Services (CRA) establishes the tariff-setting methodology. Providers set their own tariffs in accordance with this methodology (or apply to the CRA to set the tariffs a different way). Service standards are set by the Ministry of Economic Development. The Public Services Superintendent (SSP) monitors the providers to verify that they are following the tariff-setting rules and complying with the service standards. However, where private providers operate under concession contracts with a municipality, the general practice is for the contract to set service standards and tariffs, which are to be monitored and enforced by the municipality.

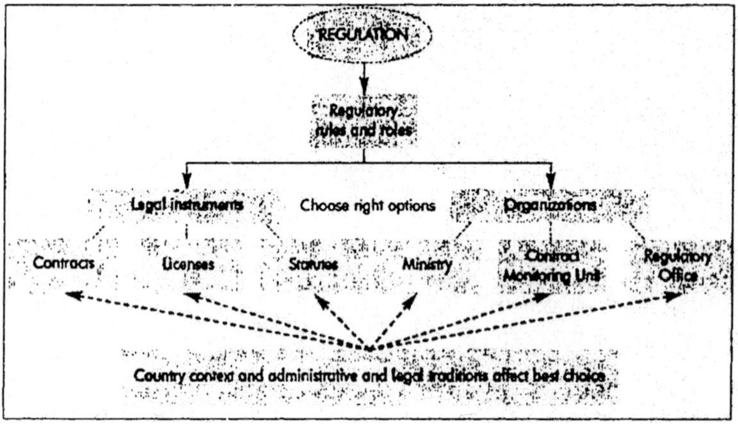

Figure 3. Selecting Legal Instruments and Organisations for Good Regulation

In Cote devoir, an affermage contract is the regulatory instrument. The Ministry of Economic Infrastructure designed, negotiated, and signed the affermage contract with the private provider. One of its departments, the Water Directorate, is the owner of the supply network and is responsible for monitoring the provider's compliance with the contract. The Directorate also leads negotiations on tariff adjustments and is responsible for granting approval for some construction projects. A separate government department monitors the costs incurred by the provider when it undertakes network renewal and extension activities.

Each of these designs represents a different regulatory architecture, but each is functionally equivalent in terms of the roles for setting tariffs and service standards that are performed.

Attributes of Good Regulation

Given that a range of functionally equivalent designs are possible, clear criteria for selecting the right legal instruments and organisations (for a specific country environment) are needed. These criteria can be thought of as attributes—the qualities that a good regulatory system should have.

The goal of regulation is to achieve good service for consumers at a price that enables providers to operate efficiently and sustainably, consistent with a clear and reasonable trade-off between service levels and tariffs. To achieve these goals, a regulatory system should have the following attributes:

1. *Coherence*. If a provider needs to meet higher service standards or to focus on system expansion, it is likely to incur higher costs, which will need to be compensated through higher tariffs or a combination of tariffs and subsidies. In contrast, if tariffs need to be lower (because the government believes the poor cannot afford water and sanitation services), but subsidies are not an option for achieving this, it makes sense that the required service standards are lower, too. The regulatory system should be able to select, and settle on the right combination of tariffs and subsidies, and service standards and coverage, such that providers are able to recover their costs, and people receive the services they are willing to pay for.

In Bogota, Colombia, a lack of coherence in regulatory decision making triggered friction and political intervention that undermined the regulator's independence and autonomy. The tariff setting methodology of the CRA (the regulator) focused on achieving full cost recovery through tariffs, partly on the assumption that municipalities were seeking political support by suppressing water rates. However, when the methodology was applied in Bogota, average tariffs increased by more than 100 percent. The municipality had included a large provision for capital works in the tariff calculation. Considerable debate ensued over whether the calculation was reasonable, with the President eventually intervening to direct the CRA's decision.

In contrast, in Senegal such tariff shocks for consumers were carefully avoided, and coherence between tariffs and services was maintained through the combination of a planned, gradual increase in consumer tariffs and guaranteed cost-recovery payments from the government to the provider. The government, having made a policy decision on the gradual tariff path, bore the risk of service costs and tariffs diverging. This risk was limited for the government as the service levels, the capital investments, and the performance of the operator were linked.

2. *Predictability and credibility.* Regulatory decisions should be time-consistent, and made on clear precedents and rules. This is essential for minimising risk to providers and, in turn, encouraging good service provision and adequate asset maintenance and capital investment.

   Many systems fail because of a lack of credible protection against regulatory expropriation. In Buenos Aires the water concessionaries suffered regulatory expropriation. Many other proposed reforms have failed because the regulatory system was not credible in assuring providers that they would be able to recover their costs. In contrast, in Vanuatu and Senegal, credibility was provided through the contract, which prevented short-term political intervention and created a predictable regulatory framework for providers. In Senegal, regulatory rules and processes that minimised the risk of steep tariffs increases also contributed to predictability and credibility.

3. *Legitimacy, transparency, and accountability.* Regulatory decisions need to be clear, widely accepted, and publicly accessible. Political and social stability is not only essential for a regulatory system's predictability; it also creates the conditions for the public to view regulation as legitimate. Moreover, beyond public scrutiny, regulatory institutions need reasons and incentives to make decisions in the long-term interests of consumers—strong, logical lines of accountability help. Accountability to the public, in turn, is essential for preventing corruption and improving legitimacy in the public eye.

   In Cochabamba, Bolivia, the lack of legitimacy and transparency in the way tariff decisions were made was a key contributing factor in the failure of the concession. The public rioted against tariff increases, largely because they lacked information on the contract and its monitoring organisations, and doubted the role of regulation in protecting their interests. As a result of intense public pressure, the government cancelled the contract.

   In contrast, in the United States, a highly transparent and participatory form of regulation is used in most states. Utilities submit applications (for example, for a rate increase) to the regulator, and any citizen or group has a right to contest the application in open hearings adjudicated by the regulator. All relevant technical and financial information is publicly available. The application of strong democratic principles helps regulation to achieve legitimacy, transparency, and accountability.

These attributes can be used as criteria for assessing the likely effectiveness of different regulatory architecture—that is, the combination of legal instruments and regulatory organisations.

Applying the Attributes to Build the Right Architecture

Each country's unique context and legal traditions should inform the way that regulatory roles are distributed amongst instruments and organisations, in order to achieve the desired attributes of regulation discussed above.

In many developed countries, an independent regulator model has worked well to achieve these attributes. For example, Of at, the water regulatory body for England and Wales, is viewed internationally as a model of successful, independent regulation. In the English political, economic, and social context—in which the government, administrators, regulators, and the general public share strong values on sector policy, and only modest changes in prices have been needed—a regulatory office like Of at has been able to regulate effectively, without direct political intervention. As this example shows, politicians are less prone to intervene where there is broad-based support for the regulatory mandate.

However, when this model is transposed to developing and transitional countries, regulatory independence is often undermined by frequent political intervention (in Manila, for example, the president intervened on tariff decisions a number of times). In an environment where there is a high risk that politicians will make decisions that focus on short-term interests and lack coherency (between tariffs and service standards), a contract can be a good legal instrument for locking in regulatory rules and achieving coherence and predictability. Many developing and transition nations have relatively effective contract law and dispute resolution mechanisms, so regulation by contract can be a credible and legitimate form of regulation. In some countries, predictability may be increased if regulation is embodied directly in statute. It is a question of finding the most appropriate instrument in a particular country context.

Contract-Based Regulation

Countries such as Senegal and Vanuatu have used contracts as an effective regulatory instrument for setting tariff rules and service standards. The legal systems in these countries were developed under influences from France, where a contract model of water regulation is widely and successfully used. As a result, in both Vanuatu and Senegal this model was well understood and respected by the government and sector participants.

For regulation by contract to work successfully, the rules must be monitored and enforced. Existing government organisations may lack the capacity or incentive to monitor performance effectively. Poor monitoring undermines customer protection, reducing the legitimacy of the regulatory system as a whole. This "legitimacy deficit" was evident, for example, in Vanuatu. Although the provider provides good services, the paucity of government monitoring has resulted in widespread concern over the lack of transparency, accountability, and legitimacy in the way the provider is controlled.

New organisational arrangements may be introduced to help increase government's capacity to enforce the rules and overcome the legitimacy deficit. This was done effectively in Senegal—where a combination of dedicated contract monitoring units, ongoing performance monitoring by the government-owned asset holding company, and timely, independent mediation on disputed issues by an outside conciliator provided the necessary support for regulation by contract to operate successfully. The combination of the rules set out in the contract, and the roles performed by monitoring organisations and government ministries created a regulatory system that was generally coherent, predictable, legitimate, and accountable to the public.

The choice of regulatory organisation must be made carefully to ensure an appropriate fit with existing institutions and with the legal instrument used for regulation. For example, a regulatory agency with broad powers and a contract may not be a sound combination, as the experience of Manila highlights. Because the concession contracts in Manila explicitly set out the tariff-setting and service standard rules for the providers, the role of the Regulatory Office was often unclear. Even Office staff became confused at times over the degree of discretion that the Office should exercise in setting and interpreting rules, or the extent to which it should focus solely on contract monitoring and enforcement. A better organisational choice may have been a contract monitoring unit with a clear mandate to monitor and enforce compliance with the regulatory rules already established in the contracts.

As the examples discussed above illustrate, a variety of regulatory architecture are possible. Although these architecture may be functionally equivalent, they are not equally successful in different country environments. Regulatory designers should choose legal instruments and organisations that form a sound overall design. The design should also be cognizant of the specific sector problems regulation needs to solve, and the particular country environment in which regulation will be seated.

Improving Regulatory Design

Since good regulatory design needs to reflect the country context, it is hard to provide singular guidelines. However, observations from regulatory successes and failures internationally, including experience from recently completed in-depth country case studies, reveal several lessons on what makes for effective regulation. These lessons point to several aspects of good regulatory design: designing-in political and context-specific features to a purpose-built regulatory model, rather than adopting a best-practice model that does not fit the country context and attempts to operate outside existing institutions.

From these lessons we have identified a number of design approaches that can help improve a regulatory regime's performance concerning the key attributes of coherence, predictability, and legitimacy.

These approaches include the following:

1. Working with the existing organisational framework.
2. Designing in the politics.
3. Limiting discretion in decision making.
4. Trading off sophistication in favour of simplicity.

These approaches are discussed in the sections that follow.

Working with the Existing Organisational Framework

Regulatory design never actually starts with a blank slate. Regulation is generally introduced in an environment where some sector organisations already exist; legal and political systems are well developed; some measures for consumer protection have already been introduced; and relationships between politicians, providers, and the public have been established. The resulting complexity of structures and incentives is not a backdrop that regulation should seek to overcome or be imposed on top of. Rather, it provides a framework for regulation to work *within.*

The choice of legal instruments and regulatory organisations should reflect the existing country conditions, but regulatory designers should also realise that these conditions may change. For example, as a country's institutional capacity and credibility improve over time, it may be appropriate for regulatory organisations to take on a stronger or more extensive role.

Sometimes such evolution is planned—initial legislation may limit the role and discretion of a new regulatory body for a limited period, but these limits may be relaxed over time (as in Victoria, Australia). Sometimes the need to modify a regulatory regime becomes apparent over time, as government policies change or weaknesses in the existing arrangements become obvious. For example, Vanuatu is currently developing a new agency to assist the government in monitoring and enforcing Port Vila's water concession contract.

In general, however, the choice of instruments (and related organisations) is a long-term one. For a regulatory system to be credible, the public and investors must perceive that it requires long term commitments and lasting structures.

Choice of Legal Instruments

A variety of legal instruments can be used to support regulation. Past approaches to regulatory design have often ignored or down-played the role of contracts in regulation. More emphasis has been placed on developing strong regulatory agencies with broad discretionary powers. However, contracts are often a good starting point for establishing clear and enforceable regulatory rules. In civil-law countries (including countries with French heritage—

such as Vanuatu and Senegal—and many countries in Latin America), contracts are seen as a familiar and legitimate tool for controlling service provision. For such countries, including service standard and rules for operator remuneration within a contract, rather than having an independent regulator set such rules, is more contextually consistent.

In some circumstances, a contract (or a contract alone) may not be the best choice. For example, if a given jurisdiction has several regulated water service providers, there may be some advantage in creating a single legal instrument, such as a statute or uniform license, that sets basic rules for all of them. Another potential attraction of setting rules in a statute is that it is generally difficult to change primary legislation. Investors may perceive regulatory risk as being lower if contractual provisions entered into with local governments are backed up by consistent laws at the national level.

Choice of Organisation

Some form of organisation will be needed to ensure that the rules are followed even where rules are set in a contract. The degree of organisational support that a contract requires will depend on the strength of existing administrative and judicial systems.

Vanuatu provides an example of a regulatory design that did not adequately consider the country's existing institutional context. The Vanuatu government had entered into a concession contract with a private provider, UNELCO. The contracting ministry was notionally responsible for monitoring the concessionaries's performance under the contract. In reality, little monitoring has been undertaken, and the government and public do not feel in control.

In retrospect, the government might have done better to give contract-monitoring responsibilities to stronger organisations. Candidates would have included the Ministry of Finance, a specially created contract monitoring unit, or a consulting firm hired for the purpose. Better contract monitoring could have increased the legitimacy of the regulatory system.

Senegal's regulatory system had a better organisational design. Regulation in Senegal worked better than in Vanuatu, largely for the following reasons:

1. The contracting party to the utility's performance contract, SONES (the state-owned, asset holding company, which had considerable technical expertise) undertook regular and thorough monitoring.
2. Dedicated contract monitoring units were established.
3. The government was active in its relationship with the utility.

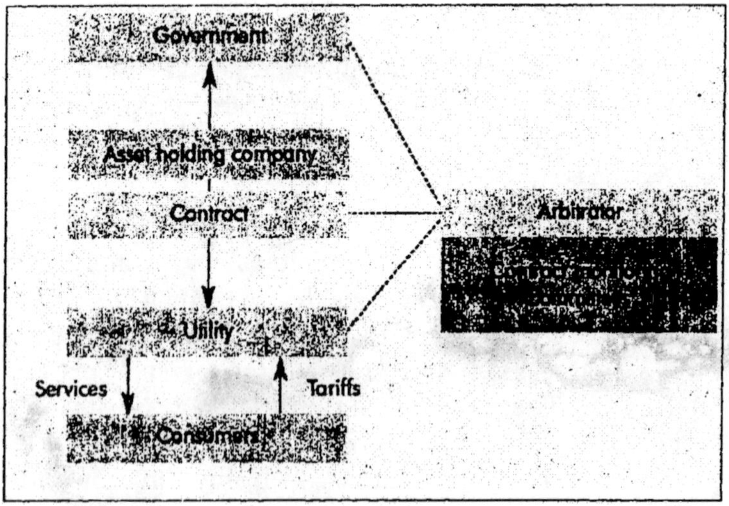

Figure 4. Regulatory Organisations Supported the Contract in Senegal

Conciliators (arbitrators) were brought in to help resolve disputes emerging between SONES and the utility (either because of contract imprecision or because of one of the parties failing on its commitments). Donors also played an ongoing and important mediating role. In summary, organisations were brought in at the potential weak points of the regulatory structure in Senegal. Regulation was more successful because the need for these organisations was identified during the design stage. A contract-based model of regulation was thus adapted to suit Senegal's existing institutional context better.

Consistency with Parallel Processes

In addition to considering the institutions that are *already* in place when regulation is designed, regulatory designers need to be fully cognizant of the institutions that are being introduced through parallel reforms. In particular, regulation is often introduced at the same time as private sector participation, which clearly influence which functions the regulatory system will need to fulfil.

Designing a package of economic regulation and contract-based private participation is more difficult than is sometimes realised. Common regulatory models were designed to work with utilities that are fully privately owned. However, private participation for WSS services is generally based on contracts between government and private companies, not outright sale of the utility. Lack of logical interface between the contract and regulatory design processes can create a mismatch between economic regulation and the private participation arrangements it was intended to support.

For example, in Manila, the Regulatory Office was not clear whether it should simply apply the rules in the concession contract, or whether it could change the rules when circumstances changed. This uncertainty contributed to a messy and confused response when a currency crisis created financial distress for one of the concessionaries. Similarly in Colombia, the relationship between rules set by the CRA (the regulator) and rules in municipal concession and lease contracts is not quite clear. This lack of clarity creates unnecessary risk for both the provider and the local government.

Create an Appropriate Role for Politics

Past approaches to regulation strove for regulatory independence with the objective of keeping politics out of regulatory decision making. Political intervention, however, may be inevitable. Moreover, politics can sometimes play a positive role. The key is to ensure that the regulatory and policy framework encourages or at least constrains politicians to make coherent decisions and honour long-term commitments. This means that the role of politics should be well defined and limited.

Governments can be made to commit to their decisions if key service and tariff provisions are locked into contracts. However, they can still be given a political safety valve to influence tariffs. For example, regulatory designers can decouple consumer tariffs and operator revenue, or provide for government-funded, output-based subsidies that can help keep consumer tariffs down.

Political Decisions

Many advisors believe that regulation should adequately balance provider cost recovery and consumer protection, and that politics can interfere by tipping the scales or by undermining the entire balancing system. One of the principal problems with politicians playing a directive role in regulation is that their decisions tend to lack long-term commitment to coherent tariff and service combinations. Politicians are often tempted to make decisions that are based on short-term interests. They may push for tariffs that only recover short-run operating costs, meaning that the provider has insufficient funds to maintain long-lived assets or make new investments. This may win favour from consumers in the short term (lower tariffs are generally popular), but in the long term it will be detrimental as services begin to deteriorate.

Alternatively, politicians may demand that services be improved or coverage increased without allowing a corresponding increase in tariffs. The lack of coherence between services and tariffs harms both the provider and consumers in the long term.

With these negative consequences of political intervention in mind, many designs have focused on reducing political involvement in regulation. Nonetheless, politics seems to rather consistently intervene, especially when it comes to setting tariffs. For example, in the Philippines and Colombia, the presidents became directly involved in tariff decisions on several occasions, even though the regulatory bodies in both countries were ostensibly autonomous. This type of intervention damaged not only the regulators' independence, but also their credibility.

Politics is especially hard to exclude if independence is combined with wide discretion to make socially and politically sensitive decisions on prices for basic community infrastructure services. This can create excessive risks for all stockholders (investors, service providers, governments, and users)—especially where the current prices are far from levels that are sustainable in the medium to long term. In response, discretion may be reduced or a transparent, accountable role for government policy provided, or both.

The threat of damaging political intervention is not the only reason that regulatory designers should, from the outset, consider a role for political decision making in regulation. There are three important arguments for giving politicians a well-defined role in regulation:

1. Politicians can make decisions that represent a collective choice on trade-offs, such as having limited services for lower tariffs, or having better quality or more widely available services for higher tariffs. People will have different preferences on these choices; a democratically accountable government could be the best organisation to make a choice that best reflects the needs of the community.
2. Politicians may have accountability to the public through the voting system. Although accountability through a democratic political system may be imperfect or diffuse, it at least provides a channel for public involvement. In the case of basic infrastructure services, this channel may be stronger for municipal or local governments than for governments at the national level. The government can exercise its accountability indirectly, by appointing independent regulators to make regulatory decisions, or directly, by choosing a coherent tariff and service standard combination on behalf of consumers.
3. If extreme events—such as a sharp increase in tariffs—occur, the public will demand that the government *does something*. A well-defined regulatory role will provide the government with a safety valve, allowing it to act in a way that minimises damage to the regulatory system while responding to the public.

These arguments point to a positive, if limited, role for politics in regulation. However, regulatory designers still need to ensure that political decision makers will take into account relevant information and advice, act transparently, and make credible, coherent, and time-consistent decisions.

Long-Term Regulatory Coherence

A well-defined role for politics should be one that commits the government to coherent, long-term decisions on tariffs and service standards. The independent regulator model attempted to achieve such commitment by limiting government involvement to setting legislation that established the regulatory body, or appointing some of the regulators. In other words, under this approach the government commits to devolve all tariff and service standard decisions to the independent regulator.

However, the independent regulator approach has frequently failed to achieve political commitment to long-term regulatory coherence. Policy makers and politicians often feel uncomfortable with relinquishing decision-making powers, and face strong pressures to intervene on tariff issues anyway. An alternative way to achieve commitment and consistency is through a contract. The government and provider could decide on coherent rules on tariffs and service standards, which would be locked into the contract, and adjusted only through well-defined periodic reviews. For example, in both Vanuatu and Monteria, the governments were involved in deciding on appropriate service standards and acceptable tariff rules when the service contract was negotiated.

Once the contract is signed, government involvement should be limited to monitoring the contract, and ensuring that the legitimacy of regulation through the contract is maintained (for example, by providing sufficient information for the public, remaining active as a contracting partner, and participating in the renegotiation of the contract if it is desired by, and in the interest of, both parties).

The government may also take part in tariff reviews, which should occur on a pre-agreed periodic basis, or be triggered by pre-agreed changes in economic or social conditions. Such reviews can create another well-defined role for political decision making, and also provide the government with a safety valve to act if shocks (the triggers specified in the contract) occur.

There may be further ways in which regulatory designers can provide a safety valve for political decision making that minimises damage to regulatory credibility. These could enable the government to influence consumer tariffs, if necessary, without influencing operator revenues. For example, in Senegal, politicians take responsibility for public welfare decisions, such as the trade-off between high service levels and high tariffs. The Senegalese government pays the provider a contractually guaranteed fee, sets consumer tariffs, and is responsible for investing in the system assets. These arrangements let the government bear the political and fiscal risks involved in setting tariffs and in influencing long-term service levels (by choosing the level of investment), while ensuring that the provider can cover its costs.

Under an alternative arrangement, the government could set consumer rates at a "socially acceptable" (but below cost-recovery) level, and make a firm commitment to grant an output based subsidy for services provided at this reduced consumer rate. This approach has been used successfully for electricity services in the Philippines, where a kilowatt-per-hour consumption subsidy is provided for poor consumers in remote areas. This subsidy is financed by a levy on all electricity consumption.

A slightly different output-based aid (OBA) approach would involve the government agreeing with the provider on service extensions to new communities, and committing to providing a connection subsidy for each new household connection made by the provider. This type of OBA scheme is currently being implemented for water service expansion in countries such as Brazil and Indonesia.

Limiting the Discretion Given to Regulatory Decision Makers

The quality of the decisions made by a regulatory organisation will depend on both the people involved in making the decisions and the rules by which the decisions are made. By *quality* we mean whether the decision helps achieve regulatory predictability, coherence, and transparency. Good decisions require competent individuals whose incentives are aligned with regulatory goals, and well-defined rules that are easy to implement.

The relative importance of the individuals and the written rules depends on how much *discretion* individual decision makers are provided—either unintentionally, through poorly formulated rules, or intentionally, through the use of regulatory principles in place of precise rules, or through organisational design.

In the spectrum from low to high discretion, a "pure" regulation by contract model is sometimes identified with low discretion, and a "pure" independent regulator (regulation by agency) model is sometimes identified with high discretion. In practice, the relationship between discretion and the regulatory instrument is more complex.

Many contracts fail to specify price reset provisions in detail. Although the process for negotiation and arbitration of price resets may be well specified, the basis for negotiating tariffs, and the various factors to be taken into account, may be quite broadly specified—creating a high degree of discretion. By the same token, it is possible to establish an independent regulatory agency with clearly limited discretion. Legislation or subsidiary instruments can specify the initial price path and key parameters or approaches to be used by the regulator during price resets.

In practice, the reset provisions under regulation by contract or agency are often vague and poorly defined, and are a source of considerable risk and uncertainty for the investor. However, a key distinction is that under regulation by contract, the new price paths are to be agreed with the operator, with recourse to arbitration in the event that agreement cannot be reached. In contrast, under regulation by agency, a new price path may be imposed upon the utility, subject to possible recourse to appeal mechanisms. In either case, it is often preferable to define clear and binding rules for price resets, which will limit regulatory discretion and reduce uncertainty for investors and other stockholders.

Levels of Discretion in Regulatory Rules

High-discretion rules—that is, price-setting provisions in contracts or legislation that are effectively principles and that include concepts that need to be defined by the decision maker—have three key advantages:

1. Precise, low-discretion rules may result in the wrong decision in some circumstances (such as if unforeseen financial shocks occur, or if base conditions change over time).
2. High-discretion rules allow a competent decision maker to consider basic policy objectives when making a decision.
3. High-discretion rules may involve lower setup costs—more precise rules will take longer to develop and gain consensus on.

In the context of a competent, independent regulatory organisation or established legal precedents that provide clear guidance on the exercise of this discretion, these advantages may make higher-discretion rules the right choice. However, if such precedents are lacking, if the regulatory organisation lacks the competence or capacity to exercise a high degree of discretion, or if the impartiality of decision is likely to be threatened by political (or provider) intervention, low-discretion rules are likely to lead to better

Low-discretion rules are likely to be a better choice for countries with limited institutional capacity and regulatory traditions, because they:

a) Make the outcomes of regulatory decisions more certain and predictable.

b) Reduce the potential for decisions to be inconsistent, biased, or arbitrary.

c) Enable each regulatory decision to be made more quickly, and with fewer resources.

The advantages listed above suggest that low-discretion rules may be a good starting point for regulatory systems that involve a large degree of decision making by an organisation (in contrast to systems that set rules in contracts, and only call for decision making by an independent organisation in special circumstances).

As time passes and experience with the regulatory system grows, institutional strength—in particular, the competence of regulatory organisations—may improve; the legitimacy of the regulatory system may be enhanced; and sector participants may discover that certain regulatory rules have not been effective or useful in all situations. If these conditions hold, the government may decide that the regulatory organisation should have a greater degree of discretion. However, the purpose of increasing discretion should be to improve the quality of important regulatory decisions by permitting more flexibility in adjusting prices to changing circumstances and incorporating lessons learned from regulatory practice elsewhere, rather than to widen the scope of regulation.

Trading Off Sophistication in Favour of Simplicity

Once decisions are made on the general regulatory framework—which organisations and legal instruments work best given the country context—attention turns to filling in the regulatory details (for example, tariff formulas and rules for calculating costs). International experience has shown that a lack of detail in regulatory rules can lead to important decisions being disputed or can reduce the effectiveness of key processes. For example, in Manila an ongoing debate arose over the role of the financial models that the concessionaries had used when submitting their bids (it was not clear from the contract whether the assumptions in the models should be binding). In Vanuatu, the contract does not clearly specify how a tariff review should be undertaken, which may have discouraged the government from entering into this process. Such examples highlight the importance of ensuring adequate details in the rules.

Conversely, the drive to provide detail should not come at the cost of simplicity and usability. Tradition and professional instinct may urge those designing regulatory systems to aim for economic optimisation. For example, an ideal set of regulatory rules would achieve full cost recovery for the provider, at the most efficient tariff, and for the most appropriate level of service, given the community's needs and willingness to pay. This, however, is a demanding ideal. Regulatory designers should not let the perfect be the enemy of the good. By creating sophisticated rules, which require large amounts of information or considerable technical expertise, designers may inadvertently reduce the effectiveness of regulation.

Predictability and credibility if adequate information is not available to effectively apply rules, or if the rules are not well understood, regulatory decisions will not be made in a predictable way, and the regulator's credibility may be undermined.

Transparency is achieved when rules are simple and clear. Overly sophisticated rules may be hard to understand and implement.

A clear example of sophistication being successfully put aside in favour of simplicity occurred in Colombia. The CRA, the Colombian water regulator, had brought in a well-known international regulatory theoretician to advise on how it could improve its regulatory methodology. The advisor's recommendations were to regulate service quality, apply penalties for noncompliance (which were to be automatically paid by utilities to customers), and open the water sector to competition by regulating bulk water prices, cross-subsidy levels, and access to distribution networks.

These ideas, which were innovative even for the water sector in developed nations, were revolutionary and unprecedented in an emerging market, such as Colombia's. Government and industry believed that the water sector was not ready for these reforms, but the CRA's leadership tried to push them through. The World Bank and other international experts explained that the proposed changes were impractical, costly, would create high regulatory risk, and would not easily solve the key water sector problems (coverage and service quality) in Colombia. Eventually, the sophisticated reforms were abandoned. A conceptually simpler, cost-based methodology was retained for setting tariffs, allowing utilities a more reliable revenue flow, and enabling them to invest in improvements to service quality and coverage.

The provision of urban water and sanitation services in many countries is poor. The services people actually get generally fall short of the services people want and would be willing to pay for. In response, governments often engage in sector wide reform to help improve services. These reforms may involve introducing economic regulation—that is, rules and organisations that set, monitor, enforce, and change allowed tariffs and service standards for water and sanitation service providers.

Economic regulation helps to ensure that utilities with natural monopoly power in water supply and sanitation services provide the services people want at reasonable prices. The government can achieve other sector objectives, such as extending service to poor consumers, or managing environmental impacts, through tools other than economic regulation (for example, subsidies or environmental regulation). Early in the reform process, the decision makers in government should set out a clear, but limited, role for economic regulation in the context of other interventions.

Having defined the role of regulation, a regulatory structure needs to be designed with an appropriate combination of legal instruments and organisations. When building this structure, designers need to consider a range of country-specific factors: the existing organisational framework, legal and political systems, and culture and traditions. In other words, there is no international best practice for regulatory design—one standard model will not fit well with, or be successful in, every country context.

Although no best-practice design guarantees these attributes, they can be enhanced by focusing on particular design features. One such design feature is an appropriate avenue for political decision making. Politics can intervene in unpredictable ways, even when attempts are made to shut it out. Such ad hoc interventions can undermine the credibility and legitimacy of the regulatory system. Political decision making, however, can be channelled into the limited areas where the government is best placed to make decisions that require collective accountability. These areas include decisions on policy-related issues, such as whether and how to provide subsidies, or which of a range of consistent tariff and service standard combinations would best serve the public's needs. Contracts can be used to enshrine government commitments to decisions it has made. With careful design, a limited, well-defined decision-making role can provide a safety valve for government involvement in exceptional circumstances (such as tariff shocks caused by a sudden change in supply costs).

Other features of good regulatory design include limiting discretion for regulatory decision makers, and using clear and simple regulatory rules. When organisations lack strength and experience, more precise rules and well-defined roles will improve the predictability and transparency of regulation. However, rules must also be easy to understand and implement. This may mean trading off sophistication in favour of rules that are easier to use in practice.

8

Analysing the Impacts of Urbanisation

Traditional measures of urbanisation based on administrative and political geographic units are inadequate to address many questions related to population settlement patterns and ecological issues that arise in recent comparative studies. National differences in the definition of urbanisation and the dependence of those definitions on administrative designations of political subunits have always made cross national comparisons difficult. In studies of the relationship between population and the environment, these differences are heightened by the ecological emphasis on the natural environment. Urbanisation is usually conceptualised as a characteristic of the population or society, but in ecological studies there is equal interest in defining urbanisation in terms of land use and land cover characteristics. While measurement differences are difficult enough to deal with when comparing the percentage of the population that is urbanised, they are much more likely to cause variation in the percentage of the land area in urban designated areas. The choice of geographic unit of analysis and definitions criteria and methodology can result in varying degrees of "over bounding" or "under bounding," sometimes within the same area . The differences in over bounding and under bounding that are annoyances in the measurement of population size become major problems for measuring the extent of urban land use.

Because ecologists often are interested in how landscapes and the environment have changed over time,. changing definitions of urbanisation within a given nation also pose difficulties for analysis. In the U.S., demographic data from past censuses are presented only for administrative and political geographic units. Identifying degrees of urbanisation in the past is made more difficult by the paucity of population and land use data for small geographic areas comparable to the "patches," or small study areas, that feature in ecological research.

The lack of detailed population and spatial information often requires use of cartographic methods for defining urbanisation; that is, reliance on mapped portrayals of urban extent. Lack of census geographic area boundary information also poses problems when linking historical demographic data for urban population with information relating to environmental processes. Portrayal of population using point data and depicting urban growth and extent through various modelling procedures can overcome problems relating to lack of boundary information.

Defining levels of urbanisation is made more difficult by the fact that it is both a discrete *phenomenon* that can be observed and measured in place at a specific time, and a *process* that occurs across space and time. The difference between urbanisation as a phenomenon and urbanisation as a process creates challenges for researchers and policy makers who base conclusions and decisions on observation and measurement of something that has happened in order to affect changes and develop policies in advance of something that will happen.

There is no easy solution to the tension created by this dichotomy—we must define and measure the thing in order to understand the process and its ecological effects.

Population and Land Area

The countries in the study, China, India, and the United States of America, are the world's three most populous countries. In the year 2000, China had an estimated population of 1.261 billion; India had 1.014 billion people; and as of April 1 the population of the United States had reached 281,421,906. While the combined population of these three countries accounts for approximately 42 percent of the world's population, the countries occupy only 15 percent of the world's land area. How these countries handle their land and population relationships will have a major impact on how all nations cope with population pressures on environmental resources.

The crudest measure of that relationship is a simple population density measure, that is total land area divided by total population. The three countries differ substantially on their level of population density. In 1998, the world's population density was almost 40 persons per sq. Km. The U. S. Population density was only 28 persons per sq. Km., a level substantially below the world average. The population density in China at 130 people per sq. Km. Is more than three times the world average, even though vast arid areas in the western part of China are sparsely populated. India is one of the more densely populated countries of the world. Its density of 307 people per square km. Puts it at almost eight times the average world population density.

Simple population density can be modified by accounting for low density land set aside for nonresidential urban uses, such as industrial, commercial, and retail uses as well as park lands. Calculation of net residential densities yields a more accurate depiction of population densities, but does not present an overall depiction of the extent of urbanisation. In addition to accounting for different kinds of land uses and land covers in the definition of urbanisation and calculation of population densities, we should also consider that patterns of urbanisation differ from one location to another depending on local topography, land use regulations, cultural preferences, and so forth. To be truly useful for ecological researchers, definitions and measurements of urbanisation should be multi-dimensional, taking into account patterns of urban development from one place to another resulting in differences in levels of population density, concentration of residential or commercial uses within specific areas, mixing of residential and commercial land uses, amount of intervening land devoted to non-urban uses, and so forth.

More important than the density of each country as a whole is the spatial variation within the country. To illustrate differences between population density calculated for administrative units and small statistical geographic areas, we have chosen one site in each country that is at or above the average population density of the nation in which it is located. The Pearl River Delta area including the major districts of Guangdong province surrounding Hong Kong, Macau, and the Pearl River has a density of 893 persons per square kilometre and an official urban population of 70 percent. South Florida is 96 percent urban but much of the population is clustered along the coast while much of the inland area reserved for national parks and conservation areas. As a result, the average density is only 172 persons per sq. Kilometre. At the other extreme, Kerala with an urban percentage of only 26 percent has a dense system of village settlement that leads to a high average population density of 749 persons per sq. Kilometre.

Administratively-based Measures of Urbanisation

Most urban definitions take as a starting point the population living in "urban places." These urban places are primarily administratively defined areas generally with recognised municipal governments. These municipal entities can vary markedly in character as well as in size between nations, within nations, and over time. For example, in the United States, laws pertaining to incorporation and annexation vary from state-to-state. In states with relatively liberal annexation laws, municipalities can annex lands with relatively low population densities, lands that otherwise would be considered rural. Such situations tend to result in over-bounding of urban population and land area. On the other hand, in states with restrictive annexation policies, state laws make it difficult for municipalities to annex adjacent densely populated territory. As a result, when this occurs outside of Census Bureau-defined urbanised areas, the extent of urbanisation often is under bounded in census publications.

The dependence on administratively defined geography to define urban population makes comparisons of levels of urbanisation difficult across the three sites. Additional problems are posed by changing definitions over time. In China the municipal definition has been changed repeatedly—the most recent change resulting in the inclusion of a large number of municipal districts with boundaries that extend well into the countryside. In India, urban population includes the population of all "towns" defined as places with a municipal corporation, municipal area committee, town committee, notified area committee, or cantonment board.

Statistically-based Measures of Urbanisation

Statistical agencies have dealt with the limitations imposed by administrative units by modifying urban definitions in various ways. In India, there has been a definition attempt to include other areas outside of "towns" that met the following qualifications: places having 5,000 or more inhabitants, a density of not less than 1,000 persons per square mile, pronounced urban characteristics, and at least three fourths of the adult male population employed in pursuits other than agriculture. In the United States, the Census Bureau expanded its urban definition in 1950 to include the population in unincorporated places of 2,500 or more and in "urbanised areas" consisting of a central place and the adjacent continuously built-up area.

In the United States and other countries there have been attempts to account for decentralisation of settlement and economic activity by defining "metropolitan areas" that include not only urbanised areas and outlying urban places but also surrounding counties that are integrated with these urban centres as measured by substantial amounts of daily commuting, even if many of these areas have densities far too low to be classified as urban. In the U.S., the metropolitan area concept does not represent an alternative urban area definition, but rather identifies a functional area influenced by an urban centre of significant population size.

Density as a Comparative Measure

These different administrative and statistical definitions make international and temporal comparisons of urban population difficult. The measures of urbanisation, average density, and land use give very different pictures of the three case study areas. In fact, given our interest in the relationship between land and population, the traditional measures of urbanisation are not sufficient to represent the spatial distribution issues. The concepts of urbanisation differ between the countries, over time within each country, and between researchers.

Urbanisation can be viewed as a characteristic of the population, as a characteristic of particular kinds of land uses and land covers, as well as a characteristic of social and economic processes and interactions affecting both population and land. Social scientists—demographers generally, but also urban policy analysts, geographers, and others—generally define levels of urbanisation in terms of population densities. Physical scientists—ecologists especially—generally approach definitions of urbanisation from the standpoint of the built environment. To these researchers, density of buildings and impervious surfaces is just as important, if not more important, as population—indeed, urban ecologists often are concerned with changes to the environment as a result of human alteration of the landscape. McIntyre *et al.* note, however, that among ecologists a wide variety of urban definitions have been used in research, ranging from any human alteration of the landscape to more precise definitions based on density and specified land use characteristics.

Alternatively, regional economists, labour analysts, and related researchers might define urban in terms of the functional area integrated with an urban centre. For these researchers, urban becomes more of a sociological and functional definition than a structural (density-based) phenomenon. Reconciling these different perceptions of what constitutes urbanisation within a single definition poses challenges for any researcher or statistical agency.

Although the authors do not have the access to the detailed level of census tabulations necessary to refine this method for all sites, an example using South Florida can serve as an exposition of how the method might function. In the U. S. Decennial censuses, population are tabulated by small-area geographical units known as census tracts as well as by administrative boundaries such as counties and towns. Census tracts are drawn so as to include approximately 4000 inhabitants and are thus smaller in densely settled areas than in less densely populated areas. The census results by tract include information on both the population and the land area of each tract. Consequently, it is possible to tabulate density distributions of both the population and the land area.

To illustrate such a method, we arranged the 800 census tracts for the seven counties of South Florida (Dade, Broward, Palm Beach, Monroe, Hendry, Collier, and Lee) by their 1990 population density. In table 1 we compare the urban and rural population that are above various density levels to see which level would give a reasonable proxy for the urban population in terms of density. At 300 persons per sq km., 5.8 per cent of the urban population and 12.4 per cent of the rural population would be mis-classified by this simple density cutoff. At 400 persons per sq. Km., 8.7 per cent of the urban population and 4.4 per cent of the rural population would be mis-classified. In fact, for this particular case, a cutoff of about 360 persons per sq. Km. Gives a result in which the percentage of the rural and urban population mis-classified is equal at roughly 7.5 per cent each.

Table 1. Distribution of Census Tracts for Counties of South Florida by Density

Population density per sq. Km	*Percent of urban population above this*	*Percent of rural population above this density*	*Percent of total population above this density*	*Percent of total land area above this density*
100	98.4	42.6	96.1	17.4
200	96.2	25.9	93.2	13.7
300	94.2	12.4	90.8	11.9
400	91.3	4.4	87.6	10.4
500	87.9	3.6	84.3	9.1
600	85.6	2.4	82.1	8.38
700	82.4	2.1	79.0	7.5
800	80.8	1.7	77.4	7.2
900	77.3	1.5	74.1	6.5
1000	73.	1.3	0.1	5.7

To compare across areas, however, a higher density level might be preferable to reduce the likelihood that high density agricultural areas might be included in the high density category. Unfortunately, data with which to assess settlement patterns at similar levels of geographic detail in India and China are limited. However, a very crude idea of how this method might work is across countries can be obtained by using the method for the larger levels of geography (districts) that are published for all three countries. Table 2 shows that a population density of 500 people per sq. Mile applied to the large scale district geography would yield 89.9 percent of the population and 74.8 percent of the land area in high density areas.

Table 2. Distribution of Districts (14) by Density for Kerala, India: 1991

Population density per sq. Km.	*Percent of total population Above this density*	*Percent of total land area above this density*
100	100.0	100.0
200	100.0	100.0
300	96.3	87.1
400	94.0	81.6
500	89.9	74.8
600	78.0	58.2
700	78.0	58.2
800	70.3	50.5
900	53.4	35.7
1000	35.7	21.5

Table 3 shows similar results for the Pearl River Delta with 84.2 percent of the population and 62.2 percent of the land area in high density areas. Given the availability of data for smaller levels of geography for the India and China sites, this measure of high density areas could be useful in making comparative studies that are less influenced by administrative and statistical differences between the countries located in high density areas that are usually thought of as "urban"—and could provide useful information on the percentage of the land area as well as the percentage of the population.

Table 3. Distribution of Districts (13) by Density for Pearl River Delta, China, 1990

Population density per sq. Km.	*Percent of total population Above this density*	*Percent of total land area above this density*
100	100	100
200	100	100
300	95.4	84.3
400	84.2	62.2
500	84.2	62.2
600	73.8	48.0
700	73.8	30.6
800	58.8	30.6
900	51.4	24.0
1000	35.6	24.0

This greater detail on the spatial complexity of each area measured at similar levels of spatial disaggregation could begin to supply the comparative data needed for ecological and other studies across many different societies and landscapes.

Analysis of Urban Population Distributions

Human adaptation to the physical environment has resulted in habitation of almost every boom on Earth yet the current rate of urbanisation represents a significant transition of the human habitat. Within the past 40,000 years the human habitat has expanded over almost all of Earth's ice-free land area. Within the past 4000 years humans have intensified settlement in areas conducive to agriculture and begun to localise in cities. Within the past 40 years the growth rate of large cities has accelerated to the point where the majority of humans will soon live in urban environments. This represents a significant recent change in the human habitat.

Physical environments favourable to hunter-gatherers are fundamentally different from those favourable to pasteurellosis and agriculturists. Similarly, urban settlements often exist in areas unfavourable for agriculture. Throughout most of recorded history the majority of humans have engaged in agriculture so the recent large scale migration to urban centres represents an significant evolutionary transition for the human species. The purpose of this analysis is to quantify the extent to which modern human settlement patterns, specifically large urban areas, occupy different physical environments and to consider the implications of this migration for the sustainability of urban centres.

The environment of a large city is fundamentally different from the environment of smaller settlements in rural settings. The environments differ in terms of physical, biological, social and cultural factors. The focus of this discussion is on the physical factors. The other factors are at least as important as the physical factors but the physical factors are probably the most amenable to simple analysis at global scales. One significant difference between the urban environment and traditional human habitats is related to the energy balance. Solar energy flux is, by far, the largest and most persistent form of energetic exchange that most humans are exposed to on a daily basis. Interestingly, most of this energy is not exploited and an increasing number of humans expend significant amounts of resources in attempts to counteract the effects of solar energy flux. In most rural environments, humans live amidst moderately abundant vegetation but in most urban environments, vegetation is relatively sparse. Vegetation cover has a profound influence on solar energy flux. Vegetation absorbs radiation in the most energetic part of the solar spectrum to conduct photosynthesis. The unused fraction of the incoming solar energy is either transpired with water or reflected at Near

Infrared wavelengths. Most building materials used in the urban mosaic absorb a significant fraction of this incoming solar energy and re-radiate it as sensible heat resulting in the Urban Heat Island phenomenon. An increasing percentage of the human population lives in urban areas where this heat induces physical stress and even loss of life during heat waves. While the average temperature difference between urban and rural environments is small compared to the range of temperatures humans have adapted to, the nature of the physical space in urban areas tends to compound the effect of the heat island. The combination of higher temperature, restricted airflow and increased ozone and particulate concentrations creates a distinct physical environment associated with urban settlements at local scales. On a regional scale, there is also evidence that really extensive urban land cover may influence albedo and transpiration enough to influence local weather patterns near large cities.

Both deliberate and inadvertent human modification of the physical environment occur at different spatial scales. For the purposes of this discussion, micro refers to scales ranging from the individual to hundreds of meters while local scale covers the range from hundreds to tens of thousands of meters and regional refers to scales between tens and hundreds of kilometres. Although humans seem to be influencing the physical environment at all of these scales, deliberate manipulation of the physical environment is limited to micro and local scales. When available, significant resources are expended on "climate control" at the scale of residences and work-spaces. Cities represent extensive habitat modification on scales of tens of kilometres but this modification rarely encompasses deliberate manipulation of physical conditions at these scales. Light levels and water flow are often controlled at local scales but human influence on air temperature and quality is largely inadvertent. At regional and global scales, human influence on these components of the physical environment is not well understood but it could not be considered direct intentional manipulation. Questions related to human modification the physical environment at regional and global scales have been the subject of extensive research within the global change research community for several years now, but the study of local scale urban environments is still a comparatively new field. A complementary, and equally important, form of global change is occurring with the expansion of these urban environments where much of the world's population now resides.

The current demographic shift from sparsely populated rural to densely populated urban environments is a distinct form of global change. It is distinct from other types of global change in the sense that a rapidly increasing number of people are experiencing environmental change, not only as result of the environment of a particular location changing, but also as a result of growth centres shifting to different physical environments.

The regional physical environment of urban areas is often different from the physical environments of its catchment areas in the rural hinter-lands so the localisation of population in cities can result in the exposure of large numbers of people to different regional scale physical environments. On a smaller scale, locations where cities evolve are generally physio-graphically distinct from those of the nearby agricultural production regions.

In some cases, this localisation may result in dense habitation of hazard-prone sites. This is often a consequence of the physiography and climate of the city's location. The following analysis will quantify the extent of this localisation and the relationship of the densely populated areas to physio-graphic and climatic characteristics of the physical environment.

In this global analysis, population distribution and density are determined from the latest Gridded Population of the World (GPW2) population dataset produced by CIESIN in 1999. This compilation of 127,105 census estimates provides a median spatial resolution of 31 km, and allows 90% of the 1990 global population to be located to within 88 km. For the purposes of a global analysis, this dataset provides more than adequate spatial resolution relative to the regional environmental variables that will be considered. Each of the 127105 census estimates links a population count to an administrative area. Dividing the population count by the area provides an average population density for that area and allows the population to be distributed evenly over the area of the administrative unit.

The spatial resolution of the population data supports inference at scales of tens of kilometres. For the purposes of this analysis, urban areas and population within the GPW2 dataset will be considered as those with a population density greater than 1000 people/sq.km. Justification for using this threshold density is provided by *Pozzi and Small.*

In addition to dense population, we will also consider the urban population living in large cities. In this case, large cities will be considered those with population greater than 1,000,000 people. The United Nations provides an enumeration of 290 cities with population greater than 1 million in 1990. The total population of these 290 cities is 795,009,000 people. By considering both administratively defined large urban areas and dense population two complementary measures of global urban population can be evaluated relative to different physical environmental factors.

Continental Physiography, Climate and Cities

Population are not uniformly distributed on Earth's landmass and neither are physical environments. Quantifying the spatial coincidence of population and environments can give some indication of the factors that may influence human settlement patterns. The spatial relationship between population and the physical environment can be quantified by calculating the distribution of people with respect to a particular parameter that characterises the environment. Environments are often described in terms of climatic parameters related to temperature and precipitation. Both of these parameters vary appreciably at different temporal and spatial scales so averages are often used to summarise the climate of specific locations. Environments are also characterised by landscape or continental physiography. Physio-graphic parameters that might be expected to influence human habitation include elevation and proximity to coastlines and rivers. All of these quantities can be measured or estimated to different degrees of accuracy and resolution and used as a basis on which to calculate global distributions of land area and population.

The distributions of global population, dense population and large cities have implications for the comparative influence of Physio-graphic and climatic components of the physical environment. This simple analysis does not account for micro-climate or the temporal components of climatic environment and, as such, should not be over interpreted. The point is to demonstrate how strongly population and cities are localised relative to Physio-graphic parameters on a global scale. Climate is obviously a very important influence on human settlement but it is presumably less of a constraint on dense urban settlements than on sparse agrarian population. This analysis quantifies the extent to which urban population are environmentally localised compared to the overall global population. The implication is that adaptation to climate change allows the expansion of the human habitat while the physical characteristics of the landscape drive a simultaneous spatial concentration of population within the expanding habitat. This impacts the sustainability of urban settlements because the Physio-graphic environments discussed here are often associated with natural hazards. Low elevation river basins and coastal zones are especially susceptible to the extreme weather events that some climate change scenarios show increases for. The tendency for cities to evolve in hazard prone Physio-graphic environments combined with the increasing shift of population from rural to urban environments implies that more people will be exposed to natural hazards as this transition progresses. Dense settlements in hazard prone locations expose large numbers of people to risk but at the same time the financial and organisational resources of some cities may allow for more effective hazard mitigation than would be possible for dispersed population. In any case, the current growth rate of urban population suggests that the impact of natural hazards on the global population may change.

9

Urban Growth and Human Development

The basic challenge facing post-industrial societies is not rural-urban co-development but sustainable development. In this perspective sustainability is the aim and rural-urban co-development one of the necessary ways. Thus, the point of departure for this note will be the connection between ecology and sustainability, followed by an introduction of society into that connection.

The World Commission emphasised the concept of sustainability in 1987. The term *sustainable development* was reshaped to describe a solution to current threats to the global society: unequal distribution of resources in time and space implying overuse of non-renewable resources besides pollution that damage natural mechanisms. Both overuse and pollution represent a fatal threat upon the future prospects of the human species and imply the need of radical changes. Sustainable development was then introduced as the headline of the necessary radical changes. In the meantime sustainability has been interpreted and used in a widespread range of contexts that infer the necessity to state the basics.

Natural Life Support Systems

In relation to natural life support systems sustainability

presumes two crucial points. One, actions that involve hazardous damage to the basic cyclical mechanisms must be avoided. Two, balance between the number of organisms - i.e., number of rabbits and amount of lettuce - must be ensured. So, we have to consider both function and capacity.

In nature, food is nothing but a biological input and the system is outbalanced by its own means. Problems do arise when one of the species (i.e., mankind) evolves and applicates skills (i.e., technology) to offset or modify the function, or to go beyond the bounds of the system's carrying capacity for instance due to overuse of resources. When so, mankind incurs responsibility in relation to *sine qua non* for fellow men in both time and space.

When human beings have entered the picture, it is also necessary to consider sustainability and natural life support systems from a social point of view and then ask: Does present social organisation support or counteract damage according to function and balance according to capacity?

Related to the latter questions complex difficulties emerge, as food in the modern world is not only a biological input but a commodity too. Then supplementary food is a source of revenue to farmers, industries, distributors, scientists, bureaucrats, etc. Besides, these actors are gathered in social institutions and are parts of societal structures. These complex structures and institutions - producing and reproducing social experience and knowledge -can support or counteract sustainability. From a social scientific point of view structures and institutions in which technology is adapted and evolved are then important analytical concepts when sustainability is studied. Structures are the material and institutions the immaterial framings of society.

ROLE OF TECHNOLOGY

Now focus is turned to human production and a couple of statements about technology are needed. It is a basic function of any society to provide and ensure means by which the members can comply their reproductive needs. These imply productive activities; technology then becomes a crucial affair from a social point of view and a sphere by which a society might be characterised.

'Technology' is in everyday comprehension most often interpreted as similarly to technical devices and matters. This implies an inadequate limitation of the conceptual meaning where crucial social dimensions are cut off. In the Greek origin the concept consist of two parts, *techne* and *logos*. *Techne* is art and craft while *logos* is knowledge.

Combining *techne* and *logos* we face productive and reproductive activities, the tools, the labour with certain skills and knowledge, and the way in which the activities are organised. Tools are technical devices as machinery, hand tools, buildings, etc.—equipment that in economics are labelled as real capital. The labour is not only the physical power of human beings but particularly their skills and knowledge provided by their individual and social experience and by research and development. Skills and knowledge pertain to the ways in which the tools are effectively used in correspondence with material and labour. Organisation of the activities, however, pertain to the social framings in which the productive activities are carried out besides the relations between the elements included in the productive activities. Putting this into an actual approach seen from a social point of view implies the necessity to understand technology as consisting of three elements:

i) Technical devices,

ii) Skills/knowledge, and

ii) Social organisation.

So, technology is related to technical matters considered in the social context; the latter being the social framings in which techniques and tools are applied and organised. In this sense technology is dealing with social organisation of productive activities and the inclusion of nature in these. In this sphere it is also determined whether the productive activities are sustainable. That is so because it is in the social organisation that the interplay between human activities and natural life support systems is determined. Just one step further is needed in the investigation of technology to underline that point.

The material structure in which the productive activities are carried out consists of two main parts: those made by nature and those moderated by man. Both are necessary conditions to carry out social production; for that reason social production must be based on two kinds of productive forces, i.e., the ecological and the social. The ecological productive forces should here cover natural capital and natural mechanisms that in unity provides the fundamental basis for human life—so ecological productive forces are the forces embedded in natural life support systems. The social productive forces—embedded in societies—should here cover the human performance by means of labour and real capital. It is important to underline that the working capacities involve a physical dimension (the labour of hands) and a mental dimension (the labour of mind)—the latter for instance the ability to co-operate and learn, cognisance, etc.

The latter dimension could also be labelled as human resources. Among the two productive forces, the ecological is claimed to take precedence over the social due to the obvious fact that the ecological forces can exist (i.e., produce and be reproduced) independent of the social forces while the opposite situation is impossible. The ability of the social productive forces to produce and reproduce is fatally depending upon the ecological forces regarding both natural capital and natural mechanisms. The human reproduction (for the individual as well as for the species) is for instance only possibly by means of biological mechanisms;

simultaneously construction of real capital is only possible by means of natural resources converted by means of human labour. As individuals, society, and species we therefore bear a fatal interest in and responsibility for maintaining the natural capital and avoiding damaging intervention in natural mechanisms when we carry out productive activities. Although the social productive forces rest upon the ecological, we have of course to be careful and bear forethought in our use of social productive forces too.

Agriculture and the Environment

From the comments above follow that technology (and then human interplay and exchange with natural life support systems) both affect and depend upon social environs. To introduce fundamentally new technologies it is necessary to alter the institutional and structural design of society. When the social design is altered rigidity occur in a new epoch and tend to keep technological evolution locked in the new direction and evaluated against the new rationality.

The peasant production system went through changes when conversion into livestock production took place in several countries around the year 1900. However, the applied technology was still founded so that the farm constituted an ecological unit part of a local and transparent cycle including livestock and grain production using very limited external inputs. This system implied a high degree of farm self supply in relation to energy and raw materials. It implied a certain consciousness too. The transparent reliance and dependence upon natural life support systems did provide the foundation for a cyclical common notion of nature as well as of society. This notion was often explicitly stated as a comprehension concerning property rights of future generations: the soil should at least be passed on to the next generation as fertile as received from the past. Basis for this comprehension was experience and knowledge; if the farmer managed his livestock or soil contrary to the biological logic of ecological cycles he would experience negative productive reactions from both livestock and soil. These negative reactions would further result in negative economic performance and then economic pressure on the family. Shortage of material opportunities could of course force the families to act as short-sighted and then to ignore long term considerations. However, without romanticising the past, one can conclude that in those times farming technology was ecological; and a functional integrity was maintained between labour (often the farmer and his family) and the local natural life support system.

The surplus from the ecological cycle—produced by means of photosynthesis, labour and natural capital (primarily soil)—could be exchanged with the external economy. However, this exchange took for a major part place at the local level implying a relatively close relationship between the producer and the consumer—in other words, the social cycle too was transparent and rather horizontal. This implied that the consumer could personally experience the ecological cycles, while the farmer simultaneously could face the consumer and receive reactions from the latter concerning the food supplied. This user-producer relationship was basis for a mutual understanding and for directly sharing of the responsibilities attached. Similarly the farmer could in general experience how the potential spill over would affect the environs and how the input to his farm was provided.

Industrialisation of Farming

After World War II industrialisation of farming was speeded up which in turn implied a rather rapid technological transformation. However, the scientific basis was for a great part already established in the mid-19th century primarily attributed to the German chemist, Justus von Liebig. He laid down the theoretical foundation for applying chemicals in agriculture stating that the plants should only be supplied with water-soluble nutrients produced in an artificial/ industrial way. In his alternative statement Liebig simultaneously and explicitly rejected the common conception of that time which stated that efficiency of the living microbes in soil was the key to adequate and efficient farming. By means of Liebig's alternative approach the dynamic comprehension of natural life support systems—as farming was understood hitherto—could be substituted by a more clinical and industrial notion of an input-output production system. This system was to a high degree designed as decoupled from local natural life support systems and potentially also decoupled from local community.

In the mid-20th century the theoretical basis as well as an affiliated notion of decoupled relations between man and natural life support systems had thus already been offered for about 100 years. So the agricultural innovation in the mid-20th century did not reflect a new scientific but rather a new social invention. The structural and institutional framework of agriculture became transformed to enable implementation of this alternative technology quite in line with the view upon technology and in line with the current social experience of that time: the evolution of fordistic industries had prepared a general heavy increase in wealth. A structural and institutional transformation was necessary why industrialisation of agriculture implied increasing amounts produced per farm besides provision of equipment and industrial intermediates. Production and distribution of knowledge had to be altered too in accordance with the alternative technology and its alternative notions.

Introducing industrial technology in farming then involved a distinct break with the up to then practised relation between man and the natural life support systems besides a similar break with attached notions. According to industrial practices and notions the peasant was transformed into a specialised producer organising his production relatively detached from the ecological cycles looking upon soil.

Direct interrelation and interaction with natural capital and biological mechanisms were to a still wider degree substituted by technical approaches enabling an endless reiteration of similar processes on similar objects. This reiteration on similar objects implied a need to adjust the objects—fields and animals—to similarity. Simultaneously the main part of the necessary inputs was reached outside the local ecological cycle and then outside the local natural life support system; for instance energy and industrial raw material. Besides, the application of various chemical inputs, such as pesticides and antibiotics, implied that biological indications of mistreatment were missed. Indications such as crop rotation and livestock diseases were no longer interpreted as symptoms of the farmer's inadequate knowledge and experience but as inevitable parts of production.

According to the new approach such symptoms should just be cured through appliance of systematic—most often chemical treatment. Finally, the detachment involved a new demarcation between crop and livestock production by which manure tended to be interpreted as troublesome waste and not as a valuable and integrated element in an efficient symbiosis between livestock and soil.

Thus, the cyclic ecological relation between man and nature was substituted by a linear relation where agriculture to a certain extent became detached from living biology and interpreted and organised as an iterative production process; input at one end and output at the other. Nature then became an outdistanced object and the functional integrity between man and nature tended to disappear. The conversion also implied new fields of experience whereafter human learning about agriculture and natural life support systems changed. Where the peasant of the past experienced that actions adverse to basic ecology (knowledge about fundamental principles of cycles in nature) would give a negative pay off, the modern farmer experienced that actions adverse to industrial logic would give a negative pay off—for instance if he avoided pesticides. Certainly, not because the nature or the logic of its fundamental mechanisms was transformed but because the social institutions and structures around agriculture were so.

Supplementary the industrialisation caused a decoupling from the local level, whereafter inputs were provided from industries around the world and the farmer lost the breath of view of the interrelated connections his farm became part of.

Thus he lost insight into the production of his inputs and the subsequent dependence on natural life support systems in various parts of the world. Farmers' horizontal integration was then substituted by vertical, international integration where the individual farmer became a tiny part in an international system hard or impossible to take in. This internationalisation also implied that farmers tended to be separated from consumers who became spread all over the world and then became rather invisible. Governmental institutions took over responsibility for the veterinary quality and thus should secure that consumers did not catch diseases from eating the food—the personal user-producer relationship then disappeared. Similarly spill over—for instance pesticides—from farming seemingly disappeared out in nowhere whether these occurred at the farms providing food to the processing enterprises or at the farms in other parts of the world producing produce as input to the former farm.

Post-industrial Society and Sustainability

Over the past decades an increasing awareness has been dawning in the so-called developed world that sustainable development is necessary to alleviate local, national and global problems afflicting the natural environment. It is suggested that this acknowledgement can be understood on the background of changes in values (related to mass belief systems) that can be attributed to the transition from an industrial to a post-industrial and post-material epoch in our rich part of the world. It is further suggested to be seen as a consequence of experiences with the irreversible and fatal environmental effects that modern technologies can result in.

The post-industrial responses to the awareness about human misuse of natural life support systems have so far been of three kinds:

1) Several local, national, and global meetings supplemented by an endless stream of documents.
2) A marginal number of green consumers and producers trying to do something in delimited sectors like renewable energy and organic food.
3) Governmental regulations *after* natural life support systems have been damaged.

To put it polemical the comments on the reactions could be:

1) Words do not make a sustainable technology. It is not by means of words but by means of actions we poison our drinking water and damage the ozone layer.
2) We do not turn society into a sustainable trajectory by eating an organic roast on Sundays and junk food the rest of the week.
3) We do not reach sustainability if we keep on fighting symptoms and leave the fundamental causes unaffected.

This is of course an unfair and derogatory judgement. The efforts made by grass root activists and well-meaning politicians and bureaucrats ought not to be underestimated -

they represent essential social actors. However, the polemic characteristic brings forward the crucial point: a more comprehensive and fundamental modification of behaviour towards sustainability has yet to be attained. This is the case although most of us presumably know—and many of us obviously know—that a good deal of our actions are not sustainable; but with the current institutional framework and the social structures within which we act, we can only hardly do otherwise.

The comprehensive modifications of behaviour have fundamental changes in social structures and institutions as a prerequisite. One of these changes is re-establishment of rural-urban co-development founded on a conscious recognition of the basics of natural life support systems; under here it is necessary to recognise that urban areas have evolved as heterotroph without adequate linkages to recipient technologies in rural areas. From a social point of view such points call for a new design of social structures and institutions where regard for function and capacity in natural life support systems is couched in the basis for the social rationale just as is the case with democracy and human rights. By the way, who would for instance seriously calculate whether the monetary benefits in current prices would exceed the monetary costs if we abandon freedom of speech?

It is asserted above that a new institutional and structural design of post-industrial society is an urgent task if serious threats to human prospects should be avoided. To gain such sustainability, respect for the ecological forces of production is a prerequisite. On the other hand it is also necessary to recognise that the purpose of society's productive efforts is to meet human needs *and* in fulfilling that task, the social forces of production are a prerequisite too. Thus we must consider two productive forces and two allocation systems related to human production and then to technology. An allocation system exists within natural life support systems that is independent of man. Due to technology and the ensuing production, humanity has introduced its own supplementary system of allocation (economy within politically established frames). The human allocation system has implications for the ecological forces of production. Ecology concerns the allocation and circulation of matter in the environment, while economy concern society's allocation and circulation of exchange value between citizens. Both ecology and economy are realities that are necessary for human production and reproduction. So, we cannot abolish ecology nor economy. Conversely we can change the institutional and structural framings for the economy and so politically determine society's trajectory.

Hence, the challenge is to design social institutions and structures so that they escape the current mismatch between the two necessary allocative systems: ecology and economy. This is as far as we can get by now, because we are only equipped with a vague sense of what that design actually should entail when carried out in practice. So it is claimed that no one—for the time being—has a final recipe. Thus, the necessary knowledge and experience must be produced. We can use inspiration from the past—for instance acknowledge lessons from the peasant system as introduced above and as included in the *principles* of organic farming. But we can not turn the clock backwards and return to previous trajectories and if we could why then abandon progress that humanity after all has endeavoured in the time between now and then?

The proper and adequate solution is to carry out social experiments to produce the necessary knowledge and experience concerning institutional and structural design of sustainable technology in a post-industrial society. In this connection it must again be remembered that technology both consists of technique and society's organisation, and that sustainability involves the relationship of technology to the ecological forces of production. Sustainability is therefore not necessarily synonymous with substitution of existing techniques—we do not necessarily have to wait for new inventions and innovations on the technical level. Evolving *organisation* of society, which is the other dimension of technology, can advance more sustainable utilisation of the ecological forces of production, even in the short-term and with the continuing adaptation of existing error-friendly[2] techniques. Here it should also be remembered that organisation of society includes the relation between rural and urban activities.

In Denmark Ecological Experimental Areas (EEA's) are suggested as means to carry out the necessary experiments. EEA are geographically specified areas where communities can conduct experiments concerning the means by which not only delimited sub-sectors but an entirely sustainable society can evolve. It is pointed out that the EEA's must be founded in existing communities because the aim is to explore how present society can evolve institutions and structures supporting sustainable technology as an entire and consistent system able to produce and reproduce. Furthermore, basis in existing communities implies experiments concerning both the process and the substance. The *process* because the findings will indicate how to evolve society from the present stage to a sustainable stage. The *substance* because the findings will indicate how to design social framings that enable a sustainable interplay between the ecological and economic allocative systems.

If such experiments are to be meaningful then they must naturally have a high degree of freedom to gain experiences via trial and error. Indeed, they must be empowered to extricate from the current social framings that are the cause of present mismatch and social traps. But it must nevertheless be maintained that there is an indispensable objective for the experiments that they must seek a suitable design of society that promotes sustainable technology in a post-industrial society. In the design of institutional and structural framings for zones as EEA it is then of fundamental importance that the ecological forces of production are consciously reintegrated, and that one is deliberate about procuring the necessary empowerment to avoid social traps.

Delimited sub-technologies such as organic agriculture and renewable energy are developed with matching partial conceptions and stand together with historical inspiration available for the experiments. The challenge is to connect these delimited sub-technologies in interaction with, and with the utilisation of, other relevant technological conquests for entire systems of human production and reproduction. In this connection it is also necessary to carry out adaptations, changes, and the further development of these conquests.

Trends in Human Development

Human beings are distinguished among all living species by their capacity to develop and think. Though development is often measured in terms of so many miles of roads, number of tall buildings, airports, cars, TVs, computers etc., it is not things and places alone that define development. Development must be people centric. Twenty years hence, the people of India will be more numerous, better educated, healthier and more prosperous than at any other time in our long history. Having eradicated the scourge of famine that plagued the country for centuries, we still confront the challenging tasks of providing a nutritious diet to all our children, educating our teeming masses, abolishing epidemic diseases and creating employment opportunities for all our citizens.

Today India is the second most populous country in the world, with about 1.04 billion people, home to a-sixth of humanity. Although it is difficult to accurately predict population growth rates 20 years to the future, we expect this number to rise by another 300-350 million, in spite of continuous efforts to reduce fertility rates. This would raise the total population to about 1330 million by 2020.

India is in the process of a demographic transition from high fertility, high mortality and stable population to low fertility, low mortality and stable population. This transition is a global phenomenon generated by the improved availability and access to modern health care that sharply reduced mortality rates and increased life expectancy. The Crude death rate has declined to one-third of its level in 1941 and the expectation of life at birth has nearly doubled during this period. Falling mortality rates have been followed by a steady decline in birth rates, but this decline has not been as steep as the fall in death rate; even after reaching the replacement fertility rates, the population will continue to grow because of large numbers of young persons entering reproductive age.

While assessing future prospects, it is necessary to take into account the vast regional differences in demographic parameters. Population growth has recently decelerated below 2 per cent for the first time in four decades, but not uniformly across the length and breadth of the country. Several States in south India have already reached, or are about to attain, the replacement level of fertility that would ensure a zero growth rate of population in the long run. On the other hand, in many states in north India, characterised by high fertility rates, it may take several decades to reach the replacement level of fertility. There are also similar differentials in levels of mortality, especially in infant and child mortality.

At the national level, two alternate scenarios for achieving population stabilisation have been considered. In the optimistic scenario, which is based on achieving the demographic goals of the National Population Policy 2000, life expectancy is assumed to rise to 71 for males and 74 for females by 2020. Under the realistic scenario, life expectancy is assumed to reach 65 for males and 69 for females by 2020. Under either scenario India's population would exceed 1.3 billion in the year 2020.

In both cases the sex ratio of population (females per 1000 males) would marginally increase from 932 in 2000 to 950 in 2020; reversing the historical trend of falling sex ratio is expected in the 21st Century. We can be more certain of the changes in the age structure of the population as given in Table 1.

Table 1. Population Projections (millions)

Year	2000	2005	2010	2015	2020
Total	1010	1093	1175	1256	1331
Under 15	361	368	370	372	373
15-64	604	673	747	819	882
65+	45	51	58	65	76

Actually, the population under-15 years is expected to increase only marginally over the next 20 years. This means that pressure for expansion of the educational system will come only from increasing enrolment and efforts to reduce drop-out rates.

The largest growth of population will be in the 15-64 year age group, which will expand by about 46 per cent by 2020 (i.e, annually by 1.9 per cent as against the population growth of much lower, at 1.4 per cent). As shown in Table 1, it is expected to rise from 604 million in 2000 to 883 million in 2020, i.e., from 60 to 66 per cent of the total population. This rise will accentuate the need for challenge of reducing fertility and increasing employment opportunities, so that the family size comes down and incomes rise.

The elderly population is also expected to rise sharply from 45 to 76 million, (i.e., by 2.6 per cent per annum) and their share in the total population would rise from 4.5 to 5.7 per cent. As a consequence of these age structural changes, the age-dependency ratio (ratio of non-working age population to working age population) is expected to fall from 67 per cent in 2000 to 46 per cent in 2020, although the percentage of elderly people to population will increase.

Food Security

The single most important implication of India's rapid population growth during the second half of the twentieth century was the threat it posed to national food security. That threat reached dangerous proportions in the mid-1960s, leading to the launching of the Green Revolution, achievement of food self-sufficiency, and subsequently, a growing stock of surplus food grains by the mid-1970s. Happily, such a threat no longer exists for the country. Growth of food production has exceeded population growth for each of the past three decades.

Statistics present a confusing picture of India's progress on food security. Both per capita food grain consumption and total calorific intake have declined slightly in recent years among all levels of the population. At the same time, grain surpluses have reached peak levels and real per capita expenditure on food is rising among all income groups. The factors influencing this trend are numerous and complex, however, it can be primarily attributed to:

i) Reduction in calorie requirement due to a more sedentary life style among both the rural and urban population. Bicycle and bus travel, mechanised pumps and equipments, access to telephones and newspapers have reduced the physical work to a greater or lesser extent for most Indians.

ii) Diversification of the Indian diet to include a larger intake of fruits, vegetables, dairy products, sugar, oil and pulses, eggs, fish and meat products, thereby reducing the required intake of calories from cereals.

However, the challenge of achieving food security for all our people remains a real one even today, and will continue to demand our attention in the coming decades. Food security depends on both availability of food and access to it. Long-term food security requires not only producing sufficient food to meet the market demand, but also ensuring that all citizens have the required purchasing power to obtain the food they need for a nutritious and healthy life. India has won the first battle, but the second still looms large. By best estimates, nearly half of the population still suffers from chronic under-nutrition. The most vulnerable are children, women and the elderly, specially among the lower income groups. While the number of children suffering from severe malnutrition declined significantly in the 1990s, the prevalence of mild and moderate under-nutrition, especially among those in the lower 30 per cent income group, is still high. Prevalence of micro nutrient deficiencies such as anemia is also very high.

The problem of chronic macro and micro nutrient under-nutrition cannot be addressed simply by increases in food production or the accumulation of larger food buffer stocks. Nor has the public distribution system been able to effectively target the most needy in an effective manner. Targeted food for work programmes and targeted nutrition programmes can alleviate the problem temporarily. But in the long run, the solution is to ensure employment opportunities for all citizens so that they acquire the purchasing power to meet their nutritional requirements. Thus, employment or livelihood security becomes an essential and inseparable component of a comprehensive strategy for national food security and must be considered as one of the nation's highest priorities. Increasing food consumption alone is not a sufficient condition for overcoming malnutrition in India. It is also necessary to address the factors responsible for the high incidence of gastrointestinal and respiratory infections as well as cultural factors responsible for faulty child feeding and weaning practices. Assured provision of safe drinking water, improved health care and education for all women are necessary elements of a comprehensive strategy to eliminate malnutrition and achieve the goal of Food for All before 2020.

India's population is still rapidly expanding. Living standards are rising and slated to rise faster than in the past. As they rise, both calorific intake and diversification of diet will increase significantly. Although a portion of this increase can and will be obtained from abroad, a fulfilling vision of India 2020 depicts this nation—with its conducive and varied climate, the largest irrigated area in the world and a vast farming population—as a major food exporter. Both as a challenge and as an opportunity, India can and must do much more to modernise and diversify its agriculture to meet the increased domestic and international demand for a wide variety of food products.

Continued growth of the agriculture sector is particularly important because it plays such a vital role in generating purchasing power among the rural population. Therefore, it is essential that agricultural development strategies for the 21st Century focus on generating both higher incomes and greater on-farm and off-farm employment opportunities.

India is now entering the fourth stage of agricultural transformation. The Green Revolution phase spread in the north-western and southern states from the mid-1960s to the mid-1980s. From the early 1980s, it spread rapidly in the central and to a lesser extent the eastern states. This, coupled with a further growth of productivity in the north-western and southern states, enabled India to achieve a 3.77 per cent annual growth rate in agricultural production during the 1980s. The overall growth slowed to 2.72 per cent in the 1990s, which was associated with a reduction in public investment in both agriculture and agricultural research, slower growth of fertilizer consumption and the area under high yielding varieties, and degradation of soils.

There is enormous scope for accelerating growth in agriculture, through improved soil nutrition and pest management, diversification into higher value-added crops, expansion and more efficient use of irrigation potential, rainwater harvesting, and infrastructure development for agro-processing industries. India's productivity on major crops ranks far below the world average. This low productivity contributes to low farm incomes and wages, lower on-farm employment generation, and relatively high food prices for all Indians. Average yields from tomato cultivation, for example, are 76 per cent higher in Mexico and more than four times higher in the USA, while average yields on seed cotton are more than four times higher in Mexico and three times higher in USA.

Even within India, some progressive farmers have achieved yields comparable to their foreign counterparts till recently; but these high achievers are a rare exception. Progressive farming must become the rule and the standard. Raising the productivity of our soil and water resources is an effective way to increase the profit margins of farmers, while at the same time reducing the cost of farm produce, so that it is more affordable to the masses. A minimum target should be to double or triple the average yields of major commercial crops. This will reduce pressure on scarce land and water resources as well as enable the country to utilise less fertile areas for other purposes.

Tapping the full potential of Indian agriculture to meet the rising domestic demand and to take advantage of the liberalisation of international trade will require, first and foremost, the recognition of the vital role that agriculture can continue to play in national development. The other necessary conditions are: greater public investment in research; expansion and development of rural infrastructure including roads, storage capacity and organised markets; improved farmer education; effective involvement of the private sector to provide technology, investment and organisational expertise for commercialisation; and modification of land regulations to achieve greater production efficiency.

A suitable land use pattern will also need to be implemented, based on the principle that each region would focus on crops best suited to their agro-climatic characteristics, soil types and water resources. Strong measures will also be needed to address the problem of land degradation that affects an estimated 45 per cent of total land area. India's objective for 2020 must not only be to produce the food its population requires but also to fully exploit the comparative advantages it possesses—agro-climatic variety, irrigation, scientific capabilities and low labour cost— to become a low cost, high profit producer for the world market.

Business-as-usual (BAU) assumes that growth of production continues at the same rates as during the 1990s. The Best-case scenario (BCS) assumes that production grows at the higher rates achieved during the 1980s. Even under the BAU, India will be able to meet the projected demand in all five food categories. This indicates that more emphasis can be placed on diversifying production to other value added agricultural products.

India needs to sustain an agricultural growth rate of 4.0 to 4.5 per cent in order to reduce food insecurity and poverty, while increasing rural purchasing power. At this growth rate, agricultural development could more rapidly diversify into horticulture, fishery, dairying, animal husbandry and other areas. It would also spur the growth of agro-processing industries in rural areas. Such an achievement is well within reach, provided there is the requisite commitment to raising crop productivity through dissemination of advanced technologies; increasing investment in irrigation, research and training; water harvesting and improved access to credit.

While food production should be able to comfortably meet the total domestic demand, there will still be sections of the population that require assistance in order to meet their nutritional requirements. In view of the high cost and inefficiency of the public food distribution system, reform should directly target the most vulnerable sections, which can be more effectively accomplished through programmes such as food vouchers or food stamps. For the vast majority of the population, food security can best be achieved by ensuring creation of gainful employment opportunities for all job seekers.

EMPLOYMENT

Population, food security, education and remunerative employment opportunities are closely interconnected. Rising levels of education and rising living standards are powerful levers for reducing birth and mortality rates. As population growth slows to replacement levels over the next two decades, India's greatest challenge will be to expand the opportunities for the growing labour force, to enrich their knowledge and skills through education, raise their living standards through gainful employment and make provisions for ensuring a good life for the aged. India has met the challenge of producing sufficient food to feed everyone, but it has yet to meet the challenge of generating sufficient employment opportunities to ensure that all its people have the purchasing power to obtain the food they require. Gainful employment is one of the most essential conditions for food security and economic security. Conversely, food security is an essential requirement for raising the productivity of India's workforce to international levels.

India's labour force has reached 375 million approximately in 2002, and it will continue to expand over the next two decades. The actual rate of that expansion will depend on several factors including population growth, growth of the working age population, labour force participation rates, educational enrolment at higher levels and school drop-out rates. Projections based on these parameters indicate that India's labour force will expand by 7 to 8.5 million per year during the first decade of this century, and will increase by a total of about 160-170 million by 2020, i.e., 2.0 percent per annum.

Total unemployment in India has been estimated to be about 35 million persons in 2002. This figure takes into account the significant level of underemployment and seasonal variations in the availability of work. It also reflects wide variations in the rate of unemployment among different age groups and regions of the country. Approximately three-fourth of the unemployed are in rural areas and three-fifth among them are educated. The recent trends towards shedding excess labour to improve competitiveness and increasing capital intensity have further aggravated the situation. A clear consensus is now emerging that major changes in economic policy and strategy will be needed to meet the country's employment needs.

Future rates of unemployment will depend on a range of factors, including the growth rate of the labour force and changes in the structure of employment between different sectors, as well as the growth rate of the economy. Adopting the higher number takes us closer to understanding the full magnitude of the challenge the country faces for providing employment opportunities for all its people. India needs to generate on the order of 200 million additional employment opportunities over the next 20 years.

The first question that inevitably arises is whether generating nine or ten million jobs a year is feasible, and that naturally begets the question of what rates of economic growth would be required for achieving this. However logical and inevitable it may sound, we believe this is the wrong way to approach the problem. The right question to ask is: How important is it to us as a nation to create employment opportunities for all? The answer here is simple. It is extremely important. It is as important to create job opportunities for all citizens in a market economy as it is to provide universal suffrage to all adults in a democracy. Access to employment is an essential component of freedom of economic choice. Absence of such opportunity means depriving our young not only of economic freedom but of hope as well. India's vision for 2020 must be founded on the premise of gainful Jobs for All. Access to employment should not only be a top priority of the government but a constitutionally guaranteed fundamental human right.

But can we possibly achieve such an ambitious goal and that too within the framework of a non-subsidised market economy? In order to answer this question, first of all we need to recognise that the economy we build over the next two decades and the jobs we create will be products of the decisions we make, not some irreversible logic of economic science. It is we, the nation, that have to decide what we want to accomplish and how serious we are about doing it, how willing we are to change our attitudes and to alter our policies to achieve this desirable goal. We conclude that if the will and determination are present, the goal is achievable.

Achieving full employment will require a reorientation of national priorities, technology policy and government action. Until now, planning to achieve national goals has been largely done on a sector-wise basis by respective ministries assigned with the responsibility. These parallel lines of planning need to be integrated around a central vision and set of goals, of which full employment must be one. As we have incorporated an environmental analysis into all our planning, every plan initiative needs also to be re-evaluated to consider its impact on employment.

Despite a persistent tendency to associate employment with large industry in the organised sector, an in-depth examination of employment potentials makes it evident that the largest share of new jobs will come from the unorganised sector. In evaluating the importance of developing each sector, we must include an assessment of its potential contribution to employment. Such an assessment will have to be made for the unorganised sector, which currently contributes 92 per cent of the country's employment and generates seven times greater labour intensity per unit of production, as compared to the organised sector. The public organised sector has been and will continue to shed jobs. Although the private organised sector will contribute significantly to the growth of the economy, its contribution to the overall employment generation will be quite modest, since total employment in this sector currently represents only 2.5 per cent of all jobs. Even if this sector grows by 30 per cent per annum, over five years it will contribute less than one per cent to the growth of the workforce.

International comparisons reveal that small and medium enterprises (SMEs) create the majority of jobs. In the USA, nearly half of the private workforce is employed in small firms, of which three-fifth have less than five employees. In Japan, 78 per cent of jobs are generated by small and medium enterprises. The small and medium manufacturing enterprises in Korea account for 99 per cent of all manufacturing enterprises and 69 per cent of employment in this sector. Therefore, the unorganised sector, including small and medium enterprises, must play a central role in the country's employment strategy. This will require modification of policies and programmes to level the playing field, improve availability of credit, increase productivity, raise quality consciousness and competitiveness, and enhance job quality.

Recent experiences of different countries in the context of globalisation also demonstrate that SMEs are better insulated from the pressures generated by the volatility of world trade and capital markets. They are more resistant to the stresses, and more responsive to the demands of the fast-changing technologies and entrepreneurial responses. Indeed, they are observed to be a very important vehicle for new technology adoption and entrepreneurial development. What is true of the most developed countries today will be true for India in 2020. SMEs will play a crucial role in ensuring India's international competitiveness and its rapid assimilation of new technologies.

An assessment of the different sectors reveals a vast untapped employment potential in a wide range of fields for unskilled, semi-skilled, skilled and professionally educated workers. Table 2 provides a list of specific sectors with the largest gross employment potential per unit of output.

The growth of food grain production may not lead to a significant growth in on-farm employment opportunities. However, there is substantial scope for creating new jobs through watershed development programmes, expansion of the area under irrigated cultivation, raising crop yields which increases labour intensity, and diversification of cropping patterns into cash crops—especially vegetables and horticultural crops. Together, these could generate upwards of 20 to 30 million new on-farm employment opportunities during the next decade.

Table 2. High Employment Potential Sectors

- Commercial agriculture
- Agro-industry & agri-business
- Afforestation for pulp, fuel & power
- Retail and wholesale trade
- Tourism
- Housing
- Construction
- Garment industry
- Other small scale & medium industries
- IT & IT enabled services
- Education
- Health
- Financial services
- Transport
- Communications
- Community services

India processes less than 2 per cent of its fruit and vegetable products, as compared with 70 to 80 per cent in countries such as Brazil, Malaysia and Philippines. The development of downstream processing, packaging and distribution activities can generate millions of additional off-farm jobs. Policies are needed to attract greater private sector participation in terms of land development, production and processing technologies, investment, management and marketing. A concerted effort to fully develop the potentials of agri-business could generate millions of additional jobs.

The recorded forest area constitutes about 23 per cent of the geographical area (about 71 million hectares) of the country, but half of this area is degraded. Hence, it is unable to play an important role in environmental sustainability and in meeting the forest produce needs of the people, the industry and other sectors. India has more than 50 million hectares of degraded wasteland that lie outside the national forests, in addition to 30 million hectares within protected areas. In spite of this huge expanse, the country is a net importer of forest products to the extent of $2.5 billion annually. Afforestation of India's vast expanse of wastelands and depleted forest areas for production of wood pulp, timber, fuel, fodder, biomass power, edible and ·fuel soil, fuel, herbs and medicinal plants for exports can create millions of jobs, while reversing environmental degradation and supporting industrial development. Every two hectares of additional area placed under plantation of forest crop such as bamboo, casuarina, eucalyptus or oil-bearing plants can generate year-round employment for one person. Development of forests can generate 10 to 15 million additional employment opportunities over the next five year plan period and increase the livelihood opportunities of low income families during the transition period, while educational levels are rising and other sectors of the economy are developing.

The contribution of primary sector employment to the total workforce has been coming down very slowly, to 56-57 per cent in 1999-2000, and should decrease to about 51 per cent by 2006-2007. This slow rate of decline is likely to continue for at least a decade, because of the hidden under-employment in the agriculture sector, partly compensated for by the vast potential for additional job creation by crop diversification and afforestation. Increasing prosperity in agriculture will naturally lead to the growth of non-farm jobs in agri-industries, agro-business and other occupations required to meet the needs of an increasingly prosperous farming community. During the second decade of the 21st Century, increasing domestic demand for manufactured products and services, coupled with more rapid mechanisation of agriculture will draw in more and more people to non-farm occupations. By 2020, total employment in agriculture may fall to less than 45 per cent, while the share of the services sector increases proportionately.

The small scale industries (SSI) sector accounts for 95 per cent of industrial units, 40 per cent of value addition, 35 per cent of exports, and 80 per cent of manufacturing employment. Registered SSI units provide nearly 18 million jobs in the country at this time. Among manufacturing sectors, the single largest employment potential is in textiles, which is slated to generate 7 million jobs over the next five years alone. More than 40 per cent of these jobs are in garment production units in the SSI sector. A healthy and rapidly expanding small sector is essential for a vibrant growth of the Indian economy as a whole. This sector serves as the field for entrepreneurship to flourish, as an entry point for new entrepreneurs who can start small and then grow, as a vehicle for extending the regional spread of industry, as a laboratory for development of innovative products and services, and as an essential support to attract large manufacturing assembling industries from overseas. Since SSIs are generally more employment intensive per unit of capital than large scale industry, they are also a source of much needed employment. Employment in the registered SSI sector has nearly tripled over the past 20 years. A repetition of this performance would generate an additional 36 million jobs over the next 20 years. A comprehensive package of venture capital, credit, liberalisation of controls, technical training, marketing and management measures is needed to ensure the continuous expansion of this sector.

By far, the largest number of new jobs will be in the services sector. Over the past 100 years, the US economy has more than quadrupled the total number of those employed, yet the percentage of the US workforce engaged in manufacturing is now back to the same level as it was in 1850, while agricultural employment has shrunk to less than 3 per cent of the US workforce. Today, the fastest growing job categories in the USA are in services industries such as financial services, insurance, education, health, construction and real estate. Rapid growth is slated for a wide range of services in India, including professional, computer-related research and development, real estate, leasing, advertising, printing and packaging, marketing, telecommunications, postal and courier, audiovisual, engineering and construction, wholesale and retail distribution, all levels and types of education, environment, banking, insurance, health, travel, sports and recreation, and all categories of transport services. By the year 2020 more than 120 million jobs will come from the services sector alone.

Tourism-related occupations, including hotels and restaurants, employ 10.8 per cent of workers globally, compared to only 5.6 per cent in India. Domestic tourism will rise rapidly as living standards increase. India's domestic tourist sector is the fastest growing in the world, but with the lowest level of investment. The potential for international tourism too has not yet been exploited properly. China currently attracts more than five times as many foreign tourists, excluding visitors from Hong Kong. Thailand, Malaysia, and Turkey attract three to four times as many. By one estimate, development of India's tourism infrastructure such as roads, airports and medium priced hotels, combined with modifications in air and hotel pricing and tax policies, could generate more than 20 million additional employment opportunities in tourist related businesses within a decade.

Numerous studies have been undertaken to assess the potentials of the IT industry and to identify specific strategies needed to accelerate development of this sector. The NASSCOM-McKinsey study in 1999 projected creation of a $70 billion IT industry, employing more than two million persons within 10 years. The worldwide market for IT services is expected to exceed $900 billion by 2010.

The recent growth of IT-enabled service businesses in India—call centres, medical transcription, technical support and back office processing, engineering and design, geographic information services, payroll and other human resource services, insurance claim processing, legal databases—is powerful evidence that the potential of IT technology and knowledge based industries extends far beyond the development of software and hardware. The US experience shows that, as the application of information technology spreads and encompasses traditional industries, it can generate new employment opportunities ten times greater in number than those directly involved in core IT industries.

IT is also a stimulant to the growth of home-based employment opportunities, especially suitable for women. The trend towards tele-working, which is growing rapidly in USA and some other countries, is just beginning in India. The lower cost and greater convenience of home-based employment is bound to open up greater job opportunities for educated women with children.

IT services will be a powerful engine of job growth, but the term 'Knowledge-based industries' includes a much wider range of commercial opportunities. It encompasses all fields in which the application of mind, judgment and skill, rather than the application of mechanised production technology is the core resource. Education, health services, biotechnology, pharmaceuticals, insurance and financial services are among the leading industries in this category. They are also among the fastest growing industries in the world. Added to these, there is enormous scope for other knowledge intensive activities such as clinical drug trials and many other types of scientific research.

The management of all types of information is emerging as a major growth industry worldwide and India is well poised to become a global leader in this field. Increasing demand for education within the country and worldwide will create tremendous demand for qualified teachers with adequate language skills. An estimated two million additional teachers will be needed in India to support 100 per cent primary school enrolment and to reduce the teacher-student ratio for improved quality of teaching. Another two million or more will be required to support higher rates of upper primary and secondary school education and to reduce teacher-student ratios at those levels. Teaching staff for vocational training and higher education need to be expanded as well.

Demand for health services is increasing worldwide. Already nurses and medical technicians are in short supply. The USA has a doctor-nurse ratio of about twice that of India. Yet the US currently faces a shortfall of nurses, that is more than three times India's total annual production of new nurses. Physicians, nurses, medical technicians and other scientific occupations will become growth industries to rival the IT sector within the next decade. Creation of new jobs in existing industries can and should be supplemented by creation of new services industries that will in turn stimulate increased employment opportunities.

It is extremely difficult to project unemployment rates 20 years into the future, when so much doubt exists even about current levels of unemployment and underemployment. However, it is clear that rising levels of education and growth of the 60 plus age group will mitigate to some extent the growth of the labour force. Combined with the enormous opportunities for creation of new employment opportunities, the incidence of unemployment should be almost eliminated during the second decade of the century.

EDUCATION

Successful population policy is directly linked to successful education policy. Success in raising literacy rates and school enrolment rates while reducing drop-out rates, especially for women, are closely correlated with the delayed onset of marriage and child birth, improved mortality for both mothers and children, and reduction in family size. In fact, a successful education policy forms the bedrock of all fields of national development—political, economic, technical, scientific, social, and environmental. Education is the foundation for a vibrant democracy in which informed citizens exercise their franchise to support the internal growth of the nation and its constructive role in the world community. It is the foundation for growth in productivity, incomes and employment opportunities and for the development, application and adaptation of science and technology to enhance the quality of life. Education is the foundation for access to the benefits of the information revolution that is opening up vistas on the whole world. Education is also the foundation for improved health care and nutrition.

Literacy, the basis of all education, is as essential to survival and development in modern society as food is to survival and development of the human body. Literacy rates in India have arisen dramatically from 18 per cent in 1951 to 65 per cent in 2001, but these rates are still far from the UMI reference level of 95 per cent. Literacy must be considered the minimum right and requirement of every Indian citizen. Vast differences also remain among different sections of the population. Literacy among males is nearly 50 per cent higher than females, and it is about 50 per cent higher in urban areas as compared to the rural areas. Literacy rates range from as high as 96 per cent in some districts of Kerala to below 30 per cent in some parts of Madhya Pradesh. Rates are also significantly lower among scheduled castes and tribes than among other communities.

These differential rates of progress leave approximately 300 million illiterate adults in the country, the largest number of illiterates in the world. For these people, the traditional avenues of knowledge dissemination through education and printed information are ruled out. These are the people who are most vulnerable to the challenges of development, because they are least equipped to rapidly expand their knowledge base. Since many of them are relatively young adults who will still be active in 2020, the country cannot afford to ignore them or leave them behind. The Government has already set a goal to achieve 75 per cent literacy by the end of the Tenth Five Year Plan. A 100 per cent literate India is of paramount importance for realising the vision for the country in 2020. Even when this goal is achieved, innovative approaches will be needed to increase knowledge dissemination through TV and other means, to literate adults with little or no formal education.

Literacy is an indispensable minimum condition for development, but it is not sufficient. In this increasingly complex and technologically sophisticated world, ten years of school education must also be considered as an essential prerequisite for citizens to adapt and succeed economically, avail of the social opportunities and develop their individual potentials. Education is the primary and most effective means so far evolved for transmitting practically useful knowledge from one generation to another.

India's education system has expanded exponentially over the past five decades, but its current achievements are grossly inadequate for the nation to realise its potential greatness. The net enrolment rate in primary schools is around 77 per cent and in secondary schools it is around 60 per cent. These compare with the 99.9 per cent primary and 69 per cent secondary enrolment for the UMI reference level. The drop out rate was 40 per cent at the primary level and 55 per cent at the upper primary level in 1999-2000. These high drop out rates from both primary and secondary school, combined with low enrolment rates at the higher levels deprive tens of millions of children of their full rights as citizens. Out of approximately 200 million children in the age group 6-14 years, only 120 million are in schools and net attendance in the primary level is only 66 per cent of the enrolment. Further, less than 7 per cent of the children ever pass the 10th standard public examination.

Apart from addressing the needs of a large illiterate population, India's knowledge strategy must also develop innovative approaches to enhance knowledge acquisition among the large community of school drop-outs. Unless something is done to drastically reduce drop-out rates, by the year 2016 there will be approximately 500 million people in the country with less than five years of schooling, and another 300 million that will not have completed high school. In other words, about two-thirds of the population will lack the minimum level of education needed to keep pace with and take advantage of the social changes occurring within the country and worldwide.

Extending the primary school system to over 500,000 villages in India has brought education to the masses. Unfortunately, this huge quantitative expansion has been accompanied by a tremendous dilution in the quality of schooling. High drop out rates in rural areas is one result of single room schools, with few teaching aids and inadequate instruction both in terms of quantity and quality. Qualitative improvement in the system can be accomplished by promoting centralised schools serving clusters of 10 or more villages, wherever distances and transportation links make that feasible. This will permit greater investment in educational infrastructure, including introduction of computers.

Achieving 100 per cent enrolment of all children in the 6 to 14 year age group is an ambitious but achievable goal for 2020. This must be coupled with efforts to increase the quality and relevance of school curriculum to equip students not only with academic knowledge but also with the values and practical knowledge needed for success in life.

A tremendous expansion of schools and classrooms will be required to support a quantitative and qualitative improvement in the country's school system.

An enormous increase in the number of teachers will also be required to achieve the alternative scenario, i.e., eliminating primary school drop outs and reducing the teacher-pupil ratio from the present high level of 1:42 down to around 1:20, which is the UMI reference level. Together, this will require an additional three million primary school teachers, more than twice the number currently employed. Similar increases will be required at middle and secondary school levels. The training of such large number of teachers will require the establishment of additional teacher training colleges and much larger budget allocations for teachers' salaries.

Qualitative improvements in education should reflect a change in pedagogical methods and lay emphasis on several dimensions, including:

i) A shift from methods that emphasize passive learning to those that foster the active interest and ability of children to learn on their own.

ii) A shift from rote memorisation to development of children's capacity for critical thinking.

iii) A shift from traditional academic to practically relevant curriculum.

iv) A shift from imparting information to imparting life values such as independent thinking, self-reliance and individual initiative that are essential for success in any field of endeavour.

An important role of education is to foster in each child the attributes and values of a responsible, capable, active and healthy member of the family and society. The rigidity of curriculum, testing and teaching methods need to be relaxed so that innovative methods and new models of education can be evolved, tested and perfected. Vocational streams have to be developed and expanded to equip larger numbers of high school students with occupation-related knowledge and skills.

Experimentation is needed with new methods for knowledge delivery. Television can be a very effective means for educating both school going and non-school going children and adults. It can deliver teaching materials in a more dynamic, entertaining, and interesting manner, utilising the nation's best teachers and multimedia teaching materials on each subject. A TV based curriculum can help slow learners to supplement classroom teaching, fast learners to learn at much faster rates than the rest of the class, drop outs to acquire knowledge they missed out in school, and adults to expand their level of education without returning to school.

New methods of delivery will be particularly necessary to augment access and improve delivery at higher levels of education. Although India's college and university network has expanded dramatically, it is able to accommodate only a tiny fraction of the college-age population. In addition, the quality of facilities, teaching and course materials leaves much to be desired. Recruitment and promotion are highly politicised; seniority rule precludes merit advancement; and the cost of delivery is beyond the means of the vast majority of young Indians.

India in 2020 must be a nation in which all those who aspire for higher education have access to college and university level courses. A national network of community colleges, similar to the highly successful American system, is needed to provide knowledge and job-oriented skills to millions of young people who lack interest in or capacity for more stringent academic studies.

The advent of computer and the Internet-based educational methods offer an exciting new learning medium that can literally transform our concept of school and classroom from physical into virtual realities. Studies in the USA project a radical reshaping of higher education over the next two decades as a result of the digital revolution. Many traditional colleges will close as more course works are delivered at a distance through alternative channels. The traditional boundaries between education and other sectors will fade, as publishers, for-profit and non-profit organisations, offer accredited, multimedia-enhanced courses directly to students, by-passing the university. The traditional classroom type of education, which is most useful for students that require personal attention and assistance and for subjects that involve hands-on experimentation, will no longer be the predominant model of education. For all other purposes, it is very costly and not very efficient in the way it uses the time of both teachers and students.

Experience shows that computer-based educational methods can lead to much faster rates and higher quality of learning, which is more inter-active and motivating for students at all levels of education from pre-school to post-graduation. It is extremely effective for enhancing reading and language skills and general knowledge among the very young and even for some sophisticated professional courses such as medicine and engineering.

Given the huge number of young students that will quest for all levels of higher education in the coming decades and the severe shortage of qualified instructors, and in the light of India's outstanding expertise in the IT industry, the country needs to embark on a massive programme to convert the entire higher educational curriculum into a multi-media, web-based format and to establish accreditation standards for recognition of the distance education so imparted.

Our vision of India in 2020 is predicated on the belief that human resources are the most important determinants of overall development. As India's IT revolution has been fuelled by the availability of a very large reservoir of well-trained engineers, its future development in many different spheres will depend on commensurate development of sufficient and surplus capabilities.

Full development of India's enormous human potential will require a shift in national priorities, to commit a greater portion of the country's financial resources to the education sector. India currently invests 3.2 - 4.4 per cent of GNP on education. This compares unfavourably with the UMI reference level of 4.9 per cent, especially with countries such as South Africa, which invests 7.9 per cent of GNP on education. A near doubling of investments in education is the soundest policy for quadrupling the country's GDP per capita.

S&T Capabilities

Literacy and general education form the base of the knowledge pyramid that is essential for rapid and sustained development in the 21st century. The continuous advancement of science and application of improved technology form the middle rung; and social ideals and spiritual values form the apex.

Technical education, both vocational and professional, constitutes the foundation for development of science and technology. India is rightly proud of the international standing of its IITs, but a handful of world class technical institutions is not sufficient. A large number of the country's approximately 500 engineering colleges need to be upgraded to quality standards nearer to those of the IITs, and given similar autonomy. Private sector initiative and investment, whether from Indian corporates or NRIs or reputed foreign universities, need to be fully encouraged. Close links need to be fostered between technical institutions and industry.

India's enormous manpower base of scientists and engineers is often coveted. President Kalam observed that

India's human resource base is one of its greatest core competencies. This is true in absolute terms, but as a percentage of the total population, we are at 1/100th of the US levels and 1/50th of the Korean level. Even China's manpower base of scientists and engineers as a percentage of its population exceeds ours by more than three times.

Absolute numbers do count, but manpower alone is not sufficient to excel in the development and application of science and technology. In terms of total investment in R&D, India's expenditure is 1/60th of that of Korea, 1/250th of that of the USA, and 1/340th of that of Japan. More significantly, atomic energy, space and defence research account for 71 per cent of all central spending on science and technology, which means that relatively little is left for investment in agriculture, energy, telecommunications and other crucial sectors within the sphere of science and technology. R&D expenditure even in India's fast-growing IT sector has been averaging around 3 per cent of sales turnover (STO), which is much lower as compared to the 14-19 per cent expended by internationally reputed software firms.

These low figures reflect on our R&D performance. India's share of global scientific output in 1998 was only 1.58 per cent of the world's total. Out of 500,000 new patent applications filed globally each year, China accounts for 96,000 and Korea accounts for 72,000, while India accounts for only 8,000. Of greater concern has been the country's inability to capitalise on our huge pool of manpower and extensive network of scientific research organisations for transferring proven technologies from the lab to the land and to the factory. Despite possessing the world's largest cadre of agricultural scientists, we have not been able to extend the momentum of Green Revolution to other regions and crops and to update the scientific practices of our farmers to levels comparable with most other nations. Crop productivity remains far below and production costs far above world averages. A similar gap exists in the application of science and technology for food processing and many other industries. High technology exports account for only 6 per cent of total manufacturing exports for India, compared to over 20 per cent for the UMI reference level.

India has a number of premier universities for scientific and technical education which produce world class scientists and engineers, but the national research system rarely produces world class results. One reason is the missing link between scientists in universities and research institutes and practitioners in agriculture and industry. Another is that non-teaching research institutes lack the continuous inflow of young talented researchers required to challenge assumptions and infiltrate new ideas and approaches. Bureaucracy, tenure and lack of accountability minimise the pressure for practical application of scientific knowledge. Other countries have done a much better job of providing optimum incentives to their scientific community and creating close linkages between science and industry. The management of technology and the administration of government require different sets of skills and a different culture. Management of technology demands innovation, global competitiveness, and wide latitude for individual freedom, characteristics that are difficult to foster under an administrative regime.

The objectives of many institutes and the mechanisms for achieving them need a radical reorientation to bring them in tune with the changing environment brought about by liberalisation of imports, technology tie-ups with foreign agencies and foreign direct investment in key sectors. If the national R&D bodies do not reorganise themselves to face globalisation and global competition, nor take into consideration the nature of the factor endowment of the country along with many existing indigenous technologies so far neglected, then they risk becoming irrelevant to the mainstream activities of industrial development. The nature of service offered by these institutions has to undergo a sea change. Grass-root consultancy and turnkey project consultancy, including project implementation and monitoring are increasingly in demand.

Another essential step is to improve the linkages between technology development and technology application by fostering close ties between basic research and business. In the USA, a large proportion of scientific research at the university level is financed by business, and most leading universities operate technology incubators designed to promote commercialisation of new products and processes. India's recent experiment with the Science and Technology Entrepreneur Parks (STEPs) has been successful in promoting application of technologies, new business start-ups, and employment. The STEPs in combination with technology incubators need to be rapidly multiplied around the country. Effective R&D management backed by suitable incentives for commercialisation are essential for bridging the gap between the lab and the land or factory.

R&D is not only essential for propelling growth in industrial fields. It can also become a growth industry on its own. Much of the work done by Indian software companies for overseas clients and parent companies rightly fall under the category of new product development. Vast potential exists for complementing India's strengths in IT with corresponding strengthening of fields such as biotechnology, pharmaceuticals, designer-made materials, and others.

India's investment in the biotechnology sector is expected to increase five-fold by the end of the current decade, from US $2 billion to $10 billion, largely as a result of growing collaboration between multinational corporations and indigenous research efforts. Huge opportunities also exist for R&D in the field of genomics, bioinformatics, DNA technologies, clinical studies and genetically modified crops. Rationalisation of procedure, backed by effective bio-safety regulations are needed to govern testing and approval of biotech products. India has the potential of converting its strong R&D infrastructure into a global research, design and development platform.

Vocational Training

The knowledge and skill of our workforce will be a major determinant of India's future rate of economic growth as well as the type and number of jobs we create. The greater that knowledge and skill, the higher will be the productivity, the better the quality, and the lower the cost of the products and services we generate. Similarly, the better the quality and lower the cost, greater will be the comparative advantage and market potential. Currently only 5 per cent of the country's labour force in the 20-24 age category have undergone formal vocational training, compared with 28 per cent in Mexico, 60 to 80 per cent in most industrialised nations, and as much as 96 per cent in Korea. A strategy to achieve full employment must include as an important component, a strategy to ensure that all new entrants to the workforce are equipped with the knowledge and skill needed for high productivity and high quality.

India has over 4,200 industrial training institutes (ITI) imparting education and training in 43 engineering and 24 non-engineering trades. Of these, 1,654 are government run ITIs, while 2,620 are private. The total seating capacity in these ITIs is 6.28 lakh. Most of this training is conducted in classroom style in the form of one to two year diploma courses. In addition, about 1.65 lakh persons undergo apprenticeship vocational training every year in state-run enterprises. If a wider definition of applied courses is taken that includes agriculture, engineering and other professional subjects, the total number receiving job related training is about 17 lakh per annum, which still represents only 14 per cent of new entrants to the workforce.

The nature of vocational skills makes it impossible for vocational schools to fully address the nation's needs. The variety of skills needed by the workforce is far too great. The changes in technology and work processes are too rapid for training courses and their instructors to stay up-to-date. The cost of training is also relatively high as it often demands full time enrolment for a prolonged period. Some vocational fields do not lend themselves to classroom or laboratory study at all. A comprehensive strategy is thus needed to enhance the nation's employable skills. It must begin by preparing a catalogue of the entire range of vocational skills needed to support the development of the country. The network of vocational training institutes and the range of vocational skills taught needs to be expanded substantially to impart those skills for which institutional training is most suitable. The private sector, which promoted the rapid proliferation of computer training institutes throughout the country, should be encouraged to recognise the commercial potential of vocational training in many other fields. In addition, it is essential to fashion more effective and efficient mechanisms for disseminating useful knowledge and skills, especially through the TV media and through computerised vocational training. The importance of computer has been widely recognised as a means to improve efficiency in business, government and formal education, but its application in vocational training is not fully appreciated.

Use of Computers in Vocational Training

i) Rates of learning on computer for both academic as well as vocational or skill-based subjects are four to ten times faster than they are in a classroom setting, and learning retention is likely to be much higher.

ii) Computers can provide multimedia, interactive, customised and individually-paced learning with instantaneous feedback and testing.

iii) It eliminates the need for producing and deputing a large number of highly skilled instructors. Course contents can be rapidly modified to reflect changing needs.

iv) For many types of vocational skills, computerised training also offers specific advantages over the live delivery of skills in a classroom.

v) Training can be delivered wherever computers are available. A nationwide network of 50,000 computerised vocational centres, run as private self-employed businesses similar to the STD booths and Internet cafes, can deliver low-cost, high-quality training to 10 million workers every year—more than five times the total number covered by existing programmes.

Although 58 per cent of Indians are engaged in agriculture, vocational training for farmers is one of the weakest links in the Indian educational system. Agricultural universities cater to the nation's need for agricultural scientists and extension officers. An extensive network of more than 300 Krishi Vignan Kendras (KVK) offers short and medium term courses for farmers on specialised subjects. The KVK network provides training to several hundred thousand farmers each year, but it can cater to the needs of only a miniscule percentage of all farmers. Agricultural education can be moved from the campus into the village by establishing a national network of farm schools, offering practical demonstration and training on lands leased from farmers in the local community. The prime objective of the schools would be to impart knowledge and skills designed to double yields on important commercial crops. Educated farmers can be trained as self-employed instructors to operate the farm schools as private enterprises on a commercial basis.

HEALTH FOR ALL

The health of a nation is difficult to define in terms of a single set of measures. At best, we can assess the health of the population by taking into account indicators like infant mortality and maternal mortality rates, life expectancy and nutrition, along with the incidence of communicable and non-communicable diseases.

According to these measures, the health of the Indian population has improved dramatically over the past fifty years. Life expectancy has risen from 33 years to 64 years. The infant mortality rate (IMR) has fallen from 148 to 71 per 1000. The crude birth rate (CBR) has declined from 41 to 25 and the crude death rate (CDR) has fallen from 25 to under 9. The couple protection rate (CPR) and total fertility rate (TFR) have also improved substantially.

Despite these achievements, wide disparities persist between different income groups, between rural and urban communities, and between different states and even districts within states. The infant mortality rate among the poorest quintet of the population is 2.5 times higher than that among the richest. Maternal mortality remains very high. More than one lakh women die each year due to pregnancy-related complications.

Like population growth and economic growth, the health of a nation is a product of many factors and forces that combine and interact with each other. Economic growth, per capita income, employment, levels of literacy and education—especially among females—age of marriage, birth rates, availability of information regarding health care and nutrition, access to safe drinking water, public and private health care infrastructure, access to preventive health care and medical care, health insurance, public hygiene, road safety, and environmental pollution are among the factors that contribute directly to the health of the nation.

Communicable diseases such as malaria, kalaazar, tuberculosis and HIV infection remain the major causes of illness in India. During the next five to ten years, existing programmes are likely to eliminate polio and leprosy and substantially reduce the prevalence of kalaazar and filariasis. However, TB, malaria and AIDS will continue to remain major public health problems. India has about 1.5 million identified cases of TB that are responsible for more than 3,00,000 deaths annually. Improved diagnostic services and treatment can reduce the prevalence and incidence of TB by 2020. About 2 million cases of malaria are reported in India each year. Restructuring the "malaria workforce" and strengthening health infrastructure can reduce the incidence of this disease by up to 50 per cent within a decade. Assessing the impact of HIV epidemic is more difficult; according to an estimate, there are about 4 million persons infected with HIV. The National Health Policy aims at achieving a plateau in the prevalence of HIV infection by 2007.

Childhood diarrhoea, another major cause of illness, is largely preventable through simple community action and public education, and deaths due to diarrhoea can be eliminated by 2010. Childhood under-nutrition, the other major area of concern, can be addressed by targeting children of low birth weights and employing low-cost screening procedures to detect under-nutrition at an early age. Given the projected improvement in living standards, food security, educational levels and access to health care among all levels of the general population, substantial progress can be made in reducing the prevalence of severe under-nutrition in children by 2020. China's remarkable success in combating disease over the past two decades is proof that a determined commitment to improving public health can dramatically reduce the incidence of infectious diseases within one or two decades.

With the demographic and epidemiological transition taking place in the coming years, non-communicable diseases are also likely to emerge as major public health problems. Modernisation of life styles will further aggravate health problems. The rapid proliferation of two and four wheel motor vehicles, increasing congestion on city roads and intercity highways have all contributed to an increasing number of deaths and serious injuries from traffic related accidents. Greater emphasis on education and enforcement of road safety rules by both drivers and pedestrians is an urgent need of the hour.

As already noted, there will be a massive increase in population in the 15-64 age group. Reproductive and Child Health care programmes must meet the needs of this rapidly growing clientele. The population in this age group will be more literate and have greater access to information. They will have greater awareness and expectations about access to quality services for maternal and child health, contraceptive care, management of gynaecological problems, etc. A major focus of vision 2020 must be on improving access to health services to meet the health care needs of women and children.

India's significant achievements in the field of health have been made possible by the establishment of a huge rural health infrastructure, along with the formation of a massive health care manpower consisting of over five lakh trained doctors working under plural systems of medicine, and a vast frontline of over seven lakh nurses and other health care workers; 25,000 primary and community health care centres; and 1.6 lakh sub-centres, complemented by 22,000 dispensaries and 2,800 hospitals practicing Indian systems of medicine and homeopathy. This infrastructure remains under-equipped, under-manned and under-financed to cope with the challenge of eradicating major threats to human life.

The inadequacy of the current health care system is starkly illustrated by the fact that only 35 per cent of the population have access to essential drugs, while the UMI reference level is above 82 per cent. Infant immunisation against measles and DPT for children under 12 years is only 60 per cent and 78 per cent compared to the UMI level of over 90 per cent for both diseases.

As a larger proportion of the population reaches middle class standards of living, an increasing number of people will turn to private health care providers. This development is welcome, because it will permit the public health care system to concentrate more resources on meeting the needs of the poorer sections. But at the same time, the level of public expenditure on health care needs to rise about four-fold from the current level of 0.8 per cent of GDP to reach the UMI reference level of 3.4 per cent. Rapid growth of the private health care system, however, requires the formulation of competence and quality standards to check and balance the increasing emphasis on health care as a business.

Criteria for a More Equitable and Effective Health Care System

i) Universal access and access to an adequate level of health care without financial burden.

ii) Fair distribution of financial costs for access and fair distribution of burden in rational care and capacity.

iii) Ensuring that providers have the competence, empathy and accountability for delivering quality care and for effective use of relevant research.

iv) Special attention to vulnerable groups such as women, children, the disabled and the aged.

Development plans for India's health care systems need to place greater emphasis on public health education and prevention. The wide dissemination of health and nutrition related information through traditional channels should be supplemented by an ambitious and persistent programme of public health education through the print, television, radio and electronic media.

Health insurance can play an invaluable role in improving the overall health care system. The insurable population in India has been assessed at 250 million and this number will increase rapidly in the coming two decades. This should be supplemented by innovative insurance products and programmes by panchayats with reinsurance backup by companies and government to extend coverage to much larger sections of the population.

The life expectancy of the Indian population is expected to reach above 65 years in 2020, which compares favourably with the UMI reference level of 69 years. Mortality rates for infants is expected to decline to about 20 per 1000 in 2020, which compares favourably with the UMI reference level of 22.5.

VULNERABILITY

Economic growth, rising levels of education among the young, expansion of employment opportunities for the working age population, slower population growth, and declining infant mortality, however, will not eliminate and may even aggravate, inequalities between different age groups, the sexes, income groups, communities and regions, unless specific corrective steps are taken for levelling the different degrees of capacity and opportunity. The Vision 2020 must have special focus on bridging the existing gaps in the various levels of development and endeavour its best to fulfil the Constitutional commitment of raising the status of the vulnerable groups vis-à-vis the rest of the society.

During the next 20 years, the aged population in India will nearly double, placing much greater demand on the infrastructure of hospitals and nursing homes, while at the same time shifting the profile of health disorders from problems of the young to those of the aged. The population above 65 years of age will increase from 45 to 76 million persons by 2020. Reference has already been made to the very high incidence of malnutrition among this group and the growing incidence of diseases associated with aging, such as cancer and cardiovascular diseases. A disproportionate number of the aged population are illiterate and living below the poverty line. While majority of these people live in rural areas where the extended family system remains prevalent, increasing urbanisation and mobility will destabilise their situation in future. The problem of coping with a larger aged population will be partially solved by a big surge in the size of the working age labour force and a reduction in the dependency ratio, meaning that there will be a larger proportion of workers to support the aged. Specific strategies will be needed to provide targeted assistance for the most vulnerable members of this group, including research on the disabilities of the aged, greater development of geriatric medicine, training of minders for the aged, and establishment of innovative support systems such as the highly successful Japanese model.

Like the aged, the disabled persons also form another subgroup that is particularly vulnerable and unlikely to benefit directly from the general advance of society, unless specific provisions are made to address their particular needs, including a special system of schools, clinics and home-based learning programmes, combined with therapeutic and institutional care.

Increasing gender equity is an important challenge of the coming years. Literacy rates for females are 40 per cent lower than for males. Females represent only 43 per cent of all students at primary level, 37 per cent at higher secondary level, and 35 per cent of those in higher education. Drop out rates are also higher for girls. The UNDP's gender development index ranks India 108th among 174 countries in terms of gender equity. It is no coincidence therefore that countries ranking highest on this index are among the most prosperous in the world. Gender equity and social development are inseparably interlinked. Reducing the disparity in nutritional, literacy and educational levels between the sexes is essential for realisation of the country's full potentials.

Children being the supreme assets of the country, the 'Rights' based approach will continue to play an important role in ensuring their 'survival', 'protection' and 'development', with special attention to the girl child. Our vision for 2020 in this regard is to see a nation free from all forms of child labour. However, complete elimination of child labour through legal means is not only difficult to implement but may also prove to be counter productive in protecting the interest of these very children. While legal enforcement can contain the demand for child labour, it may leave the poor households supplying child labour more vulnerable rather than addressing the underlying socio-economic compulsions generating the supply of such labour. Indeed, poverty eradication combined with educational reforms to provide free (or affordable) access to quality education with an interesting, innovative and job-oriented curriculum for all can effectively eliminate child labour once and for all.

The other categories of the vulnerable groups include the scheduled castes (SC), scheduled tribes (ST), other backward classes (OBC) and minorities, constituting nearly three-fourths of the country's total population. They require special attention in order to narrow down the disparities between them and the more privileged section of the population. Literacy rates for SCs and STs are 25 per cent lower than for other communities. Education enrolment rates among this group, especially for females, lag significantly behind that of other communities. Low levels of education lead to lower paying employment opportunities and lower incomes. Thus, it becomes exceedingly difficult for these communities to come out of the vicious circle. Large number of people in other communities also suffer from similar disparities.

Regional disparities in rates of development are of similar concern. Regardless of the community or the region, the overall progress of the nation will depend to a large extent on its ability to provide increasing opportunities for the disadvantaged to take initiative for their self-development. Otherwise, these disadvantaged will exact an increasing toll on the stability, well-being and development of the country as a whole. It is notable that rising levels of violence and crime in society are not so much associated with overall low levels of development, as they are with wide disparities between levels of development, which create frustration and resentment. The progress of the whole will ultimately depend on the progress of its weakest links. India's Vision of 2020 must be one in which all levels and sections of the population and all parts of the country march forward together into a more secure and prosperous future.

Bibliography

Abu-Lughod, Janet L. *Changing Cities: Urban Sociology.* Harper Collins, 1991.

Anderson, Elijah. *A Place on the Corner.* Chicago: University of Chicago Press, 1978.

Beauregard, Robert and Sophie Body-Gendrot. *The Urban Moment: Cosmopolitan Essays on the Late 20th Century City.* Russell Sage, 1999.

Borden, Ian, et al. *The Unknown City: Contesting Architecture and Social Space.* Cambridge, Mass.: MIT Press, 2000.

Bouthillette, Anne-Marie, Gordon Brent Ingram and Yolanda Retter, eds. *Queers in Space: Communities/Public Places/Sites of Resistance.* Seattle, WA: Bay Press, 1997.

Boyer, Paul. *Urban Masses and Moral Order in America, 1820-1920.* Cambridge: Harvard University Press, 1978.

Castells, Manuel. "*Theory and Ideology in Urban Sociology.*" Urban Sociology: Critical Essays. (New York: St Martin's, 1976).

Clark, Terry Nichols, ed. *Urban Innovation: Creative Strategies for Turbulent Times.* Sage Publications, 1994.

Cronon, William. *Nature's Metropolis: Chicago and the Great West.* Norton, 1991.

Cuff, Dana. *The Provisional City: Los Angeles Stories of Architecture and Urbanism.* Cambridge, Mass.: MIT Press, 2000.

Denton, Nancy and Douglas Massey. *American Apartheid: Segregation and the Making of the Underclass.*

Fischer, Claude. "*The Subcultural Theory of Urbanism: A Twentieth-Year Assessment.*" American Journal of Sociology 101-3 (1995): 543-577.

Flanagan, William. *Contemporary Urban Sociology.* Cambridge: Cambridge University Press, 1993.

Gottdiener, Mark and Ray Hutchison. *The New Urban Sociology.* McGraw-Hill, 2000.

Hannerz, Ulf. *Exploring the City.* New York, Columbia University Press. 1984.

Jargowsky, Paul. *Poverty and Place: Ghettos. Barrios, and the American City.* Russell Sage, 1997.

Kasinitz, Philip. ed. *Metropolis: Center and Symbol of Our Times.* New York: New York University Press, 1995.

Leeds, A. *Cities, Classes, and the Social Order.* Ithaca: Cornell University Press, 1994.

LeGates, Richard T. and Frederic Stout, eds. *The City Reader.* New York: Routledge, 1996.

Logan, John and Harvey Molotch. *Urban Fortunes.* University of California Press, 1986.

Low, Setha M. *On the Plaza: The Politics of Public Space and Culture.* Austin: University of Texas Press, 2000.

Macionis, J. J. and V.N. Parrillo. *Cities and Urban Life.* Upper Saddle River, New Jersey: Prentice Hall, 1998.

Mitchell, Clyde. *Social Networks in Urban Situations.* Manchester: Manchester University Press, 1969.

Mollenkopf, John. *The Contested City.* Princeton University Press, 1983.

Mumford, Lewis. *The Culture of Cities.* New York: Harcourt Brace Jovanovich, 1970.

Popenoe, David. *Private Pleasure, Public Plight: American Metropolitan Community Life in Comparative Perspective.*

Saunders, Peter. *Social Theory and the Urban Question.* New York: Holmes & Meyer, 1981.

Sennet, Richard, ed. *Classic Essays in the Culture of Cities.* New York: 1969.

Simmel, Georg *"The Metropolis and Mental Life."* In *The Sociology of Georg Simmel.* (New York: Free Press, 1950).

Smith, Michael. *The City and Social Theory.* New York: 1979.

Sorio y Puig, Arturo. *Cerda: The Five Bases of the General Theory of Urbanization.* Corte Madera, CA: Ginko Press, 2000.

Sugrue, Thomas. *Origins of the Urban Crisis: Detroit, 1940-1960.* Princeton University Press, 1996.

Tönnies, Ferdinand. *Community and Society.* C. P. Loomis, trans. and ed. New York: Harper and Row, 1963.

Wadsworth, Nancy Kleniewski. *Cities, Change, and Conflict: A Political Economy of Urban Life.* 1997.

Whyte, William Foote. *Street Corner Society.* Chicago: University of Chicago Press, 1943.

Wirth, Louis. *On Cities and Social Life.* Chicago. The University of Chicago Press, 1964

Index